Postmodern Cartographies

# Postmodern Cartographies
## The Geographical Imagination in Contemporary American Culture

*Brian Jarvis*

 Pluto Press  LONDON

First published 1998 by Pluto Press
345 Archway Road, London N6 5AA

Copyright © Brian Jarvis 1998

The right of Brian Jarvis to be identified as the author of this work has
been asserted by him in accordance with the Copyright, Designs and
Patents Act 1988.

British Library Cataloguing in Publication Data
A catalogue record for his book is available from the British Library

ISBN 0 7453 1285 3 hbk

Designed and produced for Pluto Press by
Chase Production Services, Chadlington, OX7 3LN
Typeset from disk by Stanford DTP Services, Northampton
Printed in the EC by TJ International, Padstow

# Contents

CHAPTER 1

# Introduction: A Brief History of Space

There is no country as extensive as a thought.
Ralph Waldo Emerson,
*Journals* cited in Karl (1983), p. 30

The mind is its own place, and in itself
Can make a heaven of hell, a hell of heaven.
John Milton, *Paradise Lost* (1968), p. 59

Long before America was officially charted, in the crude sketches of Enlightenment cartography, its landscapes had been discovered across the wide sargasso seas of the imagination. In his letter of 1493, the first authenticated description of the New World, Columbus reported his 'discovery' of Haiti (Hispaniola). However, during its subsequent bloody colonisation by white Europeans, this New Founde Land was seen through the template of classical, biblical and medieval mappings. American topography became a geographical palimpsest beneath which the Old World discerned traces of Atlantis and the Elysian Fields, the Garden of Eden and the Promised Land, the Happy Isles and Vinland the Good. One of the consequences of this transposition of ancient Greek, Old Testament, Norse and Celtic cartographies on to the land was the generation of profound disenchantment in some quarters. 'When you get there, there's no there there' (Stein 1996, p. 102). Émigré Gertrude Stein's wry aphorism, equally germane to bourgeois tourism and working-class migration, signposts a dilemma central to the history of her homeland: if the New World failed to live up to the legends of a terrestrial paradise, it was often depicted as an infernal wilderness. Charles Olson declared at the outset of his study of Herman Melville: 'I take SPACE to be the central fact to man born in America, from Folsom Cave to now' (Olson 1967, p. 3). One of the distinctive features to the history of the representation of this 'SPACE', is its tendency to encourage responses that gravitate towards utopian and dystopian extremes. It was the best of places, it was the worst of places, but always the land itself loomed large in the imagination of America.

The sheer geographical monumentality of the New World figures largely in the writings of early explorers, settlers, travellers and natural

1

scientists. Subsequently, during the colonial and revolutionary eras, the land often figured as a touchstone in the rhetoric of religious and political leaders. An energetic geocentricism evident in the arts throughout these times was sustained during the romantic and modern periods. It is important to emphasise the degree to which, throughout this history, relations to the land in all quarters were shaped by the ideological climate within which specific cartographies were produced. In *Landscape and written expression in Revolutionary America*, Robert Lawson-Peebles explains how 'Columbus transformed the lands he saw so that they accorded with received Christian opinion' (Lawson-Peebles 1988, p. 9). The explorer's representations of the New World were positioned within the co-ordinates of the orthodox Christian mapping of the earth, *Orbis Terrarum*. Columbus thought that he had discovered Paradise in this *Otro Mundo* because he saw it through the lens of contemporary theological and cartographic opinion. The lenses may have altered considerably, but all subsequent observers have been obliged to observe American landscapes through some form of ideological eyeglass.

## 'Never merely something to walk upon ...'

The documents produced by early explorers exhibit religious awe (New World viewed as Paradise), entrepreneurial glee (New World viewed as the Land of Plenty) and occasional spasms of sublime terror (New World viewed as Wilderness). The geographical imagination during the days of the Puritan colony stays largely within these axes. The rhetoric of the elite oscillates wildly between panegyrics to a potential New Eden and jeremiads against a cruel wasteland. Having initially inspired so much hope it was not surprising that the New World should also generate acute disillusion. Many within the Puritan theocracy encouraged their flock to look upon the land – with its poor harvests, harsh elements, insect plagues, 'savages' lurking in dark forests – as the geographical distillation of Evil. The sermons of Cotton Mather and Edward Johnson, amongst others, often depicted the land as a God-forsaken wilderness with which the Puritan faithful were required to do battle, both physical and spiritual. Clearly, the purpose behind these declamations was the institutionalisation of a Puritan worldview, within an order which saw its mission as the cultivation of an unredeemed wasteland by Christian civilisation.

Puritan cartographies provide early examples of a dystopian impulse in the American geographical imagination. Their most telling legacy, however, derives from its associated system of hermeneutics. In *Gravity's Rainbow*, Thomas Pynchon explores the inheritance left by those 'WASPs in buckled black, who heard God clamouring to them in every turn of a leaf or cow loose among apple orchards in autumn' (Pynchon 1975a, p. 281). The Puritan habit of *reading the landscape* for signs of Divine pleasure or wrath, initiates the concept of a textualised spatiality, one of the key facets of the geographical imagination to be explored in this study.

In Revolutionary America the Puritan's gloomy insistence upon viewing the New World as an unredeemed Wilderness was largely eclipsed by nationalistic celebrations of the 'Land of Plenty'. Geography was required to fulfil new needs. Thomas Paine reinterpreted the vast open spaces that had been demonised by branches of Puritan hermeneutics as signifiers of liberty and opportunity. In the process he drew an imaginative equation between topography, political economy and national character that has since been institutionalised in American mythology. This reading was confirmed in the work of de Crévecoeur and Founding Father Thomas Jefferson. Both dedicated eulogies to the soul-sustaining wholesomeness of the American landscape. The New World now promised to realise the pastoral ideals of classical civilisation, situated as it was on a 'middle ground', between the hypertrophied corruption of Old World cities and the uncultivated wilderness. Official mappings in the early days of the Republic, such as Jedidiah Morse's *American Geography* (1789) and Elijah Parish's *A New System of Modern Geography* (1810), offered academic confirmation of the beneficial social and spiritual effects of standing on hallowed New World ground.

Needless to say, the cartographies produced in Revolutionary America, like those of their Puritan predecessors, were instrumental and heavily encoded with political, economic and moral imperatives. Homages to American geographical splendour provided an ideological foundation for the promotion of a sense of national identity rooted in the land, enhancing social cohesion across vast territorial boundaries. As well as advancing the thesis that America's peoples, minus the indigenous and slave populations, were brought together by the distances between them, Revolutionary representations of the land consistently valorised certain socioeconomic practices and forms of political organisation: namely, agriculture, democracy and nationalism.

The nineteenth century witnessed an amplification of the geographical imagination, one that produced an explosive proliferation in representations of the land as diverse as American topography itself. Puritan accounts of America as an infernal wilderness reappeared in the Gothic fictions of Poe, Melville and Hawthorne. In *The Scarlet Letter*, Hawthorne explicitly echoed his ancestors' judgement on the land, describing the forest as a 'wild, unredeemed, unchristianised, lawless region' (Hawthorne 1990b,

p. 2240). Outside the Gothic mainstream, traces of a muted agoraphobia could also be detected in the popular fiction consumed by the urban middle classes, in a multitude of tales of adventure and captivity in a treacherous wilderness overrun by savages.

Alongside this thriving counter-pastoral tradition, however, the mid-nineteenth century also witnessed the rejuvenation of an essentially mystical relation to the land. In the work of the transcendentalists America once more became the New Eden. 'Yet America is a poem in our eyes; its ample geography dazzles the imagination and it will not wait long for metres' (Emerson 1990b, p. 1549). In 'The Poet' and throughout his writing, Ralph Waldo Emerson's philosophy drew on numerous sources, including the Puritan doctrine of correspondences, European romanticism and eastern mysticism. The final result, however, in many respects represented a white American corollary of pre-Columbian understanding of the land as a network of sacred spaces. The Good Gay poet, Walt Whitman, sustained this rejuvenation and sought to confirm in a spectacularly eroticised fashion, that America itself was 'essentially the greatest poem' (Whitman 1990a, p. 2713).

The transcendentalists' call for a sensuous and spiritual response to nature was of course contemporary with and inseparable from an increasingly aggressive 'development' of the land by commercial interests. The agriculturists, business leaders, river and railway companies and political leaders of Jacksonian America were sublimely disinterested in the romantics' alternative ways of seeing. One of the most savage assaults upon the hegemony of a utilitarian concept of nature's value was launched by Henry David Thoreau. The critique is at its most vehement during the passage in *Walden, or Life in the Woods*, where the earthy mystic vilifies a farmer who has dared to give his name to a local pond:

> I respect not his labours, his farm where everything has its price; who would carry the landscape, who would carry his God, to market, if he could get anything for him; who goes to market *for* his god as it is; on whose farm nothing grows free, whose fields bear no crops, whose meadows no flowers, whose trees no fruits, but dollars ... (Thoreau 1979, p. 1654)

The dominion of the utilitarian calculus extended rapidly during the second half of the nineteenth century, following the portentous declaration made by a New York newspaper editor in 1845: 'It is our manifest destiny to over spread the continent allotted by providence for the free development of our yearly multiplying millions' (Channel 4 1995, p. 3). The mythology that evolved to legitimise westward expansion fed off earlier trends and traditions in the geographical imagination (particularly the notion of the need for the civilising presence of the white man to transform the

Wilderness into a Garden). It was institutionalised by the work of Frederick Jackson Turner:

> The existence of an area of free land, its continuous recession, and the advance of American settlement westward, explain American development ... The true point of view in the history of the nation is not the Atlantic coast, it is the Great West. (Turner 1972, pp. 3–4)

The Turner thesis and its associated romantic mythologisation of the Frontier is founded upon a form of environmental determinism as simple as it is seductive: the vast open tracts of land fostered a vital respect for democracy, the essential element in American character and political economy. The mythic currency of the Frontier cannot be denied and in fact has increased steadily since it was closed down. With regard to this phenomenon David Lowenthal makes the following apposite observation: 'The Wilderness was no heritage to folk who had to cope with it; it became one only when it no longer had to be lived in' (cited in Least Heat-Moon 1991, p. 60). It must be recognised that most forms of Frontier romanticism survive only in relation to their immunity to historical actuality: all of those elements suppressed by Turner and his disciples, such as the lives of back-breaking toil and drudgery for pioneer women and men, the barbaric exploitation of ethnic and racial minorities in the 'civilising' of the Great West and the decidedly anti-democratic dispossession of the land's indigenous population.

The geographical preoccupation of American letters was sustained around the *fin de siècle* by the local colour school (Garland, Chopin, Harte, Jewett) and the naturalists (Crane, Norris, Dreiser, London). Despite obvious departures, the naturalists followed in the footsteps of their transcendentalist forebears in two major respects: a fascination with the operations of the machine in the garden and a continuation of the investigation of the social and psychological effects of life in the city, instigated initially by Poe. Both natural and urban environments in these writings were frequently seen to be the site of awesome energies and elemental principles that dwarfed the individual into insignificance.

The ensuing modernist phase in American cultural history, during the consolidation of the urban-industrial order, witnessed another spectacular upsurge in ways of seeing space. In poetry, space was a central concern for the cosmopolitan Eliot in *The Waste Land* and the more provincial Williams in his counter-epic *Paterson*. Pastoral and counter-pastoral traditions thrived in the work of Frost, Crane, the Southern Agrarians, the Black Mountain and Beat poets. In fiction, most notably, there was Faulkner's Yoknapatawpha County novels, mystic encounters with land and sea in the work

of Hemingway and Steinbeck and the city and small-town fiction
of Dos Passos, West, Lewis and Anderson. A remark made by
Faulkner in *The Hamlet* might stand as an epigraph for the encounter
with space in American writing up to and including its modernist
phase:

> geography had never been merely something to walk upon but
> was the very medium which the fetterless to-and-fro-going
> required to breathe in. (Faulkner 1940, p.242)

The *Otro Mundo* has been subjected to a range of discourses, each
of which has left its mark on the land: from pre-Columbian concepts
of the land as sacred space, to the Puritan's dread of an unredeemed
wilderness, from the commercial dreams of Virgin Territory ripe
for conquest by capital, to the romantics' dreams of a New Eden.
What is essential for the purpose of this study is a recognition of
the following: the central role that geography plays in the American
imagination and the way in which that imagination bifurcates
towards utopian and dystopian antipodes. Many of the key words
in the discourses of American history and definitions of that
nebulous entity referred to as 'national identity' are geocentric: the
Frontier, the Wilderness, the Garden, the Land of Plenty, the
Wild West, the Small Town, the Big City, the Open Road. The
geographical monumentality of the New World has inspired feelings
of wonder and terror. The discursive stratagems central to the
traditions of representing space have been consistently characterised
by a predilection for hyperbole, an excess that constitutes a polemical
impersonation of the sheer scale of New World topography. The
problematics and the promise of space lie at the heart of cultural
practices through the colonial, revolutionary, romantic and modern
eras. The intention of this study is to examine a range of
contemporary responses to the land to establish whether there is
an essential continuity in the geographical imagination, or, whether
postmodern mappings of space constitute a decisive break with
previous traditions. What are the dominant, residual and emergent
features of the geographical imagination in its postmodern phase?
Before answering this question it is first necessary to offer a brief
outline of the key areas and terminology that will be integral to this
study.

## More than words alone

*Space, place* and *landscape*: these terms are clearly central to any
analysis of the geographical imagination. Each of them denotes not
a fixed and static object so much as an ongoing process, a spatial
praxis. Spaces are not simply the passive backdrop to significant
sociohistorical action, rather they are a vital product and determinant

of that action. '[Space is] not merely an arena *in which* social life unfolds but a medium *through which* social life is produced and reproduced' (Gregory 1986, p. 451). Given the structural inseparability of space/place/landscape and social relations there can be no geographical knowledge without historical narrative. In other words, all spaces contain stories and must be recognised as the site of an ongoing struggle over meaning and value.

Space/place/landscape is always represented in relation to cultural codes that are embedded in social power structures. The three most significant power structures in contemporary American society are capitalism, patriarchy and white racial hegemony. Accordingly, the subjects of class and capital, gender and sexuality, race and ethnicity, whilst by no means exclusive of all other interests, are of critical significance to any study of the workings of the geographical imagination in postmodern culture.

Class contours are apparent across the landscapes of capital in a geography of uneven development, of stark centre-margin structures. In recent times a number of critics on the left, from different disciplinary backgrounds, have suggested that this geography is becoming increasingly protean and immune to oppositional mapping. (See Chapter 5.) Accordingly, the development and representability of the lines and nodes of capital as they are materialised in space will be a central component of this study.

In a famous passage towards the end of *The Great Gatsby*, Nick Carraway considers the dead hero's relation to the 'fresh, green breast of the new world' (Fitzgerald 1993, p. 133). One of the most conspicuous features of the geographical imagination in America is its predilection for gendered tropes. The feminisation of the land – as that which receives and nurtures (Mother Nature), but can also be dominated and exploited (Virgin Territory) – has become a subject of intense interest to feminist critics.[1] Recently, Gillian Rose (1993), Nancy Duncan (1996) and others have called for a 'spatialisation' of feminist practice and challenged the legitimacy of traditional forms of geographical knowledge on the grounds of gender bias. Some of the key insights produced by feminist geography will be utilised in this study.

In conjunction with an examination of the significance of class, capital and gender, it is also essential to recognise the colourings of contemporary cartographies. This will be attempted here with specific reference to America's largest racial minority, the black

1. The inverse of the land-as-woman trope has also been noted by feminist critics: 'In the 1840s American gynaecologist Marion Sims was describing himself as a Columbus discovering the vagina as his "New World" landscape, so that traditional definitions of landscape and geography were projected back onto the female body in gynaecological research of the time' (Westling 1996, p. 45).

community, as it is represented in the work of one of its leading writers, Toni Morrison. As well as possessing a pronounced gender bias, many of the key terms in the geographical lexicon have an ethnic specificity that is often invisible to the dominant culture. As Luther Standing Bear reminded his oppressors in the nineteenth century:

> We did not think of the great open plains, the beautiful rolling hills, and winding streams with tangled growth as 'wild'. Only to the white man was nature a 'wilderness'. (cited in Gidley 1989, p. 210).

The multiplicity of facets to the American geographical imagination cannot be underestimated, both in terms of who perceives its spaces and which spaces it chooses to see – the dialectical relationship between the representation of space and the spaces of representation. To give an indication of America's geographical diversity, this study will range from representations of the city, through the suburbs to the country, panoramic vistas and domestic interiors, spaces of abundance and of want; from nature in the raw to the second nature of technological forms that increasingly dominate large tracts of American space. In the context of this diversity it is important to bear in mind that each of these spaces is dependent upon the other. The geographical imagination is wrought from a profound spatial connectivity that Clive Bush has expressed well:

> it is impossible to divide up our experience of space. In an important sense the farmlands imply the wilderness, and the wilderness the farmlands. The city implies the countryside and the countryside implies the city. The domestic hearth implies the public domain and the public domain the hearth. Further, we divorce the geometric from the bodily, the economic from the political and the personal from the social only at a certain risk. (Bush 1989, p. 13).

In an intriguing polemical declaration, Pierre Macherey has claimed that 'the text says what it does not say (Macherey 1978, p. 83)'. Consequently, any analysis of spatial representations must seek to address the caesurae from which all cartographies are composed. Marginalised spaces are always implied and central to any map's significance, they are a clue to the ideology through which space is seen and felt. Whilst in pursuit of the fissures and faultlines in the geographical imagination, however, it is important to remain sensitive to the vital distinction Wallace Stevens once drew, whilst in contemplation of a barren snowscape, between the 'nothing that is not there and the nothing that is' (Stevens 1984, p. 10). A phrase from Clive Bush's warning, concerning the risks involved in separating the 'geometric from the bodily', introduces another critical area of concern. Whilst corporeal conceits have figured largely in aesthetic and philosophical responses to the land, traditional geographical knowledge has excluded the body as a suitable subject of concern. Feminist geographers, such as the contributors to Nancy Duncan's *Bodyspace* (1996), have challenged this exclusion, particularly in relation to the symbolic geography of patriarchy. This is a challenge that needs to be upheld. The disciplinary division between study of the body and the spaces through which it moves has become especially untenable within the late capitalist order. The body is one of the key locations on the postmodern landscape, a space subjected to colonisation, commodification and redevelopment like any other and therefore a suitable area for the consideration of the cultural geographer. Corporeal cartographies – mappings of the body – loom large on the horizon of the geographical imagination and ought to be seen as integral to postmodern spatial economy.

A final key term which requires some preliminary explication, 'postmodern', has become one of the academy's most slippery shibboleths: 'like the Toyota of thought, produced and assembled in several different places and then sold everywhere' (Zukin 1991, p. 26). Postmodernism appears as a periodising label in the arts (the postmodern aesthetic), as a means of classifying an emergent socioeconomic regime (late capitalism/post-Fordism) and as part of a diverse philosophical paradigm (poststructuralism). As such it can become a rather convenient catch-all, often applied as a defensive gesture to a disparate range of cultural practices. Nevertheless, its presence as a signpost in the landscape of discourses about the arts, contemporary social organisation and philosophy cannot be ignored and the term clearly has a selective applicability. Accordingly, without endeavouring to produce anything quite as grand as a grand narrative of the postmodern, I shall be using this term on occasion to outline dominant impulses within contemporary cultural practice.

As well as being associated with postindustrialism in the social sciences and certain tendencies in art that appear to depart from classical modernist practice, postmodernism is often associated with a third area in philosophy and literary criticism: poststructuralism. The collapsing of the boundaries between these three needs to be resisted. The notion that postmodern representations of space are, *ipso facto*, expressions of poststructuralist philosophy is grossly inadequate. The geographical imagination should not be collapsed into the often reductive orthodoxies of postindustrial cartography and poststructural philosophy. The focus of this study, of course, is the representation of space in American culture. However, this ought not to be taken as an implicit denial of the existence of terrains beyond the poststructuralists' 'textuality'. Rather, the aim is to chart the crossings between geographical actuality and the mappings of writers, social scientists and film-makers. This is not to place one's foot willingly in the poststructuralist snare of naively insisting upon the possibility of an unmediated relation to a geographical Real, but to recognise the existence of certain spatial raw materials that form the basis of any cartographic exercise and even the writing produced within the walls of academia. Borges' Library might not be built from the same rock that Boswell kicked, but like all superstructures, it consists of more than words alone.

# Part One

# Postindustrial Landscapes:
# Space and the Social Sciences

# CHAPTER 2

# All's Well in the Warfare State: Daniel Bell

Standing before the exhibits at the 1900 Chicago World Fair, Henry Adams concluded that the Dynamo was both agent and symbol of the seemingly exponential rate of change that distinguished American history. The passage from a predominantly rural-agrarian society to an urban-industrial order had occurred so rapidly that America appeared almost to outrun history itself. This sense of an unprecedented velocity to socioeconomic change was aptly captured, a few years later, by Gertrude Stein, when she pronounced herself a citizen of the world's oldest nation – a declaration founded on the premise that her homeland had entered the twentieth century at least two decades before any other country.

In what is now the rundown to an entire millennium, some critics within the social sciences have been seized by a sense of transformation on a scale sufficiently epic to testify to the efficacy of Adams' prophecy. Accounts of this metamorphosis typically start with statistics. In 1950, over 70 per cent of Americans lived in cities, 30 per cent of the labour force was employed in manufacturing and the industrial regions of the Northeast and Midwest were on the verge of an economic boom. By 1980 this economic landscape was to be transformed beyond recognition. Factories and the city were displaced by offices and the suburbs as an American's most familiar geographical experience. Simultaneously, the locus of monetary muscle began to migrate Southwest, away from the traditional manufacturing heartlands and their constituent metropolises, towards Florida, Texas and California.

Collectively, these reconfigurations in demography and economic activity have been received by many in the social sciences as evidence of the advent of a fundamentally different stage in the evolution of American political economy. The coming of a 'New Society' is the centrepiece of a thesis which appears under an array of signs: the 'service economy', the 'global village', the 'information age', the 'society of the spectacle', the 'political economy of the sign'.[1]

1. In order of their appearance within the text these particular terms are most commonly associated with the following figures: Ralf Dahrendorf; Zbigniew Brzeszinski; Marshall McLuhan; Peter Drucker; Guy Debord and Jean Baudrillard.

These labels are suggestive of some of the New Society's key attributes: this is a place in which services have eclipsed industrial production, which has witnessed an accelerated expansion of electronic technologies, forms of knowledge and information, images and media signs. Despite variations in the weighting of specific phenomena, the studies which accompany this lexicon converge on the fact of momentous *change*. The sheer number of new vocabularies seem to be testimony to a profound sense that something has passed, so that the old words will no longer suffice. One of the most ardent proponents of this view, Daniel Bell, has suggested that 'common to all sociological thought today is the sense of a profound transformation' (Bell 1974, p. 475). It is Bell who, in *The End of Ideology* (1960), provided the term which has come to subsume most of those listed above and is the most conspicuous motif for this sense of the dawning of a new age: the *postindustrial* society.

The signifier 'postindustrial' is stubbornly polysemic and contains many, occasionally exclusive, meanings. Irrespective of its semantic indeterminacy, however, what cannot be denied is the extent to which it has attained hegemonic status in many accounts of contemporary socioeconomic change. This master sign is often part of a historiography hinging upon the notion of a radical break with the past. But the postindustrial thesis is also an instrumental cartography, a mapping in which the primary ideological imperative is to erase the critical contours of late capitalism as they are inscribed in space. These cartographies disregard the labour and the grime, the class formations and conflicts of crowded cities and factories, in favour of postindustrial locations – such as the office, the university campus, assorted mediascapes and technological playgrounds – and thus seek to deny the continuing significance of capital as a force in the shaping of the American landscape. Essentially, postindustrialism constitutes a neoconservative response to the crises of late capitalism. It is a species of geographical amnesia characterised by utopian and dystopian excess. These excesses and their attendant discursive denials undermine its effectiveness as an accurate representation of space in postmodern America.

## The postindustrial playground

each sociological theorist of any pretension carries a distinctive conceptual map of the social terrain and a set of signposts to the society ahead.

Daniel Bell, *The Coming of Post-Industrial Society* (1974), p. 42

Under interrogation by one of his professors at the University of Columbia as to the precise nature of his research interests, the undergraduate student Daniel Bell rather cannily replied that he specialised in generalisations. This early predilection is evident throughout the Bell critical *oeuvre*, with its focus on macrosociological process and its drive towards memorable totalisations. In the conclusion to his early study of the history of the American Left, for example, Bell announced the advent of a radically new socioeconomic formation, but was, as yet, indecisive about an appropriate nomenclature – 'whether state capitalism, managerial society, or corporate capitalism' (Bell 1952, p. 405). This terminological indeterminacy was not finally resolved until the publication, twenty years on, of *The Coming of Post-Industrial Society* (Bell 1974). The centrepiece of this 'venture in social forecasting' is the proposition that 'the changes which are summed up in the post-industrial society may represent a historic metamorphosis in western society' (*ibid.*, p. 164).

Considering its centrality to the task of articulating the nature of this metamorphosis, the elasticity which characterises Bell's use of the generalisation, 'post-industrial society', is problematic. Bell's usage clouds the question of regional specificity: whilst it is most often applied to the situation of North America (because the processes are deemed to be more advanced and visible there), it is occasionally extended to express the inevitable trajectory of the entire western world. This geographical inexactitude is accompanied and compounded by a disconcerting chronological imprecision. Bell casually alternates between suggesting that this radically new place *emerged* in the 1950s and *will appear* 'in the next thirty to fifty years' (*ibid.*, p. x). The prefix 'post-' is stretched semantically to incorporate 'coming' and 'emerging', a 'transitionary period', an 'interregnum' and the recently experienced dawn of a new era. On occasion, 'post-industrial' is proffered modestly as an 'analytical construct' (*ibid.*, p. 483), designed to impart intelligibility to diverse changes, elsewhere it is deemed to be the very essence of the transition. Ambiguity is also heightened by the rather insouciant elision between the favoured '*post*-industrial' and '*advanced* industrial society', a term which carries entirely dissimilar connotations. Throughout *The Coming of Post-Industrial Society* semantic precision is sacrificed in the name of a utopian vision of a radically new American landscape, bursting through the husk of its industrial spatial heritage. My purpose here is to fix the precise distance between the rhetoric and the reality in the reassuring generalisations from which Bell's economic geography is composed.

In *The End of Ideology*, as part of his analysis of 'Work and its Discontents', Bell argued that 'the factory is archtypical because its rhythms, in subtle fashion affect the general character of work the way a dye suffuses a cloth' (Bell 1960, p. 248). Just over a decade later, however, he announced with equal conviction that the factory was no longer the paradigmatic geographical location for work experience:

> The rhythms are no longer pervasive. The beat has been broken ... what is central to the new relationship is encounter or communication ... the fact that individuals now talk to other individuals, rather than interact with a machine, is the fundamental fact about work in the post-industrial society. (Bell 1974, pp. 162; 166)

Bell's instrumental cartography in *The Coming of Post-Industrial Society* emerges as a diptych, in which spaces which were dominated by factories, machines and money are juxtaposed with newly peopled places. According to this mapping, America's economic landscapes are no longer under the shadow of reifying technologies and the Fordist production of goods, rather, they are the site of disalienating services, of interpersonal contact and the circulation of information. As the evanescent factoryscapes of industrial capital fade from view, individuals' primary geographical experiences are of office spaces, university campuses, places of recreation and aesthetic activity. Bell stresses that the accompanying dissolution of industrial class formation spells the eclipse of 'class' itself as a significant social categorisation. The rise of the new middle classes marks the end of class then, as previously Bell had argued that an advance in the hegemony of liberalism resulted in an 'end to ideology'. Accordingly, the landscapes of postindustrialism are largely conflict-free zones, in marked contrast to the battlefields of urban-industrial capitalism.

In support of this contention, of a bloodless revolution in sociospatial relations, Bell points to certain structural developments in occupational structure in the postwar period. The statistics, as they often can be, are impressive. In 1929, 40 per cent of the workforce was employed in the service sector; by 1967 this figure had risen to 55 per cent. The watershed year in this respect was 1956. The dominion of the factory could finally be said to have ended at that historical moment in which the United States became the first nation in which 'more than half of the employed population [was] not involved in the production of food, clothing, houses, automobiles, and other tangible goods' (Bell 1974, p. 343).

Postindustrial cartographies consistently foreground the significance of spaces occupied by the service sector and by the high-tech sunrise economies. Amongst the most popular locations are Cape Canaveral, Huntsville and Houston, the apex of the prosperous 'space triangle' and 'Silicon Valley'. With its agglomeration of computer, electronics and chemical companies, its support from and of Stanford University and its appealing setting amidst cherry, apricot and plum orchards, Silicon Valley is often figured as the paradigmatic geography of the postindustrial. These postindustrial mappings, however, contain critical geographical lacunae. They achieve their sanguine representations of a momentous reconfiguration in spatial relations only by performing certain strategic omissions, relating to the nature of white-collar labour and the structural and spatial interdependence of forms of economic activity. These exclusions need to be addressed.

Bell packages government census statistics pertaining to *quantitative changes* in occupational structure (the relative shrinkage of the industrial proletariat and the expansion of the technical and professional strata), as a *qualitative transformation* in class relations and the nature of work itself. In the process he manages to corroborate the management fantasy of office labour which service sector executives are ever anxious to promote. *The Coming of Post-Industrial Society* counterpoints the dehumanising fusion of worker and greasy machine on the factory floor, with non-reifying relations between people in air-conditioned offices. However, the postindustrial prophecy of 'all play and no work' has never seriously threatened to materialise for all but a privileged minority. Instead, throughout class structure, embourgeoisement and proletarianisation have coalesced. The bleaching of the blue collar in the postwar period has not abolished so much as confused class membership distinctions, as many of what had previously been deemed white-collar roles were subjected to the harsh discipline of scientific management and forms of control previously confined to the shop floor.

Bell maintains a strategic silence on the actual breakdown of figures involved in alterations to occupational structure. This enables him to disguise the fact that much of the so-called 'white-collar revolution' entails an expansion in 'non-productive' manual services, such as cleaning, catering and maintenance. In other words, the revolution is based upon the transfer of previously hidden and informal domestic labours from the home and the neighbourhood into the marketplace (as well as the displacement of rural labour through the rise of agribusiness and the implementation of new farming technologies). This underbelly to the white-collar revolution is obscured by Bell, as the iconography through which it is articulated is appropriated from the very top rungs of the occupational ladder – from the managers, researchers, scientists and engineers. Such a gallery diverts attention from the much larger white-collar cast who bolster the statistics, working in offices and shops where scientific management is often as rigorously adhered to as on any assembly line.

Bell ignores these places for the prestige sites of postindustrialism. In particular, the laboratory and its scientists are focused upon as the *protopos*, or ideal location, for the new social order: 'the scientific estate – its ethos and its organization – is the monad that contains within it the imago of the future society' (Bell 1974, p. 378). In his accolade to the scientific estate, Bell regularly insists upon the autonomy of the laboratory and the non-ideological nature of scientific discourse. This is verified by its positioning: 'Less than one-fourth [of scientists and other members of the 'educated elite'] are employed by business and more than half are in the universities' (*ibid.*, p. 232). The university is deemed to be liberal in ethos and thus most of its activities fall 'outside the business system ... the organization of science policy is not, in the first instance, responsive to business demand' (*ibid.*). As a corollary of his contention that knowledge is the postindustrial society's central resource, Bell suggests that there has also been a shift in the locus of power away from the business world to centres of research and learning. The places in which 'theoretical knowledge is codified and enriched, become the axial structures of the emergent society' (*ibid.*, p. 26). In fact, the university is now established as 'the primary institution of the post-industrial society' (*ibid.*, p. 116).

The proposal of an epochal realignment in the axial principles of western society towards knowledge and the nucleus of power towards the university could perhaps only have evolved and been entertained in the halls of academia. It is an alluring pipe-dream, but one which clouds the commodification of information and the continuing ascendancy of government offices, military installations and financial centres in the American spatial economy. It is also a fantasy which patently contradicts the self-image of most university authorities. The prospectus for Stanford University, for example, during the period in which Bell was insisting that intellectual institutions were uncontaminated by the flows of filthy lucre, was proudly declaring the institution's intimate association with the business community. The computer and chemical companies that this allegedly aloof and financially disinterested centre of scientific excellence affiliate with, still run on a recognisably *industrial* model. These firms may not have the *same* capital, labour and raw materials requirements as those in the manufacturing sector, but these are far from being obsolete concerns. Crucially, there is a substantial degree of continuity in their overriding goal: high profit margins. In fact, the scientific estate to the south of the San Francisco Bay region exists only because of the agglomeration economies to be gained from proximity to one another and to Stanford University. Bell's thesis ought to be confirmed by a postindustrial heartland such as Silicon Valley and yet this site stands as a testament not to the eclipse, but to the geographical extension of the logic of industrial capital.

Bell's main statistical evidence (and most of his main evidence is statistical) is 'the enormous sums spent by the US government on research' (*ibid.*, p. 247):

> The United States, by devoting 3 percent of the GNP to research and development, in the words of the OECD report on science in the United States, became a 'symbol for other countries which now regard this as a target to be reached'. From the end of the war and for the next two decades R&D expenditure in America multiplied by fifteen times. (*ibid.*, p. 250)

This signifies a new era in world history: '[Now] the *scientific* capacity of a country has become a determinant of its potential and power, and research and development (R&D) has replaced steel as a comparative measure of the strength of the powers' (*ibid.*, p. 117). Of course, R&D budgets can be interpreted as an index of a nation-state's strength, but not necessarily for the reasons which Bell is implying. First, this figure tends to coincide with industrial capacity anyway. Second, and more importantly, it is an accurate gauge because such a high proportion is associated with the military. The impressive growth in R&D expenditure after 1945 was largely attributable to the Cold War with the Soviet Union and the hot war in Vietnam. During the imperialist assault on Southeast Asia, the US Director of Research boasted that 'the Viet Nam conflict is testing almost all of the tactical military equipment and concepts developed in the last twenty years of R&D' (cited in Kolko 1988, p. 196).

It is particularly worrying that Bell is not oblivious to these facts; rather, he chooses to skim past them. *The Coming of Post-Industrial Society* notes that between 1950 and 1970, 80 per cent of all federal and 60 per cent of all other R&D was, in a rather coy expression, expenditure connected with 'external challenge' (Bell 1974, p. 253). Further on Bell even concedes that

> in 1960, these three agencies [defense, space and atomic energy] spent 91% of all federal R&D money ... in terms of evident social needs and social concerns, such as housing, pollution, environmental deterioration, and the like, there was almost no R&D effort to deal with these questions. (*ibid.*, pp. 259–61)

However, this apparently does not jeopardise the assertion made elsewhere that welfare provision, particularly in health and education, is at the head of the agenda of ethical priorities within the postindustrial society.

Simultaneously, Bell's mappings of high-tech company installations and university science parks consistently ignore the extent to which many of the key icons of the new social order have their origins in the military laboratory and on the battlefield. The first computer, ENIAC (electronic numerical integrator and calculator), originated at the University of Pennsylvania under military funding and guidance. Bell's response to the militarisation of public space, the pervasive presence of the American warfare state across the landscapes of postindustrialism, is to seek shelter in the future tense, issuing reassuring but uncorroborated promises of an imminent 'shift away from defense spending' (*ibid.*, p. 131). Twenty years on, in the wake of the Strategic Defense Initiative and aside from largely cosmetic arms reductions, this promise of a withering away of the Permanent Arms Economy shows no signs of being fulfilled. With a current estimated $3 trillion spent on 'external challenge', it is the literal combat zones of the 'New World Order', rather than those battlefields of theoretical knowledge, which remain the primary strategic concern of America's power elites.

Alongside its erasure of the pervasive shaping influence of capital and the military upon the American landscape, Bell's cartography of the postindustrial society contains two further critical geographical lacunae. The assertion of an imminent 'decline of the industrial worker' (*ibid.*, p. 35) is resoundingly silent on the nature of this fall, with the implication that this will be a smooth and painless transition. Bell's preoccupation with the postindustrial heartlands ignores the extent to which these spaces are functionally interdependent with America's industrial hinterland. This is a palimpsest in which the crises and conflicts of the frostbelt can still be detected beneath the surface display of idyllic sunbelt oases. Bell ignores the structural interdependence of the secondary and tertiary sectors and the extent to which the expansion of services has been facilitated by the growth in industrial operations. Rather than abandoning one for the other, the postindustrial society shows every indication of pursuing *both* production and services. It is essential that Bell's opposition of the two is not accepted as part of a process of painless withering away. As Sharon Zukin suggests in her exploration of *Landscapes of Power*, the crises of the automobile industry in Detroit are representative of problems faced throughout the manufacturing belt, which over the past twenty years has been riven by unemployment, labour disputes and economic strife (Zukin 1991; see especially chapter 4).

It is convenient for some American sociologists to forget that such difficulties have less to do with the excellence of their own economy, as it progresses to a higher postmanufacturing base, than with overseas competition from the Pacific Rim and Europe. This crisis has been exacerbated by the migration of industrial operations. The myth of a postindustrial United States is largely founded upon the redeployment of manufacturing activities to developing host countries replete with enticing free trade zones and a non-unionised labour supply. The geographical mobility of the secondary sector

permits the affluence of the postindustrial centre, which retains
control and performs the hygienic administrative functions whilst
the 'dirty work' is done abroad. The 'deindustrialisation' of the
American landscape must be seen in the light of an international
recomposition of the industrial working class – the workers of
those countries in Central and Latin America, Asia, Africa and
Eastern Europe, with whom the postindustrial core has established
exploitative ties of dependence. These places are conspicuous by
their absence from the myopic mappings of postindustrial
enthusiasts.

## Mapping in the future perfect

> Inevitably, a post-industrial society gives rise to a new
> Utopianism.
>
> Daniel Bell, *The Coming of*
> *Post-Industrial Society* (1974), p. 488

Discussing the origins of his key term, Bell admits that, in 'Leisure
and Work in the post-industrial society', David Riesman used it
marginally earlier than himself, but goes on to claim, quite correctly
(if a little immodestly), that it is from his own work that it has gained
much of its currency (*ibid.*, pp. 37–8). In a rather scornful footnote
Bell criticises Arthur Penty, the originator of the term in 1917, for
his naive utopianism. Penty, a guild socialist and disciple of William
Morris, coined the term 'postindustrial', in the wake of the First
World War, to denote a possible future society. At the heart of this
utopian mapping was a vision of a renaissance in the small artisan
workshop, replacing the factory in a socioeconomic order
characterised by the decentralisation of power. The irony of Bell's
censure of this vision, as Krishan Kumar has noted, is that there
is a far greater degree of convergence between the post-First World
War and Second World War versions of the postindustrial thesis
than the Harvard sociologist would probably care to admit (Kumar
1978, p. 314). Bell is consistently hostile towards the romantic shades
of a classical Marxist mapping of a possible postcapitalist space and
yet his own cartography displays key elements of socialist aspiration:
the overthrow of a military-industrial complex, the withering away
of capital and the social ownership of welfare.

Postindustrialism often manifests itself as a utopian geography.
That Bell is keen to distance himself from the ecstatic fringes of
this tendency is evident from his attack on Kahn and Wiener's *The
Year 2000*. This work predicted the arrival of a post-scarcity
economy by the turn of the millennium. It was packed with
reassuring visions of futuristic landscapes across which cybernetic
automation technologies permit 'almost unlimited productive

capacity' (Bell 1974, p. 38) and the only difficulties confronted were to do with the administration of abundance. Bell dismisses this thesis as simply a science fiction of the 1960s, one which was brought back to earth by the sudden rediscovery of the limits to growth in the early 1970s. However, much of his own argument is founded upon a similar assumption of progressive affluence: '[western society] has mastered a secret denied to all previous societies – a steady increase of wealth and a rising standard of living by peaceful means' (*ibid.*, p. 274). Bell's own utopian leanings are also manifested in a vision of the coming of a great 'Scientific City of the future' (*ibid.*, p. 213), comparable to Bacon's 'Salomon's House', the key institution of a 'New Atlantis' (*ibid.*, pp. 44–5).

As it moves towards its conclusion this cartography becomes increasingly fanciful and appears to generate a momentum of its own. Bell posits three distinct stages in human history which have culminated in a contemporary epochal 'change in consciousness and cosmology' (ibid., p. 487). The first stage was the era in which man moved only in the natural world. Next came the time of *homo faber* – man the maker – when the environment was transformed into a manufactured second nature, a world of machines. Now, in the postindustrial age, the 'constraints of the past vanish with the end of nature and things' and as man is returned to himself, life becomes 'a game between persons' (*ibid.*, p. 488). There are three concomitant geographical ontologies in this evolution: originally, reality was defined as nature; during the industrial age it became 'technics', an environmental second skin of mechanical forms; but, in the postindustrial age, it has become nothing less than the social world itself. As its vision of the passage from the necessity of nature and the reign of machines to a non-alienated social world emerges, Bell's cartography of the postindustrial society suggests nothing less than the imminent conquest of reification.

If it provides a critique of contemporary shortcomings and recognises the possibilities for radical change, utopian writing can be an oppositional cultural practice. However, as previously mentioned, the most disturbing feature of Bell's utopian mappings is that he does not miss the underside of postindustrial landscapes so much as choose to marginalise it. Bell sees the migration of industrial functions, but continues to insist on its absolute disappearance. He sees the bureaucratisation of science, but continues to valorise the laboratory. He sees the marginalisation of women, the working classes, different racial and ethnic groups, but chooses to compose eulogies to those forces for 'inclusion' which are supposedly sweeping the postindustrial society. He sees the militarisation of public space in the Warfare state, but chooses to insist upon the emergence of a peaceful communal order.

As he casually sweeps aside crisis and conflict, poverty and waste, insisting that life has become a 'game amongst people', *forgetfulness* is revealed as the prime requisite for acceptance of Bell's mapping of postindustrial space. The subtitle of this work – 'a venture in social forecasting' – and its final section – 'an agenda for the future' – illustrate one of the devices by which this condition is encouraged. Postindustrial societies are often mapped in the future perfect; they distract from the real places of today with an enticing grammar of expectancy. Written during the war on Viet Nam and on the brink of energy crisis and economic recession, it is easy to understand how Bell's projections could have gained such currency in some quarters. This, of course, simply explains rather than excuses a methodology built upon the exclusion of all awkward contemporary sociospatial details for a utopian historiography of the future. The ideological imperative behind *The Coming of Post-Industrial Society* is the provision of a comforting vision of the future of America, placating anxieties fuelled by the problems suppressed within its analysis. Finally, Bell's own definition of ideology, as 'a set of formal justifications masking a reality', is perfectly applicable to his own thesis (*ibid.*, p. 386). The coming postindustrial landscape is a suburban sociological romance which achieves assurance through a culpable critical amnesia.

# CHAPTER 3

# How I Learned to Stop Worrying and Love the Mediascape: Marshall McLuhan

> The new media are not bridges between man and nature: they are nature.
>
> Marshall McLuhan,
> *Understanding Media* (1964), p. 14

Whilst Daniel Bell's mapping of the postindustrial landscape condones a selective critical amnesia, that of Marshall McLuhan encourages a condition approaching unconsciousness. The media guru's pronouncements on those technological forms which increasingly dominate space and its perception – television, radio, telecommunications, the automobile and an array of consumer gadgetry – undoubtedly contributed to their establishment as creditable components in the study of culture. However, a large part of his success in this respect can be traced to the blind visionary optimism which informs his work. His *oeuvre* reveals the development of a faith which enabled him to transcend the role of mere cultural analyst, for the mantle of a Whitmanian Poet-Priest, ecstatically embracing, magically and mythologically, the each and all of a high-tech second nature.

In terms of this development *Understanding Media* is the key document, since it represents the moment of McLuhan's conversion. This is the text in which he succumbs publicly to the exhilarations of futurism and learns to love the new technological hyperspace without question. Whilst Bell was insisting upon the increasing obsolescence of industrial machinery across the landscapes of postindustrial America, McLuhan was romanticising the rapid multiplication of new devices whose collective effect was to transform the knowledge society into a worldwide spiritual community, the 'global village':

> During the mechanical ages we had extended our bodies in space. Today, after more than a century of electric technology, we have extended our central nervous system itself in a global embrace,

abolishing both time and space as far as our planet is concerned. (*ibid.*, pp. 3–4)

McLuhan's understanding of mediascapes are traced back in an ambitious historiography to Genesis. In the time before the written word, speech, music and dance, acoustic and architectural space, were fused in an Edenic, mythic space. With the arrival of the serpentine phonetic alphabet, however, man was cast out from this prelapsarian utopia. Literacy is not interpreted by McLuhan as simply the ability to read and write. The 'technology' of the word, reinforced through print, traces all experience through the stencil of linearity, uniformity and repeatability. The result was the formation of a repressive 'Gutenburg Galaxy', of landscapes dominated by these principles, which culminated in the alienating spatial economy of industrialisation and the assembly line.

Throughout *Understanding Media* it is evident that McLuhan's interest in the effects of technological forms is not primarily social, nor political (in any direct sense) and certainly not economic. By their omission each of these aspects are reduced to epiphenomena. Instead, he concentrates upon the direct *physiological* impact of technology, the *places* it subsequently produces and their *spiritual* integrity. Thus, the phonetic alphabet, with its 'excessive' visual orientation, is seen to be the determining factor in the evolution of industrialised, spiritual wastelands. The written word, according to this crude semiotic determinism, fostered the formation of profane places in which 'Typographic Man' is divorced from the environment and from his own senses. This is elucidated by a favourite quotation from Yeats:

> Locke sank into a swoon;
> The garden died;
> God took the spinning jenny
> Out of his side. (cited in McLuhan 1964, p. 25)

The Lockean swoon is that hypnotic trance induced by the ascendancy of the visual component to sensory experience, concomitant with the evolution of print. This is why the garden (symbol of unified consciousness and pre-Gutenburg harmony) died. Its demise, however, corresponds to the dominance of *mechanical* technologies only (the spinning jenny of industrialisation), and with the arrival of new postindustrial electric media the garden is restored to bloom.

Alongside Yeats, McLuhan makes use of the work of a number of artists in his analysis, especially James Joyce. One quotation from *Finnegan's Wake* appears no less than six times: 'The West shall shake the East awake/ While ye have night for morn' (p. 35 *et al.*). This phrase is appropriated as a Whitmanesque prophecy that the

westernisation of the east shall be accompanied by an orientalisa-
tion of the west by new technology. Across the mediascape westerners
are shaken out of their typographic trance by electronic implosion.
Consequently, this resurrects 'the spell and incantation of the tribe
and the family to which men readily submit ... [returning us to]
the charmed circle of tribal magic' (McLuhan 1964, pp. 185–6).
As well as blurring the boundaries between east and west, civilised
and tribal places (in McLuhan's macrogeographical, colonialist
formulation), the new mediascapes are the site of a collapsing of
distinctions between art and lifestyle, since, in the global village,
there is no true art because everybody is engaged in making art.
McLuhan goes on to exceed even these extremes of technopastoral
idealism, advancing beyond Daniel Bell's belief that the differences
between art and business, campus and community are diminishing,
to assert that, from the launching of the first satellite, the globe itself
has been aestheticised, 'translating the entire world into a work of
art' (*ibid.*, p. 97):

> If the work of the city is the remaking or translating of man into
> a more suitable form than his nomadic ancestors achieved,
> then might not our current translation of our entire lives into
> the spiritual form of information seem to make of the entire globe,
> and of the human family, a single consciousness? (*ibid.*, p. 61)

Beyond the rhetorical extravagance of this vision, McLuhan's
major claim, concerning the actual material benefits of life in the
global village, is essentially twofold. *Understanding Media* proposes
that the new planetary spatial economy is distinguished by greatly
increased levels of participation and the rapid decentralisation
of power:

> Electric speeds create centres everywhere. Margins cease to
> exist on the planet ... In an electric structure there are, so far
> as the time and the space of the planet are concerned, no
> margins. There can, therefore, be dialogue only among centres
> and among equals. (*ibid.*, pp. 91; 273)

Collectively, these assertions of a 'third technological revolution'
illustrate the extent to which McLuhan attempts to confuse an ideal
with the actual state of affairs. There is validity in the claim that
new vortices of power are evolving. However, the vision of a
decentralised and participatory global hyperspace obscures the
economic and military colonialism, as well as the scientific and
technological imperialism, which is at the core of the international
restructuring of capitalist spatial relations. The migration of
industrial capability to the developing world, discussed in relation
to Bell's mappings, has resulted precisely in the accentuation of a
core-periphery model of economic geography.

What can make some of McLuhan's propositions seem appealing is his apparent attention to the specificity of those forms of media which constitute a second nature. McLuhan draws intricate distinctions between print, telegraph, radio and television and their iconic impact upon space, both physical and perceptual. However, these media are never really understood as *practices*. Instead, they are interpreted as catalysts to psychospiritual ways of seeing. Media are understood as devices which impact upon generalised human organisms in generalised physical environments, as opposed to specific groups in specific geographical locations. The cartographic imagination which informs *Understanding Media* is essentially idealist and fails to recognise the determining significance of material conditions. In parts, there is even an unmistakably metaphysical tinge to McLuhan's superficially materialist account of past and present mediascapes. *Understanding Media* concludes by proclaiming an end to history itself in the golden age of the global village. It is both ironic and disturbing that this utopian vision is projected from a methodological base which is largely immune to geographical and historical actuality. As with the utopian impulses in Bell's postindustrial mappings, McLuhan's discourses on the future perfect need to be recognised less as a means of analysing space, than as a means of sanctioning its contemporary restructuring. The recourse to utopian celebration in both Bell's and McLuhan's cartographies constitutes a covert suppression of real places and a calculated cancellation of contemporary struggle. During the 1960s and early 1970s, as McLuhan prophesied the advent of a harmonious global village, the social benefits of contemporary technological advance were being associated with a range of crises: hot and cold wars, environmental waste and pollution, changes in working conditions, economic and cultural imperialism and the centralisation of control over information. Within this context McLuhan's mappings can be read as an attempt to massage away anxieties with promises of a not-too-distant future of community, participation and stability. Ultimately, McLuhan is significant less as a sociologist than as a sociological phenomenon.

*Understanding Media*'s account of the third technological revolution insists upon the arrival of a new age of information, on the depoliti- cisation of society, the dissolution of capital and class structure and the unlimited productive potential of automation. Each of these facets must be interpreted as a signifier of the continuity between the cartography of the global village and Bell's postindustrial society. Although McLuhan's currency as cultural capital has depreciated dramatically since the early 1970s, representations of technology as a universal panacea for all sociospatial difficulties continue to flourish. Understanding McLuhan therefore can be a useful starting point from which to begin to demystify post-McLuhan formulations of this mythology.

The cornerstone of many postindustrial mappings of American space, a belief in the obsolescence of capital and its associated conflicts, should not be misconstrued as simply part of an abstract academic debate. Since the monopolisation of political power by the New Right in North America and the UK in the 1980s, there has been a degree of convergence between governmental economic policy and visions of the postindustrial future. Reaganism, Thatcherism and (to a lesser extent) their successors, have involved economic strategies entirely consonant with the imperatives of the global village and the information city. For example, in both their rhetoric and practice, western governments and multinational corporations have used variations on this thesis to legitimate the 'shedding' (a favoured naturalising metaphor) of jobs in the manufacturing sector.

Most of the homages to a brave new postindustrial world were produced during the period of postwar long-wave growth, before the widespread economic and energy crises of the early 1970s. But, at the apex of the boom–bust cycle during the 1980s, such ideas witnessed a resurgence. In 1987, in a *New Society* article, Daniel Bell could pick up where McLuhan left off and once again declare with confidence that

> by 2013, the third technological revolution –the joining of computers and telecommunications ... into a single yet differentiated system, that of the 'wired nation' and even the 'world society' – will have matured. (Bell 1987, p. 42)

The utopian vision of an essentially static futureworld, composed of landscapes across which massive computer-programmed, self-reproducing cybernetic systems whirr away unattended – providing all possible goods and services and leaving the post-work force surfing the Net in a creative, labour-free existence – is a science-fiction fantasy utilised both in the halls of academia and the corridors of power.

The self-imposed class myopia of the prophets of postindustrialism prevents them from having to examine the damaging side-effects of advances in technology. By isolating it from its central position in economic organisations geared towards the maximisation of profit and military institutions involved in the manufacture of death, they can confidently proclaim the imminent universalisation of landscapes serviced by automation. However, in a world economy characterised by gross inequalities in the distribution of wealth and resources, the developed regions, with their superior postindustrial economies, are likely to employ all their advantages to strengthen the relations of dominance and dependence between themselves and the developing world.

In *Late Capitalism*, published in the same year as *The Coming of Post-Industrial Society*, Ernest Mandel provided a detailed account of the actual, as opposed to the promissory composition of commodity production as a 'contradictory unity of non-, semi-, and fully-automated enterprises' (Mandel 1975, p. 206). He also proposed that automated industry represents, if anything, a purer and more refined stage in the evolution of capitalism; not its successor but its saviour:

> Late capitalism, far from representing a 'post-industrial' society, thus appears as the period in which all branches of the economy are fully industrialised for the first time ... mechanisation, stan-dardisation, over-specialisation and parcellisation of labour, which in the past deformed only the realm of commodity production in actual industry, now penetrate all sections of social life. (*ibid.*, pp. 191; 387)

Essentially, the postindustrial society, like the global village, must be read as a neoconservative cipher which cloaks the extension of the logic of industrial capital into superstructural spaces. To rest content with the utopian promises of Bell and McLuhan, by learning to love the media and accept the ideology of the end of ideology, is to provide precisely those conditions under which the extension of this logic into previously uncommodified areas will continue.

CHAPTER 4

# Everything Solid Melts into Signs:
# Jean Baudrillard

In a review of *Understanding Media*, for *L'Homme et la Société* in 1967, Jean Baudrillard reproached McLuhan for his crude technological determinism. He was especially critical of the celebrated slogan, 'the medium is the message', which he deemed to be 'the very formula of alienation in a technical society' (Baudrillard 1967, p. 227). Since this early article, however, once radical fervour within the French intelligentsia was dampened by the disappointments of 1968, Baudrillard's interpretations of the technical society have increasingly insisted upon the obsolescence of critical terminology associated with the concept of alienation and have converged with many of McLuhan's key formulations. In some intellectual cadres Baudrillard has emerged as the heir to McLuhan's mantle of the postindustrial society's pre-eminent media guru. My intention in this section is to trace the loci and lacunae of Baudrillard's seductive postmodern cartographies. I begin with a synopsis of their evolution, as an interpretative frame through which to view *America*, a key text for the maturation of mappings of the postindustrial landscape.

## The semioticisation of space

Summarising Baudrillard's ideas is a difficult task. His writing, since the mid-1970s in particular, has been characterised by an aggressively anti-hermeneutic stance. Baudrillard's work glides vertiginously through protean political positions, flaunting its indeterminacy, resisting reasoned analysis. It dispenses, when it is expedient, with the critical orthodoxies associated with Enlightenment rationality. Nonetheless, given his currency as cultural capital, it remains imperative to grasp the central elements of his cultural (anti-) theory. The curve of Baudrillard's career mirrors aspects of both Bell's and McLuhan's – specifically, the former's abdication of critical responsibility and the latter's embrace of a highly aestheticised cultural theory. The centrepiece of my argument is that Baudrillard's development, from a recognisably neo-Marxist perspective, to a postmodern pataphysic, constitutes the contemporary culmination and dystopian mirror-image of postindustrial cartography in the social sciences.[1]

In the early works *The System of Objects* and *Consumer Society*, Baudrillard insists upon the postwar appearance of a profoundly original geography. In the new environment, dominated by a second nature of technological forms and artificial materials, consumption is the axial principle. In the wake of the Second World War, advanced industrial societies achieved the full implementation of a spatial and economic model which surfaced initially in the 1920s in North America, but was postponed by the Depression and global conflict. This model entailed a fundamental shift in the ruling logic of capitalism's production of space, away from the mass manufacture of goods to the generation and control of mass consumption. Crucially, in these early texts, Baudrillard interprets the extension of the process of rationalisation, from the realm of productive forces into that of consumption, as a continuation of the logic of industrial capital. In his critique of an *advanced* industrial society, Baudrillard describes a spatial economy within which all objects are defined and related by the code of commodity consumption. It should be stressed that, according to this critique, the consumer is a produced object among produced objects.

This thesis utilises the Saussurean schema of *parole* (as a system of self-differentiating signs) in relation to the explosive expansion of commodities in advanced industrial societies. Baudrillard also supplements the critical concepts of exchange- and use-value with that of 'sign-value'. At this early stage in his work Baudrillard's formulations are not intrinsically anti-Marxist; rather they can be interpreted as an effort to integrate radical social theory with semiology. However, in Baudrillard's subsequent work, social relations and economic activity are increasingly marginalised by a fixation on the signification of the commodity as opposed to the commodification of the sign. Production is dislodged from centre-stage by an emergent regime of signification and the combination of signs and codes which programme the social order are deemed to possess an autonomous logic. The era of capital makes way for the time of the sign. This ditching of human agency in the production of space is reminiscent of McLuhan's insistence upon the self-regulatory logic of technological development and represents the

---

1. My use of the term 'pataphysics' is indebted to Douglas Kellner's analysis in *Jean Baudrillard: From Marxism to Postmodernism and Beyond* (1989, pp. 162–5). Kellner draws a fascinating and largely convincing parallel between Baudrillard and Alfred Jarry: 'Baudrillard's universe is a totally absurd place in which objects rule in mysterious ways, and people and events are governed by absurd and ultimately unknowable interconnections ... Like Jarry's, Baudrillard's universe is ruled by surprise, reversal, hallucination, blasphemy, obscenity and a desire to shock and outrage' (pp. 162–3).

moment of Baudrillard's departure from a recognisably Marxist
critical tradition.

The turn to language itself, to an interrogation of sign, discourse
and text in cultural studies and the social sciences, is typically
appraised in one of two mutually exclusive ways. First, it is seen
as a radical return to the very roots of cultural politics, to that through
which history is always already articulated. Alternatively, it is
viewed as a reactionary introversion, inspired by a French
intelligentsia disillusioned by 1968, when the perceived inability
to intervene effectively in the material world, initiated a mass
retreat to the material word. Whilst Baudrillard's focus upon the
semiotics of the consumer city of signs may have initially been
galvanised by the promises of the first position, the extent of his
subsequent fixation upon the sign certainly owes something to the
disappointment of the second position.

That the Baudrillard thesis is a variant on classical postindustrial
cartography is clear from the importance he ascribes to the transition
from a 'metallurgic society' (in which space is organised around
industrial production) to a '*semiurgic* society' (in which spatial
relations are decentred by the flow of signs and information)
(Baudrillard 1975, p. 185). In 'Design and Environment, or How
Political Economy escalates into Cyberblitz', the transformation
is traced back to the Bauhaus. The German school of architectural
design, whose own origins are left uninvestigated, is seen to have
initiated the practice of relating to objects as 'pure signs' (as
opposed to commodities) and thus to have begun a 'universal
semantisation of the environment' (*ibid.*). Political economy is
therefore displaced by a multiplicity of semiotic codes which
dominate all areas of sociospatial organisation:

> Everything belongs to design, everything springs from it, whether
> it says so or not; the body is designed; sexuality is designed,
> political, social and human relations are designed ... this 'designed
> universe' is what properly constitutes the environment. (*ibid.*,
> p. 186)

In this regime of signification, designer signs have floated free
from any material base and in a moment of sublimely poststructural
vertigo, Baudrillard suggests that the sign 'no longer designates
anything at all ... [but] refers back only to other signs. All reality
then becomes ... a structural simulation' (Baudrillard 1988b, p. 125).
Everything solid melts into signs; all extratextual realities are
dissolved into insignificance. It follows that the Baudrillardean
mapping of the landscapes of consumer capital constitutes a far more
monolithic and totalising design than the classical Marxist paradigm,
which much of his work during the 1970s was devoted to attacking.
The 'code' represents a master narrative entirely destructive of the

*différance* Baudrillard seeks to valorise elsewhere: it is a form of semiotic determinism at least as reductive as McLuhan's technological determinism.

In *The Mirror of Production* (1981), Baudrillard turns his back completely on Marxism as the disenchanted horizon of capital. Around the time of *Symbolic exchange and death* (1986b), he begins to suggest that truly revolutionary critics must not limit themselves to seeking simply a good use of the economy, but must become dedicated to the destruction of the very principle of production. To this end he offers 'symbolic exchange' as an authentically oppositional critical practice. In so far as it is defined, symbolic exchange would appear to be an anti-utilitarian credo, one which consists of the cherishing of whatever is deemed by the dominant culture to be without worth. It involves a lyrical evocation of 'waste', 'excess', 'sacrifice' and 'destruction', all that which is polysemic and founded upon 'ritual', 'repetition', 'seduction', 'defiance' and 'death'. As is characteristic of his work after the mid-1970s, Baudrillard adroitly avoids the provision of singular, determinate definitions of key terms in the lexicon of symbolic exchange. Apparently it is not necessary either to explain precisely how symbolic exchange will prove to be subversive. Tantalisingly, it is suggested that this is a practice which was central to the social activity of pre-industrial communities. Baudrillard and McLuhan cross over once more, with a vision, beneath all the futurist trappings, of the overthrow of a productivist economy as a reinstatement of tribal spaces, as a revolutionary *return* to the conditions of pre-industrial existence.

Behind Baudrillard's nostalgic reclamation of a land ravaged by productivism through symbolic exchange – indeed, behind much of his later writing – Nietzsche is clearly a major presence. Examined from the perspective of Bloom's 'anxiety of influence' thesis, one might suggest that Baudrillard, during his *Mirror* phase, replaces one intellectual father (Marx) for another (Nietzsche). There is considerable irony in this oedipal textual drama. As he sacrifices socialist science for Nietzchean play, Baudrillard fails to see that his radical antidote to capitalism reflects its fundamental dynamic more clearly than the Marxist mirror of production. Symbolic exchange, with its valorisation of waste, destruction and death, sacrifice, expenditure and excess, is simply consumer capitalism distilled into its purest form. The original meaning of 'consume', of course, is 'to lay waste'. Each year, across the landscapes of North America, consumer capitalism conducts its symbolic exchanges on a scale which Baudrillard could only dream of.

In *The System of Objects* Baudrillard's proclamations about the changes taking place in advanced industrial society were tethered to a sense of an underlying continuity:

Everything is in motion, everything is changing, everything is being transformed and yet nothing changes. Such a society, thrown into technological progress, accomplishes all possible revolutions, but they are revolutions upon itself. Its growing productivity does not lead to any structural change. (Baudrillard 1968, p. 217)

In his writings since the early 1970s, an acute semiotic and technological mesmerisation loosens this mooring and a sense of irrevocable rupture with the past comes to the fore. The era of industrial capitalism geared towards production and accumulation *has* passed. In its place stands a society saturated by signs and simulacra, bombarded by cyberblitz and undergoing implosion, moving in time to the pulse of new electronic technologies:

The city is no longer the politico-industrial zone that it was in the nineteenth century, it is the zone of signs, the media and the code. (Baudrillard 1981, p. 60)

In his attempt to articulate the conditions which accompany the transition from modernist landscapes of industrial production to a postmodern hyperspace of electronic simulation, McLuhan becomes an increasingly conspicuous presence in Baudrillard's work. Both subscribe to a technological formalism which freezes analysis at the point of the device itself. The signs of the culture industry, like all other signs across the textualised hyperspace of postindustrialism, exchange exclusively amongst themselves. Under the guise of a technological materialism, the perspective which privileges the medium over the message seeks to suppress the materiality of relations within the culture industry. Simultaneously, it ignores the specificity of media practices by reducing them to a single form with a universal sensory impact, and thus once more reinforces that obliteration of difference which Baudrillard laments elsewhere as a consequence of high-tech implosion.

It is important to emphasise that Baudrillard's appropriation of key McLuhanite ideas does not extend to an embrace of his predecessor's futuristic exuberance. In some respects Baudrillard is less McLuhan's successor than his nemesis. The mediascape is figured as a place of futility and despair, one in which cybernetics and telecommunications have colonised social space, reconstructing it in their own conditioning image. When Baudrillard proclaims the 'end of alienation', it is indicative of his sense of the passing of a 'self', as conventionally defined, with which to experience alienation in the first place. Baudrillardean nihilism is at least the equivalent in its intensity of McLuhanite optimism: the post-alienation electronic utopia, the global village, in which humans fuse with each other and their technologies in a spiritual homecoming, is supplanted by an anti-Eden, whose subjectless subjects are programmed by the signs, simulacra and media they have loosed upon themselves.

One of Baudrillard's key borrowings from McLuhan is the concept of 'implosion'. This is understood as the abolition of the space between the real and its reproducible representations. Telecommunications technology has obliterated private and public spaces. Consequently, possibilities for social interaction have disappeared, as industreality has imploded into the transparent depthlessness and instantaneity of the mediascape. It follows that the media does not simply transmit an *a priori* reality; rather its signs are doubly real, or, as Baudrillard has it, 'hyperreal'. In this context he interrogates the symbolic imperatives of Disneyland, as a geographical testament to the reign of the hyperreal. This is a place which consists of 'simulacra' (the perfect copy for which no original has ever existed) and which promotes its fantastical status as a cloaking device

> to conceal the fact that it is the 'real' country, all of 'real' America, which *is* Disneyland ... Disneyland is presented as imaginary in order to make us believe that the rest is real, when in fact all of Los Angeles and the America which surrounds it are no longer real, but of the order of the hyperreal and of simulation. (Baudrillard 1983, p. 25)

Initially Baudrillard's project involved the deconstruction of Marxist and Freudian paradigms – to smash the mirror of production with symbolic exchange and the mirror of desire with simulation. These models are founded upon a nineteenth-century hermeneutic of suspicion, a paranoid quest for the hidden sign which is inappropriate to the postindustrial time of the sign, to a postmodern hyperspace, in which everything is obscenely and ecstatically visible. In his work during the 1980s, Baudrillard's increasingly hermetic and cynically apolitical *écriture* has come to be dominated by this fatalism and the notion of *'le cristal se venge'* – the revenge of the object upon the subject. That this situation should be greeted by Baudrillard with a distinctly Jacobean glee is not surprising when one considers that he had been conducting last rites over the subject for more than a decade. *'Le cristal se venge'* is simply the culmination of a tendency evident from the outset of his career: the subject has consistently been dwarfed by the spaces into which s/he is inserted, be that the realm of the commodity, the sign or code, the media, simulacra or the hyperreal. As his work has assumed a less ashamedly metaphysical caste, this process is now translated as an ahistorical abstraction known simply as *'le cristal'*.

*Fatal Strategies* focuses the issue: 'The desire of the subject is no longer at the centre of the world, it is the destiny of the object' (Baudrillard 1984, p. 11). Baudrillard's 'progression', from an examination of the *system* of objects to a declaration of the *destiny* of the object, constitutes a recuperation of a mystical perspective. The roots of the object's destiny are traced to its own 'evil genius', to powerful forces beyond human agency which shape history. Such a development was latent in his early writing and more particularly in the conviction that the system could never be interpreted from the point of view of the subject, who ought to be recognised as an ideological mirage produced for the sustenance of the code. However, *Fatal Strategies* also invokes the logic of the reversal. Baudrillard invites the reader to submit completely, to pass over to the side of the object, but to do so with the promise that the perfection of reification will entail its inversion (*ibid.*, p. 181). This fatal strategy is reminiscent of McLuhan's injunction to go with the (high-tech) flow. Both positions are delivered from a perspective so Olympian that the politics of the ultra-radical and the ultra-reactionary become practically indistinguishable. Nowhere is this convergence more evident than in Baudrillard's mappings of America.

## On a road to nowhere

The reader's passage through *America* begins with a warning: 'Caution: Objects in the mirror may be closer than they appear' (Baudrillard 1988a, p. 1). This prefatory remark signals two key elements of the ensuing textual journey. Baudrillard's appropriation of the sign written on the mirror of his rented Chrysler is an indication of his intention to pursue an aestheticised approach to cultural analysis. Concurrent with this implicit formal declaration, the message itself can be decoded as the *raison d'être* of the entire journey – for this is the land in which the evil genius of the object is most spectacularly realised. America is offered as a mirror into which the western world can gaze and watch its future rapidly accelerating towards it. Its cities, in particular New York and Los Angeles, are deemed to be 'at the centre of the world' (*ibid.*, p. 24), but, in accordance with the dictates of an aesthetic approach, the criteria for this judgement is withheld. In the context of Baudrillard's previous writings, it might be assumed that this is in no sense a reference to the economic position of the United States. Rather, it would appear that America is located as the globe's paradigmatic geography, that space in which the developments which Baudrillard charted elsewhere can be encountered in their purest form. Landscapes here exist as photography, events as television: 'America is neither dream nor reality. It is a hyperreality' (*ibid.*, p. 28). This land 'has something about it of the dawning of the universe' – a dawning practically indistinguishable from an apocalypse to

Baudrillard's millennial vision (*ibid.*, p. 23). Baudrillard works hard to generate an ambience of mystery around the places he surveys and to reveal the landscape's inherent hostility to cartographic precision. To trace the contours of American space, it seems, is to outline the shape of things to come, which will entail a decimation of everything that has previously been known.

The tour begins with Baudrillard speeding across the desert, over the sierras of New Mexico and the Texan hills. Somewhere between Las Vegas and Salt Lake City, poised on the geographical cusp of narcissistic indulgence and Puritan restraint, Baudrillard is visited by a vision of the desert's 'geological monumentality' and 'magic'. Such a spectacle inspires a question: 'What is man if the signs which predate him have so much power?' (*ibid.*, p. 3). The source of the landscape's power lies in the fact that its signs are 'void of all meaning, arbitrary and inhuman, and one crosses without deciphering them' (*ibid.*, p. 127). Far from being a radical antipode to the social spaces of the American city, Baudrillard offers the desert as a paradigm for the necessary negation of the social, the 'ideal schema of humanity's disappearance' (*ibid.*, p. 19). This crossing thus becomes a rite of passage in which celebrants can pass over to the side of the object, achieving

> deliverance from the organic ... [into a] phase of death in which the corruption of the body reaches completion ... the desert is a sublime form that banishes all sociality, all sentimentality, all sexuality. (*ibid.*, p. 41)

Surprisingly, Baudrillard chooses to forget that the prime touristscapes he is surveying, Death Valley and the Texan hills, are already inscribed with social significance through their innumerable media reproductions. Instead, in the desert sun, everything races towards a terminal vanishing point and the speed with which Baudrillard glides over arguments reproduces the automotive mode of motion. This is analysis on the road (to nowhere). The driver records the sights through the windscreen as a 'marvellously affectless succession of signs' (*ibid.*, p. 5). The movement of the car facilitates an experience of instantaneity over time as depth, of landscape surfaces over their histories. Driving becomes a 'spectacular form of amnesia' (*ibid.*, p. 8). Since one leaves no trace, one partakes of an 'aesthetics of disappearance' and the 'evaporation of meaning' (*ibid.*, p. 9). Baudrillard's kenotic drive is fuelled by a lexicon of disconnected signifiers as evocative as they are indeterminate: silence, absence, disappearance, purity. Of course, to inquire into their precise meaning, or to challenge the key terms in this cartography, is to reintroduce precisely those ideological chimera whose dissipation *America* is devoted to. Baudrillard's lyrical repetitions are designed to sacrifice analytical depth for

emotional charge, as the tourist contents himself by playing with
America's mythological surfaces (the Desert and the City, Space,
Speed and Movement).

When Baudrillard leaves the desert for the city, discarding the
'driver' persona for that of the postmodern *flâneur*, America's
urban spaces are interpreted exclusively as the reproduction of a
mythical desertscape, as the 'finished form of the future catastrophe
of the social' (*ibid.*, p. 5). Los Angeles does not exist in contradistinction to the wilderness that encloses it; rather, it mirrors its
absences. The city is mapped through the stencil of a purifying
extermination of all human meaning, a liturgical expulsion delivered
with near-visionary intensity. To go along for the ride here is to be
a hostage to Baudrillard's coercive vision of America as an emblem
for everywhere, rather than the nowhere he has built around
himself.

> It is because you are delivered from all depth there – a brilliant,
> mobile, superficial neutrality, a challenge to nature and culture,
> an outer hyperspace with no origin, no reference-points. (*ibid.*,
> p. 124)

Leaving his Chrysler behind, to stroll through the parks of Los
Angeles, provides Baudrillard with the opportunity to repackage
another hegemonic fable – California as the 'Land of Plenty':
'Curiously, in this world where everything is available in profusion,
everything has to be saved and economised' (*ibid.*, p. 40). Ecological
concern, exercise regimes and dieting are grouped together as
hangovers from Puritanism, anorexic reactions to overabundance:

> Of course our basic problem today is how to avoid becoming
> overweight ... [due to] the ease with which we now live ... we
> no longer have any awareness of death, since we have passed
> over to a state where life is excessively easy. (*ibid.*, pp. 42–3)

Baudrillard's view of the state of California, enforced through
collusive and coercive pronouns, is only made tenable in the
mappings of *America* by some critical geographical omissions.
During his travels through the Sunshine State, Baudrillard takes
in the postindustrial heartland only – the parks, the mall and the
media, the suburbs and the loci of yuppie culture. There are no
detours through those allegedly obsolescent relics from the 'orgy
of modernity': he steers clear of the industrial frostbelt and the poorer
inner-city regions. The tour is confined to the scenic deserts and
its postindustrial oases, to sanitised white suburbs and centres for
Sunshine economic interest. Baudrillard's mapping then, like those
of Bell and McLuhan, privileges those places in which the mundane
crises of late capitalism can be forgotten: Irvine, the 'new Silicon
Valley', the Salk Institute, university campuses, the Bonaventure

Hotel and Disneyland. His soundbites – 'life is excessively easy' –
can only be entertained by choosing to forget the margins of
capitalist geography: the spaces occupied by the Los Angeles'
underclass, the sites of the thriving sweatshop industry, police and
gang violence, drug problems and collapsing infrastructure.

Upon his arrival in New York there is little indication of any
memories returning of the underside of the postindustrial geography
of hyperreality. Baudrillard continues to forget the crises confronted
by the American city. New York remains one of the world's leading
financial centres and is home to the headquarters of powerful
media corporations. However, the core of the 'Big Apple' is rotten.
The city is increasingly the site of scenes of squalor and deprivation
traditionally associated with the Third World: squatters' camps,
mass homelessness and unemployment, deteriorating infrastructure.
It is precisely these aspects of the city which Baudrillard chooses
to ignore. New York is represented as 'the centre of the world', a
'place of total electric light' (*ibid.*, p. 14). The postmodern *flâneur*
cruises the streets and revels in the scenes and signs that surround
him: 'it is always turbulent, lively, kinetic and cinematic' (*ibid.*, p.
16). There is an accumulation of asides which refer rather obliquely
to the city's urgent socioeconomic difficulties, but they are hurriedly
relegated to instances of local colour. Thus, he notes that 'modern
demolition ... [is] a marvellous modern art form' (*ibid.*, p. 17); that
queues outside soup kitchens rival those outside the fashionable
restaurants; and that the mad seem to have been let out on to the
streets – casually erasing the significance of housing shortages,
hunger and cut-backs in federal welfare provision. Whilst Bell
chose to ignore the conditions of urban crisis and McLuhan to
transcend them, Baudrillard, on the rare occasions that it merits
attention, actively seeks to aestheticise them. The city 'acts out its
own catastrophe' and the spectator gleefully relishes its 'sparkle and
its violence', devouring the 'insolent beauty' of urban crisis (*ibid.*,
p. 18). Walter Benjamin, in his account of modernist *flânerie* in the
cities of industrial capital, suggested that the aestheticisation of
politics and history was an essentially fascist impulse. Baudrillard's
mapping of the landscapes of hyperreal America are undoubtedly
consonant with the totalitarian dismissal of the country's disinherited
and its least habitable regions by the New Right who were enjoying
political ascendancy during his visits.

The explanation given for the turn to an aestheticised cultural
theory in *America* centres upon a hostility towards conventional
academic modes of inquiry:

> No one is capable of analysing it [hyperreal America], least of
> all the American intellectuals shut away on their campuses,
> dramatically cut off from the fabulous concrete mythology

> developing all around them ... Where the others spend their time in the libraries, I spend mine in the deserts and on the roads. Where they draw their material from the history of ideas, I draw mine from what is happening now, from the life of the streets, the beauty of nature. (*ibid.*, pp. 23; 63)

Whilst one cannot analyse landscape, one can be initiated into its mysteries by, in a celebrated American gesture, becoming the Wanderer. Somewhat unexpectedly, Baudrillard aligns himself with an American romantic and anti-intellectual tradition. Drawing a distinction between the immediacy of lived experience and its theoretical signifiers (something which the early Baudrillard would surely have frowned upon), he appears to suggest that, even in the context of total simulation, some spaces and forms of experience are more real than others. Baudrillard's anti-intellectualism valorises an alternative way of seeing which fuses elements of Emersonian transcendentalism and Beat philosophy. He leaves the library behind to go on the road and, like the Pranksters on the bus, he gives out cool advice to each and all – 'abdicate normal rules – go with the flow of images' (*ibid.*, p. 23).

*America* thus sanctions the transition to aesthetic modes of perception and persuasion, an exotic intermingling of the literary and the sociological. At precisely the same time, however, *America* also attacks the notion that the aesthetic possesses a radical cultural instrumentality:

> art no longer contests anything, if it ever did ... [modern art] is an art of collusion *vis-à-vis* the contemporary world. It plays with it ... it never disturbs the order, which is also its own ... truly, art can no longer act as radical critique or destructive metaphor. (*ibid.*, p. 48)

The extension of this claim to Baudrillard's own aestheticised social theory might provide a rationale for the abdication of critical responsibility in the cartography of *America* and for its ecstatic embrace of a playful nihilism. 'It has all been done ... It has destroyed itself. All that remains is playing with the pieces' (*ibid.*, p. 123).

The essential impulse behind Baudrillard's playful mapping appears to be self-erasure. Throughout *America*, ideas and images incessantly cancel each other out. One of his favoured tropes is the oxymoron: thus, the repeated 'fragile meta-stability' (*ibid.*, p. 118 *et al.*). The land is described as a 'paradise', a 'utopia', a seductive and exhilarating postmodern playground of signs. It is also a land of death, of excrement and repression, a graveyard of meaning and representation. The US is the 'utopia of wealth, rights, freedom, the social contract and representation'; it is also the 'end of representation ... the subject, the neutralisation of all value, the death of culture' (*ibid.*, p. 118). It is, in other words, whatever Baudrillard wishes it to be. The flaunting of an anti-hermeneutic such as this is occasionally provocative, more often it is simply perplexing. It is, however, always geared towards the emptying of meaning from *America* and America. Ultimately, Baudrillard seems to yearn for a purifying silence, the stillness of the desert, for something beyond the clatter and babble of simulated sights, sounds and signs.

*America* opens with a vanishing point and closes with a silent centre-point of absence in the desert: the signs in between are saturated by an aesthetics of disappearance, the desertification of significance. The land is reduced to a 'giant hologram', a 'special lighting effect', high-tech metaphors which are indices of this cartography's contiguity with classical postindustrial cartography. It is a place where things seem to be made of 'a more unreal substance' (*ibid.*, p. 64). America's materiality is thus dissolved into a self-referential play of ghostly images and this etherealisation is the aim of *America*. A revised version of consensus is produced, in which all social relations, the circulation of capital and desire, all crisis and conflict, struggle, promise and hope dissipate in the white heat of a semiotic phantasmagoria. If the social logic of pre-industrial communities exhibited a marked fetishism of natural objects (moon and stars, sea and trees) and the industrial age was characterised by a fetishism of commodities (which failed to detect the machinations of capital beneath its seductive second skin), the postindustrial period has witnessed an increasing tendency towards the fetishisation of the privileged signs and images of a second nature.[2] In this respect Baudrillard's mapping of America as everywhere and nowhere is the culmination of tendencies evident throughout postmodern culture. All that is solid melts into signs – only to asphyxiate in simulation. *America* is the terminus of postindustrial mythology. This is the way the global village ends; not with a bang, but a simulated whimper.

2. The phrase, 'second skin', in relation to a description of the commodity, is borrowed here from Wolfgang Fritz Haug. In *Critique of Commodity Aesthetics: Appearance, Sexuality and Advertising in Capitalist Society*, Haug describes the commodity as a 'promissory second skin' (Haug 1984). I intend to utilise this suggestive definition in my readings of Pynchon, Auster, Phillips and *Blade Runner*.

# CHAPTER 5

# Mapping on the Left:
# Jameson, Harvey, Soja, Davis

If we want things to stay as they are, things will have to change.
                    Giuseppe di Lampedusa, *The Leopard* (1960), p. 47

Prophesy now involves a geographical rather than historical projection; it is space not time that hides consequences from us.
                    John Berger, *The Look of Things* (1971), p. 45

Bell, McLuhan and Baudrillard have viewed the landscapes of North America from divergent methodological perspectives. There is, however, a considerable degree of convergence between the representations of space allowed by neoconservative sociology, media mysticism and postmodern pataphysics. In postindustrial cartographies certain aspects of landscape and ways of seeing are foregrounded repeatedly. There is a remorseless standardisation of space as a consequence of the focus on totalised macrogeographical process (the postindustrial society, the global village, the political economy of the sign). This inability to attend to the geopolitics of microspaces is a necessary precondition for the millennial excesses, the utopian/dystopian extremes encouraged by these mappings. There is also an insistence upon the profound originality of contemporary developments, the subsequent obsolescence of conventional terminology within social science discourses (class and capital are no longer imposing presences in a spatial economy that has witnessed an end to ideology and alienation) and the need for aesthetic modes of contemplation.

The proponents of postindustrial cartographies follow the new middle classes in their mass migration to the suburbs. They insist that flows of capital have been replaced by a sea of signifiers and information, mediascapes and IT superhighways loom large, whilst factories and manufacturing industry have withered away. This ignores the extent to which many of the most conspicuous icons on the postindustrial horizon themselves originated on the factory floor. As Alex Callinicos argues in *Against Postmodernism*:

> The proliferation of phenomena of 'reproduction' (fashion, media, publicity, information and communication networks)

requires a vast expansion of material production; the greater circulation of images depends upon a variety of physical products – television sets, video-recorders, satellite discs and the like. More fundamentally, people do not live by MTV alone, but continue to have mundane needs for food, clothing and shelter which makes the organisation and control of production still the major determinant of the nature of our societies. (Callinicos 1984, p. 148)

Bell, McLuhan and Baudrillard all deny the structural integration of secondary and tertiary sectors, the interdependence of spaces devoted to production and consumption. In this, as in other respects, postindustrial cartographies are clearly consonant with the mappings of dominant ideology outside the academy. They provide institutional alibis for right-wing political hegemony through selective amnesia. Of course, such mappings have not existed in isolation. In fact, there has been an impressive resurgence of the geographical imagination amongst social and cultural critics on the left, especially since the late 1970s. Many of the places and people conspicuous by their absence from postindustrial cartographies are brought in from the margins by these critics.

In *Postmodernism, or, the Cultural Logic of Late Capitalism*, Fredric Jameson, a figure at the forefront of the current spatialisation of the Marxist critical tradition, declares:

I think it is at least empirically arguable that our daily life, our ·psychic experience, our cultural languages, are today dominated by categories of space, rather than time, as in the preceding period of high modernism. (Jameson 1991, p. 16)

In the original article of the same name, Jameson's recognition that any attempt to understand contemporary conditions and cultural production would 'necessarily have to raise spatial issues as its fundamental organising concern', led him to call for a 'new aesthetic of cognitive mapping', a cartography of a rapidly evolving 'postmodern hyperspace' (Jameson 1984a):

a new kind of spatial imagination capable of confronting the past in a new way and reading its less tangible secrets off the template · of its spatial structures – body, cosmos, city. (Jameson 1991, pp. 364–5)

This call has been echoed and answered by a number of prominent Marxist geographers and cultural critics. Ernest Mandel fuses geographical materialism with the more traditional historical variety in his investigation of the dynamics of uneven development in *Late Capitalism* (1975). David Harvey utilises a spatial hermeneutic in an economic geographer's perspective entitled *The Condition of*

*Postmodernity* (1989). In a study that admirably fuses the personal and the political there is Marshall Berman's (1982) mapping of three modernist cities (Petersburg, Paris and New York) as spaces in which 'all that is solid melts into air'.

In *Postmodern Geographies*, Edward Soja has analysed the work of these writers in terms of a 'geographical renaissance', overturning the subordination of space to history in post-Enlightenment social thought (Soja 1989; see especially chapter 2). Each of these writers focuses upon the persistent shaping influence of capital and on the fundamental politicality of space. To understand this and view space as a social product can be difficult. Dominant ideology enforces the physicalist conception of the geographical, which sees it, or rather fails to see it as anything other than a context for significant action. This is absurd when one considers how much of the environment is wo/man-made, a direct result of social action, translation and experience. But the physicalist perspective continues to dominate. Whilst the terms 'historical', 'political' and 'economic' all resonate with human action, the term 'spatial' typically evokes a geometrical image, something external to social context. 'Landscape' suffers a similar fate. Its common usage, derived from the visual arts, denotes all that which is not body or action, suggesting it to be neutral, asocial, passive. This conventional definition needs to be challenged by tracing the origins of the word. 'Land', in its early Gothic meaning, signified a 'plowed field', a human-worked or defined space; 'scape' meant a 'composition' or 'collection'. The term 'landscape', when used in critical cartographies on the left and in this study, is intended to denote this original sense, of landscape as a 'composition of socially constructed spaces'. As Soja argues, echoing John Berger and calling for a 'radical spatial praxis':

> We must be insistently aware of how space can be made to hide consequences from us, how relations of power and discipline are inscribed into the apparently innocent spatiality of social life, how human geographies are filled with politics and ideology. (Soja 1989, p. 25)

In *Place and the Politics of Identity*, Stephen Pile and David Keith term the proliferation of Marxist and neo-Marxist mappings and of geographical metaphors in a range of academic disciplines, a 'spatial vogue':

> There is a sense in which the geographical is being used to provide a secure grounding in the increasingly uncertain world of social and cultural theory. As some of the age-old core terms of sociology begin to lose themselves in a world of free-floating signification, there is a seductive desire to return to some vestige of certainty via an aestheticised vocabulary of *tying down*,

*mapping* our uncertainties and looking for *common ground*. (Pile and Keith 1993, p. 12)

Pile and Keith recognise the phenomenon, but offer little in the way of explaining it. The implication appears to be that in an indeterminate 'world of free-floating signification' (presumably Lyotard's postmodern society, with the carpet of master narratives whipped out from under it) this is largely an autonomous institutional response.

An alternative reading might suggest that this trend is part of a transatlantic exchange between intellectual traditions within left-wing writing dating back to Marx. Berman's studies are clearly indebted to the work of Walter Benjamin, particularly his eclectic readings of Paris and the figure of the *flâneur* in the poetry of Charles Baudelaire. Soja's comments on the politicality of space are often close to being verbatim transcriptions of the work of Henri Lefebvre, particularly *The Production of Space* (1991). Jameson's work, in tone if not always in substance, might similarly be seen to be indebted to the writing of Michel Foucault. In 'The Eye of Power' and elsewhere in his analyses of specific heterotopias and institutional spaces (the asylum, the clinic, the prison), Foucault regularly insisted upon the need to address the imbalance between history and geography in the academy:

> A whole history remains to be written of *spaces* – which would at the same time be the history of *powers* – from the great strategies of geopolitics to the little tactics of the habitat. (Foucault 1980, p. 149)

To trace the origins of this resurgence of the geographical imagination on the left to an independent institutional search for a new grand narrative, or, to an Old World tradition of critical cartographies, is, however, inadequate on its own. It is necessary to historicise the spatial vogue.

Amongst critics on the left the turn to geography has been universally applauded as a radical and emancipatory challenge to the hegemony of historicism and of capitalist spatiality. It can also be read, however, as symptomatic of a crisis of faith in the grand narratives of classical Marxist prophecy. It may be far from coincidental that the upsurge in interest in spatial politics follows rapidly on the heels of a series of devastating disappointments for the left on the historical stage: the failure of 1968 in France, the rise to politicocultural hegemony of the New Right since the late 1970s and the collapse of various communist regimes. Given these historical conditions, the classical Marxist narrative, based on the imminent collapse of capitalism and the inevitable seizure of the means of production by an enlightened proletariat, is jeopardised.

The displacement of attention from the temporal to the spatial must itself be interpreted, in part, as a historical phenomenon. The foregrounding of the processes by which capitalism restructures across space relieves the Marxist critic from the onerous responsibility of prophecy, of dating the demise of a devastatingly durable economic order.

This is by no means the only problem associated with the current vogue for mapping on the left. There is little or no consensus on the use-value (as opposed to its exchange value as cultural capital), of the term 'postmodern'. Soja claims to draw specifically postmodern cartographies, whilst Jameson and Harvey share a barely disguised disdain for all things postmodern and Berman practically denies its existence. This disciplinary migration has also involved the importation of what is often a rather crude reinvention of the classical Marxist base/superstructure paradigm. Jameson collapses a totalised 'postmodern hyperspace' into the economic system of late capitalism with minimal regard for the precise mechanisms of mediation and causality: market capitalism produced the spatial logic of the grid; monopoly capitalism produced a figurative space; and multinational capitalism produces a schizospace characterised by disorientating ruptures and fragmentation (Jameson 1991, p. 347). Similarly, beneath the stunning studies of David Harvey there lies a relatively elementary hypothesis: the instability of money within a flexible Fordist regime of accumulation promotes instability in space–time relations and instability in postmodern cultural production. The geographical, economic and cultural orders in left-wing cartographies are all too frequently folded into one another in conjunction with a totalised notion of 'experience'. All places become simply a palimpsest for Capital. These mappings have all of the weaknesses and strengths of traditional base/superstructure analysis. Like their neoconserv-ative counterparts producing reassuring (or, in Baudrillard's case, reassuringly apocalyptic) visions of postindustrial, post-capitalistic places, the broad brush strokes of macrogeographical models tend to obscure critical details and differences.

At the same time, there are disturbing elisions between the visions of place offered by the left and the ultra-right that need to be addressed. Jameson and Harvey often appear mesmerised by the awesome incorporative power of late capitalism and indulge in flights of distinctly Baudrillardean pessimism. Whilst insisting upon the necessity for action there is often doubt about the precise form that strategies for resistance and change must take and their possible effectiveness. Jameson's call for a new 'aesthetic' of cognitive mapping seems dangerously close to Baudrillard's own insistence on the need to switch to aestheticised modes of social theory.

Even more damning criticisms of mappings on the left focus upon their own telling lacunae: particularly gender and race. The almost universal marginalisation of sexual politics from discussions by male academics of 'postmodern hyperspace' might be read as a retreat, both from the disappointments of recent history and the challenge of feminism. Gillian Rose has attacked Edward Soja for suggesting that spatiality has been universally disregarded in favour of historicity. This ignores the fact that

> geography was central to anti-colonial movements from the eighteenth century onwards and as countless feminist historians argue, feminist projects too have been organised over geographical networks, have used institutional spaces in which to try and create women's culture, and have struggled against the patriarchal spatial imagery of the public/private division. (Rose 1991, p. 118)

In consideration of Harvey's work, Rose goes further and suggests that Marxist mappings reproduce phallocentric spatialities through a gynophobic demonisation of postmodern geographies:

> the postmodern [is] frothy, seductive, fecund, disruptive, charismatic, local, passionate, titillating. Harvey seems able to make sense of postmodernism only as a feminine Other, and hence his fear, his fascination and his rejection. (ibid., p. 120)

In *City of Quartz: Excavating the Future in Los Angeles*, Mike Davis reinforces the marginalisation of a specifically sexual politics within the consideration of postmodern geographies, but does manage to avoid many of the other drawbacks associated with critical cartographies on the left. First, Davis manages to combine an analysis of macrogeographical process with a meticulously researched attention to local detail. One of the advantages of this approach is that he is sensitive to the possibility of producing utopian/dystopian revisions of space that implicitly sanction political passivity:

> Soja and Jameson ... in the very eloquence of their different 'postmodern mappings' of Los Angeles, become celebrants of the myth [L.A. as dystopia]. The city is a place where everything is possible, nothing is safe and durable enough to believe in, where constant synchronicity prevails, and the automatic ingenuity of capital ceaselessly throws up new forms and spectacles – a rhetoric, in other words, that recalls the hyperbole of Marcuse's *One-Dimensional Man*. (Davis 1990, p. 86)

Second, as in the work of a number of postcolonial geographers, such as bell hooks, Davis recognises the critical significance of race and ethnicity to the sociospatial structuring of the postmodern American city. *City of Quartz* traces the reproduction of imperialist segregation at home. Whilst Jameson selects the Bonaventure

Hotel as the epicentre of postmodern hyperspace, Davis suggests that it is the savagery of its insertion into the city which captures the true spirit of urban renaissance. Jameson's views of landscape often seem to come from *within* the centres of luxury and affluence. Davis examines such sites in relation to the intensification of inequality and class and race conflict across Fortress LA.

*City of Quartz* provides a useful methodological paradigm for those interested in mappings of American space. It is essential to integrate analyses of micro- and macrogeographical processes – to uncover the specificity of individual sites (streets, suburbs, nature and second nature, national and individual bodies) whilst understanding their position within larger spatial systems. The following chapters offer an examination of the dialectical relations of power and resistance within these systems in the mappings of recent fiction and film.

# Part Two

# Plotting Postmodern Landscapes: Space and Fiction

CHAPTER 6

# Notes from Underground:
# Thomas Pynchon

Maps are too important to be left to cartographers alone.
J.B. Harley, 'Deconstructing the Map',
(1992), p. 231

In the task of establishing a radical political culture, spatial concerns
have become increasingly central. As mentioned in the last chapter,
Fredric Jameson explicitly recognises the significance of geography
in his work on postmodernism. The final clarion-call of his seminal
essay, 'Postmodernism, or, the Cultural Logic of Late Capitalism',
is for a series of maps of the new and rapidly evolving postmodern
hyperspace. In this Jameson may be missing a crucial point. The
dilemma facing the critic of late capitalism may not be an absence
of maps, so much as an inadequacy in our own cartographic skills.
I would suggest that the maps are already there, if we are prepared
to look for them. In fact, they can be uncovered in precisely those
postmodern art works Jameson spends much of his essay denouncing
as complicit with the (il)logic of late capitalism. The following
chapters will be devoted to an investigation of the geographical
imagination in works of postmodern fiction which constitute a
dissident remapping, of variable effectiveness, of the hegemonic fable
of North America as a postindustrial society.

Traditionally, maps, like the spaces they represent, have been
assumed to be fairly neutral affairs – objective and impartial
accounts of the external world. This notion needs to be challenged
at the outset of any attempt to map the landscapes of postmodernity
in recent fiction. Between 1650 and 1750 a 'reformation in
cartography' took place in Europe. This necessitated

> measurements of arcs of the meridian, to ascertain the size and
> figure of the earth; astronomical observations to determine
> accurately the position of a great number of places on the
> earth's surface, in latitude and longitude; and survey of large
> areas, by triangulation from precisely measured bases and with
> improved instruments. The number of positions accurately
> fixed increased from 40 in 1682 to 109 in 1706 (and by 1817
> to over 6,000). (Skelton 1972, p. 18)

51

This reformation is partially attributable to advances in the technologies of measurement and graphic reproduction, but it is also intimately connected to developments in the needs of merchants and monarchs, the Church and the State. During the Renaissance geographical knowledge became a valued commodity and maps evolved accordingly as instrumental tools, rather than purely objective guides. The rational representation of space must be related to the rise of a bourgeois-capitalist economic order. The mapping of the globe enabled space to be interpreted as available for appropriation by private ownership and established part of the material basis for the imperialist expansion of capitalist economic systems and social relations. Maps were not a capitalist invention, but the ones designed since the Renaissance were of a markedly different order: stripped of all elements of fantasy and religious significance (previously their primary function), devoid of any sense of the experiences involved in their production. Maps became strictly abstract and functional systems for the factual ordering of phenomena in space, defining territorial boundaries, property rights, trade and communication routes, domains of administration and of social control.

The central objective of any strategy of plotting postmodern landscapes in and through the landscapes of postmodern fiction, must be to assert, against the apparent neutrality of the map, the fundamental politicality of space. Space needs to be made visible by foregrounding its ideological content, to illustrate how it can be made to hide consequences, how relations of power and discipline are inscribed into the apparently innocent spatiality of our environment. For, as Lefebvre has argued:

> If space has an air of neutrality and indifference with regard to its contents and thus seems to be 'purely' formal, the epitome of rational abstraction, it is precisely because it has been occupied and used, and has already been the focus of past processes whose traces are not always evident on the landscape. (cited in Soja 1989, p. 62)

## Molemanship in the early fiction

In the opening paragraph of 'Postmodernism, or, the Cultural Logic of Late Capitalism', Jameson briefly mentions Thomas Pynchon, alongside William Burroughs and Ishmael Reed, as a 'postmodern author' (Jameson 1984a, p. 89). Given the frequency with which this label is attached to his writing, both by supporters and detractors, it might be more accurate to suggest that Pynchon is the quintessential postmodern author. In their collaborative study, *Writing Pynchon*, Alec McHoul and David Wills make a persuasive argument in favour of this suggestion and go on to assert that

> Pynchon's fiction may be more contribution to CLT (contemporary literary theory) – particularly under the name of Jacques Derrida and the later Roland Barthes – than 'object text' for it. (McHoul and Wills 1990, p. 2)

In illustration of their argument they link the strategic non-resolution of the code of enigma in Pynchon's *V* (where we never definitively discover who, or what, 'V' is), to the Derridean concept of 'adestination' (the fact that a letter can never truly arrive). Whilst it is advanced from an antithetical critical perspective (poststructuralism), this 'writing' of the author is precisely analogous, in both tone and resolution, to Jameson's argument that the postmodern text is that which is centreless, without destination or direction, literally pointless (although, unlike McHoul and Wills, he finds little to applaud in this). Both interpretations disregard the fact that Pynchon's quintessentially postmodern fiction is unified by a very precise sense of direction and purpose.

In Pynchon's first ever published work, a short story entitled 'The Small Rain', Nathan Levine describes himself as a Wanderer, one concerned with 'the essential problems of identity, not of the self so much as *an identity of place* and what right we really had to be anyplace' (Pynchon 1985, p. 49; emphasis added). This signals an acute geographical awareness in Pynchon's work from the outset, one which manifests itself not in 'adestinationality' or directionlessness, but in a continual movement *underground*, towards the critical contours of the postmodern landscape. Pynchon's fictions gravitate towards the contraries and contradictions of uneven development, towards the spaces occupied by the underclass and the disinherited and towards the omnipresence of forms of waste, which, potentially, may become oppositional objects once situated as anti-commodities.

In Pynchon's second published short story, 'Low-Lands', a discontented middle-class professional called Dennis Flange decides not to go to work, but to stay at home drinking and chatting with the garbage man. They are kicked out of the house by Flange's irate wife and seek refuge at the local garbage-tip, where they meet the black watchman/king of the dump, Bolingbroke, who, after telling them a series of fantastic sea-stories, puts them up for the night. Flange is gently awakened from his slumber by a midget called Nerrissa, who leads him to her underground room, through a labyrinth of secret tunnels, constructed during the Depression years by a terrorist group called 'The Sons of the Red Apocalypse' and currently occupied by gypsies, where, as the story ends, Flange decides to stay, 'for a while, at least' (*ibid.*, p. 75).

Plotting Flange's movement away from established society then, he leaves the world of the PMC (Professional-Managerial Class) for the company of eccentric non-conformists; he departs a mock-English cottage in the suburbs, furnished with unused $1000 stereo units, for the homes of the marginalised, of social derelicts and ostracised groups who, like gypsies, are defined in social terms as 'white trash'. Flange's geographical descent (from his house built above sea-level, to the dump and then on to Nerrissa's subterranean hideaway) is simultaneously a class descent. This 'molemanship', as he dubs it, through various strata of society's rubbish and its waste, into contact with the underclass and life in the low-lands of capitalist geographies, is the path typically chosen by each of Pynchon's major characters and the characteristic curve of all his subsequent plottings.

This gesture is repeated initially in the two short stories that followed 'Low-Lands'. In 'Entropy', we move from the neat, obsessively orderly penthouse apartment of Callisto to the lease-breaking party of messy Meatball Mulligan downstairs. Similarly, in 'Under the Rose', a spy drama, we meet Porpentine, self-acclaimed 'champion of cobwebs, rubbish, offscourings' (*ibid.*, p. 112). (This is just one of many potential saviours in Pynchon's work associated with the anti-commodity: Benny Profane in *V* and Tyrone Slothrop in *Gravity's Rainbow*, spend much of their time in sewers – literal, fantastical and metaphorical.)

The last of Pynchon's early short stories, 'The Secret Integration', like Samuel Clemens' seminal rites-of-passage tale, *The Adventures of Huckleberry Finn*, is concerned both with contemporary racial politics and the awkward passage from innocence to initiation. The narrative follows the adventures of a group of children in a small West Massachusetts town as they plot against the 'scaled-up world adults made' (*ibid.*, p. 135). The geography of this condensed *Bildungsroman* is organised around the structural opposition between a new housing estate which embodies the dominant principles of the 'world adults made' and the children's hideout. The rebellious gang plan their various campaigns from deep within a derelict mansion, the 'Big House', a place protected by a ghost and an exotic history which elicits a powerful 'feeling of ceremony' (*ibid.*, p. 156). The Big House can only be negotiated by passing through doorways 'where old velvet hung whose pile was worn away into maplike patterns, seas and land masses taught in no geography their schools knew' (*ibid.*, p. 157). This is the children's haven away from the stifling monotony of shopping malls and suburbs, epitomised by the new development on the edge of their town:

> But there was nothing about the little, low-rambling, more or less identical homes of Northumberland Estates to interest or

to haunt ... no small immunities, no possibilities for hidden life
or other worldly presence: no trees, secret routes, shortcuts,
culverts, thickets that could be made hollow in the middle –
everything in the place was out in the open, everything could
be seen at a glance; and behind it, under it, around the corners
of its houses and down the safe, gentle curves of its streets, you
came back, you kept coming back, to nothing: nothing but the
cheerless earth. (*ibid.*, p. 150)

The centrepiece of this story is the events that follow the arrival of
a black family, the Barringtons, into this world. The white adults
behave hysterically at this unwanted intrusion into their sanitised
suburban 'community' and as part of a sustained campaign of
intimidation, they cover the front lawn of the Barrington house with
trash. When the children discover this they begin 'kicking through
it, looking for clues' (*ibid.*, p. 182) and this reveals that the refuse
comes from their own homes and is both embarrassing and
incriminating. Following this discovery, when they return home to
'hot shower, dry towel, before-bed television, good night kiss', it
is now also to 'dreams that could never again be entirely safe'
(*ibid.*, p. 185). The bigotry of their parents has also put an end to
the gang's own secret integration, since they lose their imaginary
playmate, Carl Barrington, an attenuated ghost-son for the town's
token black family. Pynchon's description of Carl Barrington's
origins is noteworthy:

> [He] had been put together out of phrases, images, possibilities
> that grownups had somehow turned away from, repudiated, left
> out at the edges of towns, as if they were auto parts in Étienne's
> father's junkyard – things they could or did not want to live with
> but which the kids, on the other hand, could spend endless hours
> with, piecing together, rearranging, feeding, programming,
> refining. (*ibid.*, p. 184)

Waste is all that which a culture casts away in order to fix its outer
limits and thus define that which is not itself. In Pynchon's fictions
the anti-commodity at the margins is *the* critical geographical text,
one charged with a history, memory and feeling absent at the core
and thus priceless in a sense those adults who would deny all secret
integrations are unable to perceive.

## From supermarkets to sacred sewers

Spatial concerns are similarly at the heart of Pynchon's first major
novel, *V* (1975b). The narrative of this vast, encyclopaedic work
is structured around five episodes of history since 1899 (all involving
international espionage): the Fashoda incident, disturbances in

Florence connected with a Venezuelan rebellion, a native uprising in German southwest Africa in 1922, an account of the siege of Malta during the Second World War and events in Paris on the brink of the First World War. Each of these episodes is interpreted by Herbert Stencil, attempting to plot the historical geography of imperialism, alongside a series of episodes in the lives of various people living in contemporary America, self-dubbed the Whole Sick Crew, centring on Benny Profane. Stencil is lost in the labyrinths of the past; Benny is astray in the streets of the present. Both come across 'V' in its/her many manifestations: a series of gendered forms (Victoria, Venus, Veronica); a series of factual and mythical places (Venezuela, Vesuvius, Valetta, Vheissu, the V-note); a series of incidental geometries (the shape made by spread thighs, or street lamps stretching to the horizon). However, neither Stencil nor Profane can definitively define V. The hope of plotting each of V's vectors to a point of original divergence or convergence is continually thwarted.

Focusing exclusively upon the text's metasemiotic code, McHoul and Wills declare that $V$ is 'about signification in a world where the transcendental signified is absent ... it is a deconstruction of hermeneutics and teleology' (McHoul and Wills 1990, p. 163). According to this reading $V$ signifies a tract on the arbitrariness of the signifier, the fundamental inability to plot or stencil the signified with any degree of certainty. Such a reading promotes the confession of Fausto Majistral to master discourse within the text. Certain Majistral proclamations resonate distinctly with those at the centre of poststructuralist thought:

> the fiction of continuity, the fiction of cause and effect, the fiction of a humanised history endowed with reason ... The word is, in sad fact, meaningless, based as it is on the false assumption that identity is single, soul continuous. (Pynchon 1975b, pp. 306–7)

Any account of Pynchon's fiction which sought to ignore the prominence of its metasemiotic code would obviously be inadequate. However, to foreground its presence to such an extent that it occludes all other narrative possibilities is to risk simulating the standardisation and sterility of Northumberland Estates at the level of critical analysis. There is little doubt that $V$ is openly hostile towards the principles of Enlightenment rationality. This hostility at no point, however, spills over into an ecstatic abandonment of associated concepts such as identity, meaning and soul. Instead, $V$ is haunted by a dread as pervasive as the cryptic signifier that gives the text its name. As the narrative performs its rhythmic temporal and geographical displacements, the one constant that is encountered is the drift into insensate ways of being, a remorseless and deathly 'falling away from what is human' (*ibid.*, pp. 321; 405). Paul Maltby rightly notes that the human for Pynchon is not a transtemporal essence; rather 'it is a precarious cultural construct that, under certain historical conditions, may disappear' (Maltby 1991, p. 131). Enlightenment precepts may be placed *sous rature* in *V*, but there is still a large emotional and political commitment to certain premises which would be anathema to the orthodox poststructuralist sensibility. This commitment is most obviously expressed in the text's representations of space.

Pynchon's geographical imagination assumes a variety of forms in *V*. First, there is an impressive number of maps present in the work: of Florence and the Uffizi, of the New York sewers and underground where Benny spends much of his time, of German southwest Africa and Malta. The mythical island of Vheissu is so mysterious specifically because it is unmapped. In *City of Words*, Tony Tanner, unlike McHoul and Wills, notes the significance of landscape in the Pynchon novel, but suggests that this dimension is interesting finally only in so much as it provides a 'composite image of the various areas of human consciousness' (Tanner 1971, p. 166). Tanner's tendency is to reinscribe place in these texts as allegories of the mind, thus deflecting from their ideological significance and submerging social conflict in depoliticised geometries. Accordingly, he ignores the presence of the underclass and the anti-commodity in *V*, those hidden geographical texts of the postindustrial landscape. This suppresses the ways in which Pynchon continually foregrounds the marginalised and the dispossessed, plotting the contours of the social relations of capitalism as they are inscribed in space.

The escalating hegemony of the 'inanimate' is evident across the landscapes of *V*. Stencil traces its designs in the imperialist history of reducing places to colonies and people to subjects. Outside, on the street, Benny experiences at firsthand the metastasis of reifying technologies and commodification in a culture laid waste by consumerism: 'He walked; walked, he thought sometimes, the aisles of a bright, gigantic supermarket, his only function to want' (Pynchon 1975b, pp. 36–7). Imperialism and consumerism, according to Pynchon's plottings, are part of a continuum. In southwest Africa, in 1922, Herr Fopl murders and maims native Hereros, reducing them to props in his orgiastic re-enactment of the 'spirit of '04'. Forty years on, in North America, consumers fall in love with their cars, have nose jobs and wire themselves up to the television set. *V* splices together Old World *fin de siècle* colonialism and the colonisation of subjectivity and desire in the brave new world of commodity capitalism. Both are seen to be involved in an insidious annexation of the animate and subsequent subjugation of moral consciousness.

In his search for a way out of this 'bright, gigantic supermarket', Benny Profane is driven underground, beneath the streets, to the waste and promissory darkness of the New York sewer system. Here, as evidence of that instinctive affiliation with the oppressed which typifies the Pynchon schlemiel, he joins up with a gang of poor Italian immigrants hired on subsistence wages to track down and kill the city's subterranean alligator population. In the realm of the anti-commodity and those who are literally this culture's *under*class, Benny, like Dennis Flange before him, finds himself more at home. The sewer is portrayed allegorically as an underworld, vernacular geography of secret spaces and 'sewer stories' which go beyond truth, falsity and the rationalism of the alienating capitalist cityscape above. When he confronts a cornered prey, Profane's flight threatens, briefly, to become a pilgrimage:

> He waited. He was waiting for something to happen. Something otherworldly, of course. He was sentimental and superstitious. Surely the alligator would receive the gift of tongues. (*ibid.*, p. 122)

Benny's expectation of a revelatory glossolalia remains unfulfilled. Subsequently, when he has cornered a critical clue in his search, Stencil is left similarly disappointed, when the promise of the 'gift of tongues' is thwarted and he is left wondering 'what gift of communication could ever come from a woman' (*ibid.*, p. 472). As if in answer to this question *V* culminates, like *The Crying of Lot 49*, with Pentecostal possibilities: a figure in black, with a mutilated face and a 'curiously sentimental, feminine motion of the wrist', waves to the seabound Sidney Stencil from the wharf at Fort St Elmo: 'He called something in English, which none of the observers understood. He was crying' (*ibid.*, p. 467).

Throughout *V* the gift of tongues, 'communion', St Elmo's fire and all forms of otherworldly experience are denied to Profane and the Stencils, father and son. Their yearning for such experience, however 'sentimental and superstitious', must be interpreted as an implied critique of the vehement desacralising forces that drive Benny underground. Pynchon's geography of the fall away from what is human hinges upon the expansion of profane places – for as colonial dependencies and supermarkets are built up, so too are all spaces of myth and magic razed to the ground. This is the driving force behind the respective quests of the schlemiel and the scholar and that which imparts a sacred significance to Benny and Stencil's search. This religious dimension is a critical component of Pynchon's mappings, but it rarely converges with orthodox scriptural authority. The sacred in *V* persists as a shorthand for forces aligned against the disenchantment of the world by an unholy trinity of capital, technology and technical rationality.

Throughout *V* one of the forces that furthers the integration of religious, political and moral apostasy is tourism. Tourists are defined as 'lovers of skins', of surfaces, images and simulacra:

This is a curious country, populated only by a breed called 'tourists'. Its landscape is one of inanimate monuments and buildings; near-inanimate barmen, taxi-drivers, bellhops, guides ... More than this it is two-dimensional as is the Street, as are the pages and maps of those little red handbooks ... Tourism thus is supra-national, like the Catholic church, and perhaps the most absolute communion we know on earth: for be its members American, German, Italian, whatever, the Tour Eiffel, Pyramids, and Campanile all evoke identical responses from them; their bible is clearly written and does not admit of private interpretation; inconveniences; live by the same pellucid time-scale. They are the Street's own. (*ibid.*, p. 273)

Baedeker discourses infiltrate ways of seeing and responding to place. This is indicative of a systematic *flattening* out of space, its reduction to an anaemic picturesque. Pynchon's analysis of tourism, as a means of responding to place which accentuates depthlessness, is directly analogous to Jameson's classification of the 'supreme formal feature of all postmodernisms' (Jameson 1984a, p. 62). In his essay 'Reification and Utopia in Mass Culture' Jameson defines the tourist as an archetypal postmodern persona, one who

no longer lets the landscape 'be in its being', as Heidegger would have said, but takes a snapshot of it, thereby transforming space into its own material image. The concrete activity of looking at a landscape – including, no doubt, the disquieting bewilderment with the activity itself, the anxiety that must arise when human beings, confronting the non-human, wonder what they are doing there and what the point or purpose of such a confrontation might be in the first place – is thus comfortably replaced by the act of taking possession of it and converting it into a form of personal property. (Jameson 1986, p. 138)

I quote at length here because of Jameson's exact description of Pynchon's 'Baedeker world' and of the situation of the central characters of narratives such as *V*, one of an increasingly disquieting bewilderment when confronted by postmodern landscapes. This illustrates the distance between Benny and Stencil and the delineation here of a postmodern persona. In this respect, Pynchon's work should be seen less as a target of the Jamesonian critique than as a fictional analogue to it. Both are engaged in an assault upon lovers of skins.

## Transcending the hieroglyphic streets

Broadly speaking, (which, in the context of Pynchon's fiction is still to speak narrowly), *The Crying of Lot 49* (Pynchon 1979) concerns Oedipa Maas, whose 'disquieting bewilderment' grows to gargantuan proportions after she learns that she has been named executor of the estate of Pierce Inverarity, a deceased Californian real-estate mogul. As she sets about exploring this estate she becomes ever more entangled in a web of clues which seem to point to the possible existence of an underground (yet again) anarchic organisation called the Tristero. This covert syndicate possesses a tortuously complex history, originating in various political conflicts in Europe during the Renaissance and appears to oppose all official lines of communication. The Tristero may also have developed its own secret communications infrastructure which, perhaps, is flourishing in contemporary California. 'Seems', 'possible', 'perhaps' – all of this is highly provisional however, since Oedipa can never be entirely certain whether she is discovering a real organisation, is the victim of a gigantic hoax, or is wildly hallucinating. She begins by trying to map Pierce's estate, which leads to the Tristero, which perhaps leads to the legacy which is America. But Oedipa can never be fully confident that she has finally confronted anything more than her ex-lover's 'need to possess the land, to bring new skylines into being' (*ibid.*, p. 134).

Initially Oedipa is 'insulated', with only a vague sense of her entrapment, but then her cosy suburban bubble is pierced by Inverarity's will. As she attempts to decipher its contents she encounters an array of texts – wills, stamps, Jacobean revenge tragedies – and their variants, editions, revisions and counterfeits, she is forced to read mysterious graffiti and even the streets of the city itself. Oedipa becomes cryptologist, code-breaker, literary critic, archaeologist, author – but neither she nor the reader is permitted to know finally whether she is discovering things or creating them, whether she is mapping a real phenomenon (or a real hoax), or like Stencil, simply mapping the contours of her own fantasies and obsessions (since the unmapped island of Vheissu may be read as 'V-he-is-you'). According to the Manichean mind-set which informs her quest, the labyrinth of 'zeroes and ones' (*ibid.*, p. 135), Oedipa may have stumbled across alternative channels of communication, or, be the absolute victim of those who control the official communications infrastructure. These perfectly poised possibilities remain unresolved and produce the narrative's peculiar mixture of revolutionary hope and paranoid dread. The only escape from this double bind is the frightful possibility that a new world is only a new mind, that, like Borges' cartographer, the increasingly detailed map which she is composing will finally coalesce to reveal only the contours of her own face.[1] At the close (which is precisely not the end), we are left alongside Oedipa at an auction, awaiting the crying of lot number 49 – an event which may, but just as easily may not, resolve whether the Tristero is a plot against her, a plot against America, or a plot dreamt by a madwoman.

In their interpretation of *Lot 49*, McHoul and Wills have few reservations about appropriating this work exclusively as a poststructural *Ur*-text. In the context of a narrative which focuses on the relations between a character whose nickname is 'Oed' and one whose forename, Pierce, clearly references the American founder of semiotics, it would clearly be reductive to deny the significance of this dimension. *Lot 49* is concerned with the activities of detecting significance, imposing meaning and interpretation in a Borgesian labyrinth of signs. However, the quest which is the narrative's organising structural principle takes place on more than one level and to ignore its social and symbolic potential is to sustain that semiotic fetishism bemoaned by the producer-actor Driblette: 'Why is everybody so interested in texts?' (*ibid.*, p. 53). The encounters with spurious shibboleths and what Pierce-Yves Petillon calls 'semiotic shenanigans' (Petillon 1991, p. 162) take place in the physical milieu of Southern California: in the narcissistic suburbs, the phalocratic military-industrial complex and the margins occupied by the underclass.

Oedipa Maas encounters both the meaning of meaning and the meaning of America. In the process she learns that there is more to disinheritance than the loss of Enlightenment grand narratives and chimerical master signs. At the same time, Pynchon might be seen to suggest a relation between the absence of transcendental signifiers and the development of transnational information economies. The hypertrophy of quaternary production and consumption has resulted in a volatile multiplication of signs, information and media images in the global village. Oedipa's pursuit of the Tristero can be read as a parable of disorientation and the liminality of the *logos* in the extravagantly textualised spaces of the postindustrial landscape. This is not to confirm the Baudrillardean thesis of a displacement of capital's primacy within a political economy of the sign, but to recognise an intensification in the commodification of the symbolic. For present purposes I should like to discuss two main areas of this text: the work's religious dimension as a response to the historical geography of late capitalism, and the Tristero organisation as part of a continual affinity

1. The phrase 'a new world is only a new mind', comes from the William Carlos Williams poem 'To Daphne and Virginia', in the collection *The Desert Music* (1954). Borges' tale of the cartographer is entitled 'El hacedor' (1960).

in Pynchon's fiction with the disinherited and an exploration of the omnipresence of forms of waste across postindustrial landscapes.

Driving a rented Impala into the city of San Narciso, Oedipa Maas sees the houses and streets beneath her almost magically take on the form of a circuit card within a transistor radio, there is 'a hieroglyphic sense of concealed meaning, of an intent to communicate' and she feels as though 'a revelations also trembled just past the threshold of her understanding' (Pynchon 1979, p. 15). Later, she is to describe her experiences 'as if (as she'd guessed that first time in San Narciso) there were revelations in progress all around her' and to wonder if 'all the gem-like clues she had stumbled across were only some kind of compensation. To make up for her having lost the direct, epileptic Word, the cry that might abolish the night' (*ibid.*, p. 81). These phrases, repeated often in the Pynchon narrative (one could also note the repetition of 'communion' in *V*), are indices of the fact that concurrent with all the ultra-contemporary concerns for IT, cybernetics and all the characteristic Pynchon technologese, there is an ultra-traditional religious discourse within this work. Metasemiotics in *Lot 49* is accompanied by a deep concern for spirituality. As Phillipa Berry suggests in 'Deserts of the Heart', this combination is not uncommon in contemporary cultural production: 'the trace of the holy survives within postmodernism in persistent echoes of that cultural legacy to which it declared itself the murderous heir' (Berry 1990, p. 7).

Religious discourses have always been one of the most effective means of plotting the physical universe and the place of the individual within it. For the believer who subscribes to scriptural authority, the environment and each event that occurs within it can be fixed in relation to the will of a divinity. Puritanism offered one of the most authoritative and authoritarian forms of spiritual cartography. Its mappings encouraged the American faithful, upon arrival in the New World, to read every landscape detail as a potential sign of His Will. Subsequently, Puritan hermeneutics, founded upon the doctrine of correspondences, were reinscribed in Emersonian transcendentalism, with its insistence that physical facts were symbols of spiritual truths and that each and all were interconnected through an infinite ethereal network (the 'Over-Soul'). In part, the prominence of the need to map and connect in Pynchon's fictions is a testament to the legacy of Puritan ideology and American romanticism. Whilst the Puritan faithful and the disciple of transcendentalism read nature as God's Book, the second nature of postindustrial landscapes is interpreted by paranoid plotters, like Oedipa Maas, as texts which promise revelations concerning secular masters and the path to new forms of redemption.

The term most frequently used to describe the landscapes of *Lot 49* is 'hieroglyphic' and this is continually linked to a sense of and the need for 'patterns of revelation'. As previously noted, the streets of San Narciso, from above, contain 'a hieroglyphic sense of concealed meaning'; a map of Pierce's housing developments flashed on to the TV screen seems to contain 'some promise of hierophany' (the theological term denoting the manifestation of the sacred in a profane world) (Pynchon 1979, pp. 15; 20). At street level, as she wanders through the Dock Bay region of San Narcisco at night, Oedipa comes across a series of hieroglyphic signs. Towards the close, she describes her entire quest as a passage through a labyrinth of 'hieroglyphic streets ... behind which there would either be a transcendent meaning, or only the earth' (*ibid.*, p. 125).

In *The Image of the City* Kevin Lynch was one of the first geographers to begin to consider landscape as narrative by addressing the question of a city's 'legibility' – the ease with which an urban landscape could be read, its parts recognised and organised into a significant pattern. San Narciso is described in *Lot 49* as 'less an identifiable city than a grouping of concepts' (Pynchon 1979, p. 14) and the persistent description of the streets as 'hieroglyphic' could be read both as a crucial component of its existential cartography and as a critique of the illegibility of the postmodern urban landscape. Oedipa's inability to get her bearings in the disorientating hyperspace of the late capitalist city is a function of its dispiriting opacity, the invisibility of the forces which mould it.

As well as offering an implicit critique of the illegibility of the postindustrial landscape, Oedipa's desire for revelation suggests a continuation of Pynchon's hostility towards the desacralising of space. Throughout his studies of various urban areas Edward Relph has compiled an exhaustive typology of spaces, including primitive, perceptual, abstract, architectural, existential, cognitive and that which he feels has been systematically eliminated in capitalist societies – sacred spaces (Relph 1976). A sacred space is replete with symbols, centres and meaningful objects – it is rarely functional, being structured instead according to myth, ritual, ceremony and magic as a physical embodiment of communal history. These are precisely the sorts of places that characters search for across the profane landscapes, the cheerless earth of Pynchon's fiction. They long to discover a place in which, to paraphrase Marcuse, people no longer recognise themselves in their commodities, finding their soul in an automobile, in which spaces are no longer organised along increasingly rational lines for increasingly irrational ends (Marcuse 1966, p, 9). Commodification and rationalisation is felt as an insidious falling-away from what is human. Oedipa's quest for a Word in the litter, a revelation or form of transcendence behind the 'hieroglyphic streets', is an attempt, conscious or otherwise, to establish a dialogue with the mute capitalist cityscape, to acquire the gift of tongues which will permit communication with prelapsarian places. Her intent is to achieve a level of disalienation and reinscribe the rational-illegible-alienating postmodern urban landscape with magic and myth, relocating its sacred spaces.

Despite a continuing affinity with the marginalised within a capitalist economic order, it is important to note in any assessment of the counter-hegemonic potential of his dissident mappings, that Pynchon's fictions do not formulate the kind of collectivist and programmatic response to that system which is traditionally favoured by the left. Pynchon's relation to radical politics is equivocal. The hostility to capitalism expressed in his work owes less to classical Marxist understandings of its workings than to a neo-Weberian critique of the disenchantment of the world. Oedipa yearns to plot a path out of the spatial economy of postindustrial Southern California, 'a real alternative to the exitlessness, to the absence of surprise to life, that harrows the head of everybody American' (Pynchon 1979, pp. 117–18). This 'absence of surprise' is articulated in the need to hear a 'direct, epileptic Word' (*ibid.*, p. 81). Etymologically, this stunning phrase is oxymoronic, since it combines the loss of rational consciousness with the *logos*, or original Greek term for 'reason'. Such a combination can be read as an expression of Pynchon's Weberian contempt for the rampant rationalisation of economic activity and social life. Capitalism is despised first and foremost as a manifestation of this process. Its origins lie in the asceticism of Puritan Protestantism and its main consequence is the elimination of the possibilities for magic, spirituality and surprise. Oedipa's plottings are valorised less as the literalisation of poststructural orthodoxies, than as an urgent *re-enchantment* of the profane geographies of technical rationality.

## 'Holy shit!'

At the outset of her search Oedipa believes the Tristero might be a malign conspiracy of various mysterious business organisations, such as the Yoyodyne corporation. But, as her quest takes her beyond the silicon landscapes of sunbelt California, to the Dock Bay region of San Narciso at night, she begins to wonder whether it might not be a silent conspiracy of the disinherited, the isolates (picking up on Melville's term), that the Tristero may be a second, hidden America plotting against the society she has previously known. As with Flange in 'Low-lands', Oedipa undergoes a disembourgoise-ment. An Orange County Republican and suburban housewife moves from the eclectic bric-a-brac of middle-class Californian society and into the company of tramps, outcasts and exiles within the system, people plotting in the invisible interstices of her culture. During her 'night town' odyssey she meets a facially deformed welder, a scarred black woman, a soap-eating night-watchman and a sailor suffering from the DTs. The Tristero sign 'decorates each alienation, each species of withdrawal' (Pynchon 1979, p. 85) and becomes a banner for the underclass, for the poor, racial minorities, political extremists, homosexuals, the mad, lonely and frightened.

The class contours to Pynchon's geography of California are critical. It is only when Oedipa enters the low-lands, the spaces occupied by the disinherited, that the possibility of revelation becomes imminent. The religious quest is inseparable from a social odyssey which reveals those groups who may form the basis of a secret revolution. The existence of an oppositional communications network may be an entirely delusory utopian fantasy, but the actuality of the people Oedipa meets is not in doubt. Once she moves beyond the suburbs, Oedipa's spiritual sensitivity is a catharsis to an historical and political consciousness. The epileptic 'Word unheard' that haunts her quest must be read both in an Eliotean sense and as a sign of the muted voices of the underclass, signifying the possibility both of revelation and revolution.

Throughout *Lot 49* and each of Pynchon's fictions, religious and political discourses are inseparable. This is particularly evident in the equation which is continually drawn between that which is without value to commodity capitalism and that which is, or could be sacred. One of the coded messages employed by the Tristero is 'W.A.S.T.E' – a cryptogram Oedipa decodes as 'We Await Silent Tristero's Empire'. This is discovered on the side of a trash can which is also, perhaps, a post-box for the disinherited, part of an extensive unofficial communications system. Pynchon associates waste (one of the dominant characteristics of a throwaway society of instant obsolescence) with fantasy and possibilities for opposition. In *Lot 49* Mucho Maas is plagued by memories of the junk people used to bring him as part-exchange when he was a car salesman. He is extremely sensitive to waste and sets off on an elegiac evocation of each car's history, how, in marked contrast to the commodity which seeks to suppress the history of its manufacture, the anti-commodity is inscribed with its human traces, residues and experiences. Oedipa illustrates a similar empathy when she is able to read the sorry tale of the life of a drunken down-and-out sailor, suffering with delirium tremens, from the dirty, stained old mattress that he dies on.

Waste, in all of its manifestations, is a crucial component of Pynchon's third major novel, *Gravity's Rainbow* (Pynchon 1975a). The waste of millions of lives on the war's assembly line; the waste of the underclass in the ongoing war of a capitalist economic order geared towards the maximisation of profit; the wasting of the environment through pollution and the over-consumption of non-renewable resources, all the junk and detritus of a consumer culture mass-producing throwaway commodities:

> Taking and not giving back, demanding that 'productivity' and 'earnings' keep on increasing with time, the System removing from the rest of the World these vast quantities of energy to keep its own tiny desperate fraction showing a profit: and not only most of humanity – most of the World, animal, vegetable and mineral is laid waste in the process. (*ibid.*, p. 412)

But, somewhat paradoxically, waste is also envisaged as a potential weapon of the preterite against the malign alliance of Technology, Thermodynamics and Them – a series of objects which, like the hieroglyphic streets, require decoding:

> kicking endlessly among the plastic trivia, finding in each Deeper Significance and trying to string them all together like terms of a power series hoping to zero in on the tremendous and secret Function whose name, like the permuted names of God, cannot be spoken ... plastic saxophone reeds *sounds of unnatural timbre*, shampoo bottle *ego-image*, Cracker Jack prize *one-shot amusement*, home appliance casing *fairing for winds of cognition*, baby-bottles *tranquillisation*, meat packages *disguise of slaughter*, dry-cleaning bags *infant strangulation*, garden hoses *feeding endlessly the desert* ... but to bring them together, in their slick persistence and our preterition ... to make sense out of, to find the meanest sharp sliver of truth in so much replication, so much waste ... (*ibid.*, p. 590)

Tchitcherine's mission, as an agent of Stalin in Central Asia, is to advance this process of disenchantment, to lay waste to the magic of folk culture, undermine the authority of the shamans and extinguish the 'Kirghiz Light' (*ibid.*, p. 541). In the process he comes to the conclusion that there must be a counter-force in the Zone: 'Who was the soviet intelligence agent who showed up in the fiasco in the clearing? Who tipped the Schwarzkommando off to the raid? Who got rid of Marvy?' (*ibid.*, p. 542). The answer to all three questions, intentionally or otherwise, is Lieutenant Tyrone Slothrop. There is a case for arguing that Slothrop *is* the counter-force in the zone. Significantly, this saviour rises not from the dead, or the sea, but from a dumpster – 'covered from head-to-toes in eggshells, beer cans, horrible chicken parts in yellow gravy, coffee grounds and waste paper' (*ibid.*, p. 598). In a text that pays such close attention to the semiology of slang and expletives ('ass' as shorthand for 'soul' and the etymology of the famed 'shit'n'shinola'), Seaman Bodine's exclamation at the sight of his saviour may be of deeper significance than first appears: 'Holy shit, Rocketman, it really is' (*ibid.*).

Throughout his quest Slothrop is associated with garbage in general and with excrement in particular – in the toilet bowl–sewer–Malcolm X episode from his teenage years; disguised as a pig rolling around in the manure of a sty as part of the festivities in a small village in the Zone; addressed by Them in characteristic mock-sinister typography: 'You Think You're Good But You're Really Shit And We All Know It' (*ibid.*, p. 603). Like Oedipa, Slothrop stumbles across *objets trouves* and takes these signs for wonders. Because they are untouched by the logic of commodification and technical rationality they reveal the possibility for other ways of being in the world:

> He used to pick and shovel at the spring roads of Berkshire ... picking up rusted beer cans, rubbers yellow with preterite seed, Kleenex wadded to brain shapes hiding preterite snot, preterite tears, newspapers, broken glass, pieces of automobile, days when he could *make it all fit*, seeing clearly in each an entry in a record, a history: his own, his winter's, his country's ... and now, in the Zone, later in the day he became a crossroad, after a heavy rain he doesn't recall, Slothrop sees a very thick rainbow here, a stout rainbow cock driven out of pubic clouds into earth, green wet valleyed Earth, and his chest fills and he stands crying, not a thing in his head, just feeling natural ... (*ibid.*, p. 647)

Following Mailer, Burroughs and a number of other American novelists – especially after the publication of Norman O. Brown's influential *Life Against Death* – Pynchon explores personal waste, the politics of scatology, and draws a series of equations between faeces, capital and the Word. From his early short stories, like 'Lowlands' and 'The Secret Initiation', to *Vineland*, Pynchon's fiction explores the possibilities of waste as a redemptive force, investigating the potential of the anti-commodity, in a poignant and provocative narrative poetics of junk amidst the extreme hygiene of America's air-conditioned nightmare. It struggles awkwardly, but persistently, towards that moment when waste refusal might just become the refusal of waste. The above epiphanic passage from *Gravity's Rainbow* reveals the extent to which Pynchon's hostility to capitalist geographies elicits a return to archaic forms of religious and pastoral mysticism. The key question in assessing the counter-hegemonic potential of such visions is determining the extent to which such utopianism is inspirational or simply mystifying and ultimately counter-productive, in that it distracts from the physical realities of place in postmodern America. The following section will seek to address this question in relation to *Vineland*.

## Territories of the spirit

Every part of this soil is sacred in the estimation of my people
... these shores will swarm with the invisible dead of my tribe,
and when your children's children think themselves alone in the
field, the store, the shop, upon the highway, or in the silence
of the pathless woods, they will not be alone. In all the earth
there is no place dedicated to solitude. At night when the streets
of your cities and villages are silent again and you think them
deserted, they will throng with the returning hosts that once filled
them and love this beautiful land. The White Man will never
be alone.

Let him be just and deal kindly with my people, for the dead
are not powerless. Dead, did I say? There is no death, only a
change of worlds.

Chief Seattle, Speech delivered at
the signing of the Port Elliot Treaty, 1855

Only the historian will have the gift of fanning the spark of hope
in the past who is firmly convinced that *even the dead* will not
be safe from the enemy if he wins. And this enemy has not ceased
to be victorious.

Walter Benjamin, 'Theses on the Philosophy
of History', *Illuminations* (1982), p. 257

A ghost, though invisible, still is like a place
your sight can knock on, echoing ...

Rainer Maria Rilke, 'The Black Cat' (1987), p. 65

*Vineland* (Pynchon 1990) is a tale of crossings. The temporal focus
of the narrative slips back and forth, between the late 1960s and
the mid-1980s, as it follows the actions and inaction of four main
figures: Zoyd Wheeler, a living relic from the 1960s' hippie
subculture, on the run in Reagan's America; Frenesi Gates, Zoyd's
ex-wife, who crossed over from the counter-culture to collaboration
with state authority; their child, Prairie Wheeler, who is hunting
for clues to the identity of her mother whilst being hunted down
by a Department of Justice taskforce; and Brock Vond, State
Attorney and fascist schemer at the head of the search for the
disunified members of this attenuated family unit. The life-stories
of each of these figures intertwine as a telling micronarrative of the
politicocultural sea-change which America experienced during this
period. In various capacities, Zoyd, Frenesi, Prairie and Brock are
implicated in the nexus of power relations connected to the
dissolution of counter-cultural activism associated with the New
Left in the 1960s and the subsequent conservative counter-
revolution, which propelled Reagan and the New Right to political
ascendancy in the 1980s. *Vineland* is a tale of incorporation,

complicity and routine betrayal. The betrayal of friends and family, of ideals and the promise of the 1960s' rebellion. However, it is concerned with more than one variety of crossing and contains moments which appear to fulfil the criteria for Jesus Arrabal's definition of a miracle in *Lot 49*: 'You know what a miracle is? ... another world's intrusion into this one' (Pynchon 1979, p. 104). Two questions haunt this tale, like the Thanatoid ghosts who drift around Shade Creek: will betrayal go unavenged? And will the Trail of Tears that leads from the 1960s to the soulless neofascism of Reagan's America mean a world without miracles, a permanent exile from the home that Pynchon calls 'territories of the spirit' (Pynchon 1990, p. 317)?

*Vineland* opens in 1984, the year of Reagan's re-election and the metastasis of a virulent conservatism in the socioeconomic, religious and military spheres. Pynchon resists the temptation, in this context, to romanticise the era which witnessed the flowering of various liberal and radical movements dedicated to change. In retrospect the 'Mellow Sixties' may have seemed 'a slower-moving time, predigital, not yet so cut into pieces, not even by television', but it was also the time of those atrocities with which Civil Rights campaigners, feminists, the New Left, environmentalists and anti-war protesters were in productive opposition: 'War in Vietnam, murder as an instrument of American politics, black neighbourhoods torched to ashes and death' (*ibid.*, p. 38). There is a directness to the political history in *Vineland* which was not always evident in Pynchon's earlier work. Whilst, for example, *Lot 49* dealt in allegorical representations of counter-cultural resistance (the Tristero), *Vineland* draws out selective strands of its historical actuality. At the same time there is far less opacity surrounding the nature of the enemy. No longer a mysterious and maybe even a metaphysical Them, it is now quite straightforwardly the State, the Government, the Department of Justice, the police and Ronald Reagan, with his programme to 'dismantle the New Deal, reverse the effects of World War II, restore fascism at home and around the world, flee into the past' (*ibid.*, p. 265). This programme is the centrepiece of what DEA officer Hector Zuniga calls 'a *real* revolution ... a groundswell, the wave of History', as opposed to the New Left's 'fantasy hand-job' (*ibid.*, p. 27).

*Vineland* may eschew the soft-focus sentimentalism of 1960s' nostalgia and possess a challenging explicitness in its drawing of the lines on the battleground of contemporary political history in the US, but its account of the forces underlying the eclipse of the Yippie by the Yuppie is often fragmentary and obscure. The dissolution of the counter-culture and the passage to a second term in the Presidency for the ex-Screen Actors' Guild spokesperson appears to be attributed to a confused admixture of the machinations of the state and various internal weaknesses, partly structural (a divisive factionalism) and partly psychosexual (a predisposition towards masochism) in the New Left.

Brock Vond, the authoritarian villain in *Vineland*, offers his own interpretation of the counter-cultural activists whom he seeks to subjugate. This reading is founded upon the premise of an inescapable reactionary subtext to all narratives of radical action:

> Brock Vond's genius was to have seen in the activities of the sixties left not threats to order but unacknowledged desires for it. While the Tube was proclaiming youth revolution against parents of all kinds and most viewers were accepting this story, Brock saw the deep – if he'd allowed himself to feel it, the sometimes touching – need only to stay children forever, safe inside some extended national family. (*ibid.*, p. 269)

The cartooning of 1960s' radicals as, at root, only 'children longing for discipline' (*ibid.*), is corroborated by Frenesi's masochistic compulsion to obey Brock, her helpless turn towards him as an image of authority. It also tallies with his view of political history which, like his fascination with subcultural physiognomy, is based upon the work of the nineteenth-century criminologist, Cesare Lombroso, particularly his notion of misoneism:

> Radicals, militants, revolutionaries, however they styled themselves, all sinned against this deep organic human principle [misoneism], which Lombroso had named after the Greek for 'hatred of anything new'. It operated as a feedback device to keep society coming along safely, coherently. Any sudden attempt to change things would be answered by an immediate misoneistic backlash, not only from the state but from the people themselves – Nixon's election in '68 seeming to Brock a perfect example of this. (*ibid.*, p. 273)

For much of *Vineland* the narrative voice appears dedicated to the promise of revolutionary change, to the possibility of 'a world sprung new, not even defined yet, worth the loss of everything in this one' (*ibid.*, p. 117). However, this dedication is undercut by the authority which gravitates towards the voice of Brock Vond. The most disturbing part of Pynchon's chronicle of contemporary American political history is the degree to which Vond's voice begins to assume metanarrative proportions. Far from contradicting the Vond/Lombroso historiography, *Vineland* often appears to conspire to confirm it. The Vondian dismissal of radicals as 'children longing for discipline' is validated by the exclusive attention to white student activism in favour of other branches of 1960s' political dissidence. According to this reading those involved in Civil Rights sit-ins and Freedom Rides in the Deep South were actually longing for the discipline meted out to them by the police. Similarly, the workers, veterans, women's and gay rights activists on demonstrations at this time were secretly desirous of the violent police clamp-down which their protest encountered. The infantilisation of the left through telling factional lacunae is reinforced by their persistent referencing as 'children' involved in adolescent posturing and 'left-wing kiddie games' (ibid., pp. 197–8; 214; 239). Sanction is also provided by ex-members of the counter-culture, like Frenesi Gates, who dismisses her involvement with 24fps as nothing more than 'running around like kids with toy weapons' (ibid., p. 259), living in a 'wraparound fantasy' that was 'cheesy and worthless' (ibid., p.346).

Vineland reveals a key facet of Pynchon's own political preferences. Whilst wholly committed to the plight of the dispossessed, he is far from unequivocal in his enthusiasm for the possibility of collective political programmes. He is hostile to the State as an agent of oppression and to the New Right in particular, but seems unwilling to advance those forms of organised mass resistance which are surely the most effective means of challenging either. If there is an endorsement of any strategy for resistance here it is for micropolitical activities which are more spontaneous and anarchic than those traditionally favoured by the left. This would seem to align Pynchon with fringe elements in the New Left which Vineland simultaneously discredits. There is, however, an alternative to the bipolar political philosophies offered within the text; an alternative which might be inspirational, or might guarantee the continued ascendancy of those forces Pynchon opposes. To determine the efficacy of this alternative it is necessary to turn now to the critical geographical dimension of this narrative.

The historical passage which Vineland surveys and the solutions it tentatively offers are figured in spatial metaphors which are continuous with the cartographic imagination displayed in Pynchon's earlier work. Places in the narrative are parabolic, history is related through the juxtaposition of spatial stories. Following a period in American history when 'revolution went blending into commerce' (ibid., p. 231) and entering the Reagan era of 'greed and its ennoblement' (ibid., p. 308), the suffusion of a malignant conservatism is seen to leave its mark on the land. Vineland is Pynchon's representative geocultural entity for Reagan's America, the site of an almost entirely successful neofascist counter-revolution. In the 1960s this place was a haven for runaways like Zoyd Wheeler from the 'Nixonian Repression', but, as the 'Repression went on, growing wider, deeper, and less visible, regardless of the names in power' (ibid., p. 145), Vineland becomes far less secure.

Zoyd Wheeler can see that 'the signs are there on street corners and shop windows' and he attempts – forlornly, as is the case with most of Pynchon's earnest but bewildered schlemiels – to read them, to 'locate landmarks, anything that'll give a clue' (*ibid.*, p. 40). The signs point to the Repression that dominates space in Vineland. Most obviously there is a dramatic intensification in martial manoeuvring, a militarisation of public space. The stepping-up of military and police presence in Southern California, which Mike Davis has charted in *City of Quartz*, has expanded here to the coastal communities and redwood hillsides of the Northwest. Vineland is a strategic site in the Reagan administration's War on Drugs, a war which is traced in the text through the iconographic stencil of imperialist aggression in Viet Nam (with aerial assaults launched upon marijuana plantations, dawn patrols, violent dispossessions and camps designed for Political Re-Education Programmes).

Pynchon explicitly associates the overt fascism of endo-colonisation with the dominant demographic trends in the region. Brock Vond's personal taskforce make 'an industrious roar that could as well have been another batch of designer condos going up' (*ibid.*, p. 191). If the plans of commercial interests are realised this roar would be heard across the land: 'All born to be suburbs, in their opinion, and the sooner the better' (*ibid.*, p. 319). What begin as 'little crossroads places', 'pre-suburban citrus groves and pepper fields', are rapidly developed into uniform leafy housing tracts where 'the rates of human affliction in all categories zoom' (*ibid.*, p. 38).

In conjunction with militarisation and suburbanisation, the other prevalent geographical process in the region is the rapid expansion of spaces devoted to shopping and commerce. The malls which bracket the city appear to exert a gravitational attraction for the residents of Vineland; drawing them towards shopping complexes like the 'Noir Centre', where Prairie witnesses 'yuppification run to some pitch so desperate that [she] at least had to hope the whole process was reaching the end of its cycle' (*ibid.*, p. 326). The mediascapes manufactured by the Tube play a central role here. Simultaneously they are seen to naturalise the operations of the police and the military, 'turning agents of government repression into sympathetic heroes' (*ibid.*, p. 345), and intensify the commodification of space by peddling the romance of the suburbs and channelling desire towards the mall.

Pynchon's alternative to the politics of the New Left and New Right is articulated through a palimpsest of resistance beneath the official maps of Vineland, a counter-hegemonic cartography located between the interstices of the Repression. Beyond the auspices of state authority and military aggression, beyond the suburbs, malls and mediascapes, there is another world in this text, 'Vineland the Good' (*ibid.*, p. 322). This is a significant phrase, borrowed from documents of pre-Columbian Icelandic voyages to North America such as the *Laudamabok* and the *Kristni Saga*. '*Vinland* the Good' clearly signals within the text the initial utopian promise represented by the New World, the kind of home America might have been. *Vineland* is torn between a dystopian dread of the inexorable spread of totalitarian control and the possibilities for spaces of accommodation, for the plight of those dispossessed like Zoyd Wheeler, struggling to 'get back his own small piece of Vineland ... out here on the periphery, in motion, out on one of the roads that had taken him away from home, and that must lead back' (*ibid.*, p. 374).

The official mapped zones are shown to contain some prospects for transgression. Zoyd refuses to live in a 'developer condo' and gradually adds, in a familiar gesture for the Pynchon schlemiel, to a small used trailer, from the waste he encounters:

> using lumber washed up on the beaches, scavenged from the docks, brought home from old barns he helped take down, transition fittings and adapter pieces that could take whole days ... at the great Crescent City Dump to find. (*ibid.*, p. 358)

The 'Great South Coast Plaza Eyeshadow Raid', in which two dozen girls on roller skates ventured on a notorious shoplifting expedition, allegorically suggests the possibilities for bricolage in the malls and across a consumer culture. Similarly, the relationships between viewers and the Tube suggest the existence of creases in the contours of a consumerist mediascape. The Tube is not portrayed exclusively as a repressive tool of social control. Many of the touchstones in the conversations between Zoyd and Prairie, even about her mother, a subject about which they 'never joke' (*ibid.*, p. 40), are from Tubal discourses. Zoyd's relations with the media suggest the possibility of reversing the manipulation to receive money from the State, whilst Frenesi's parents display a highly critical engagement with Tubal propaganda. Television is also responsible for occasional 'defects of control' (*ibid.*, p. 279), even amongst the likes of Brock Vond, who, once, 'not many years ago, sober, wide awake [had] begun to laugh at something on the Tube' (*ibid.*, p. 278). Media representations belong in part to the realm of fantasy, and fantasy can assume a variety of guises, not all of them necessarily repressive.

Beyond the mediascapes, the mall and the suburbs there are also places in Vineland, due to its rugged topography, where the Repression can be eluded: 'Half the interior hasn't even been surveyed – plenty of redwoods to get lost in, ghost towns new and old ... Indian trails for you to learn' (*ibid.*, p. 305). Ghost towns 'new and old' is a signpost pointing to the two places at the heart of *Vineland*'s alternative cartography: Thanatoia and the Yurok's Forest. In Reagan's own back garden of sunshine and simulacra,

Pynchon plots a path to where the bodies are buried. Thanatoids, Vineland's living dead, are depicted in a seriocomic Gothic: 'We are assured by the *Bardo Thodol*, or *Tibetan Book of the Dead* that the soul newly in transition often doesn't like to admit – indeed will deny quite vehemently – that it's really dead' (*ibid.*, p. 218). They inhabit another world, a geographical palimpsest which occasionally becomes visible to the living. Their status and function within the text is ambiguous. Thanatoid behaviour, their vehement reluctance to admit that they have died, by continuing to watch TV, go to work and hold conventions, in a text so dense with eclectic reference to media mythologies, may suggest the zombies in Romero's *Dawn of the Dead*. Mark Jancovich has argued that

> zombification is also connected to the processes of rational control through a preoccupation with the media and consumerism. [In *Dawn of the Dead*] ... the zombies are mindlessly drawn to the film's central location, a shopping mall, by the last remnants of the conditioned habits of behaviour and desire associated with consumerism. (Jancovich 1992, p. 91)

The Thanatoids' listless repetition of conditioned habits raises the possibility that they are, like Romero's zombies, allegorical representations of the living dead wandering through the malls and addicted to the Tube in those spaces beyond Shade Creek. What undercuts this reading is Pynchon's insistence that Thanatoia is the borderland of the betrayed – a territory occupied by those who have been turned in, cheated on, lied to and finally murdered. On the other side of this borderline, 'invisible but felt at its crossing, between worlds' (Pynchon 1990, p. 228), are the 'unavenged dead', like Weed Atman, whose assassination led to the collapse of the People's Republic of Rock'n'Roll. In *Gravity's Rainbow* Pynchon drew a metaphorical equation between the history of dispossession and ghosts. Towards the end of his odyssey Slothrop becomes increasingly ethereal, drifting off among 'the Humility, among the grey and preterite souls, adrift in the hostile light of the sky, the darkness of the sea' (Pynchon 1975a, p. 742). The Thanatoids at Shade Creek can be read as Pynchon's own vehement refusal to allow the history of injustice to be forgotten, an allegorical manifestation of the need for their persistence given that, as Walter Benjamin asserts, '*even the dead* will not be safe from the enemy if he wins' (Benjamin 1982, p. 257). 'What was a Thanatoid, at the end of the long dread day, but memory?' (Pynchon 1990, p. 322). Benjamin's recommendation to the historian who seeks to rekindle 'the spark of the past' is extended in *Vineland* beyond the Thanatoid ghosts of the recent dead, to the region's initial victims of dispossession, the Yurok tribe.

In her analysis of the text Deborah Madsen suggests that *Vineland* presents repression as normal and entertains no illusions of transcendence ... Hapless citizens can only submit to the pressure exerted by the long and gun-toting arm of the federal law, by the mass media, through television, magazines and novels, popular music, movies and the like, by the manufactured 'mindscape' of the shopping malls and freeway system that dominate American space. (Madsen 1991, p. 126)

My own readings of Pynchon's mappings of American space so far have attempted to illustrate his concern for the means of resisting repression. Madsen's account of the geography of Vineland ignores these spaces of and strategies for accommodation and suppresses the critical significance of the Yurok tribe to this narrative mapping which contains moments of transcendence with explicitly Emersonian echoes. *Vineland* constitutes what the native American writer William Least Heat-Moon calls a *Prairyerth*, or 'deep map', a multilayered cartography which pushes beneath the malls and freeways towards the mythical heart of this locale – beyond Thanatoia, in the depths of the redwood forest lies Tsorrek, at the end of the Ghosts' Trail, the Yurok Land of the Dead (Least Heat-Moon 1991). This dead centre of Vineland's cartography is the site at which Pynchon chooses to locate those sacred spaces for which his characters so devoutly search, in magic realist visions inspired by aboriginal myth:

Everything had a name – fishing and snaring places, acorn grounds, rocks in the river, boulders on the bank, groves and single trees with their own names, springs, pools, meadows, all alive, each with its own spirit. Many of these were what the Yurok called *woge* ... Some went away physically, forever, eastward, over the mountains, or nestled all together in giant redwood boats, singing unison chants of dispossession and exile ... Other *woge* who found it impossible to leave withdrew instead into the features of the landscape ... Vato and Blood, who as city guys you would think might get creeped out by all this, instead took it as if returning from some exile of their own. (Pynchon 1990, p. 186)

The geographical myths of this place's indigenous population are recovered by Pynchon and used to articulate a 'call to attend to territories of the spirit' (*ibid.*, p. 317). Brock Vond, the character who is least attentive to this call, is finally spirited away to Tsorrek in a passage which has deep intertextual resonances. First, it represents a fulfilment of Jesus Arrabal's definition of a miracle. Second, it is a realisation of the Emersonian doctrine of Divine Justice, quoted by Jess Traverse (a name suggestive of crossings) at the annual Traverses–Beckers reunion in the redwood forest:

> Secret retributions are always restoring the level, when disturbed, of the divine justice. It is impossible to tilt the beam. All the tyrants and proprietors and monopolists of the world in vain set their shoulders to heave the bar. Settles forever more the ponderous equator to its line, and man and mote, and star and sun, must range to it, or be pulverised by the recoil. (*ibid.*, p. 369)

Third, Brock's demise appears to be an exact consummation of the prophecy made by Chief Seattle, in 1855, at the signing of the Port Elliot Treaty restricting the Suquamish and Duwamish tribes to poor-quality reservations a few hundred miles up the west coast from the Yurok's territory. The White Man is not alone on the highway or the forest, the land is suddenly teeming with the dead in an epiphanic moment of repossession which repeats the classic geographical gesture in Pynchon's writing – a journey underground:

> Once down under the earth, there would be no way to return. As he stared out the window, Brock realised that around them all this time had been rising a wall of earth each side of the narrowing road ... And soon, ahead, came the sound of the river, echoing, harsh and ceaseless, and beyond it the drumming, the voices, not chanting together but remembering, speculating, arguing, telling tales, uttering curses, singing songs, all the things voices do, but without ever allowing the briefest breath of silence. All these voices, forever. (*ibid.*, p. 379)

Brock's voice, which had threatened to become the master discourse of *Vineland*'s history, is finally silenced by the tongues of a ghost community of the original dispossessed. But how should this silencing be received? This miracle may be intended as a triumphant reclamation of spaces of magic and myth, a reversion to mysticism designed to inspire in the battle against the repression practised by the likes of Vond. However, it seems more likely that this recourse to pre-capitalist narrative forms is largely symptomatic of Pynchon's inability to endorse any form of materialist praxis in his history of a land that could have been Vineland the Good. Jameson's definition of narrative, which is heavily indebted to Levi-Strauss' anthropological analyses of aboriginal myth, is entirely appropriate here. Pynchon reverts to the provision of *symbolic* resolutions to actual historical problems (see Jameson 1981, p. 9). To achieve this symbolic resolution he also has to ignore much of the historical actuality of the Yurok peoples.

The Yuroks were and still are, though in severely depleted numbers, a native American salmon-fishing tribe located near what came to be known as the northwestern Californian coast, in a heavily forested area dominated by redwoods and Douglas fir. The miracle which Pynchon relates in *Vineland* may be partially based upon two episodes in Yurok history. In the late nineteenth century the Ghost Dance, based upon visions in which the dead would flock back to the earth, was introduced to and assimilated by tribal folk culture. More recently, in December 1964, heavy rains and a major flood along the Klamath river, the 'river of ghosts' (Pynchon 1990, p. 186), washed away a number of Yurok cemeteries exposing the bones of the dead. Many of the tribespeople interpreted this as a supernatural response to government action in 1962 when the Division of Highways had violated a sacred space by cutting a road through a mountain.

There are many aspects of Yurok custom and social relations which would no doubt appeal to Pynchon's political sensibility and provide a telling comparison with the political economy of contemporary Vineland. According to historians there was no overall power structure within a Yurok community or at the tribal level; in fact the structure and organisation of social life represented a form of contained anarchy. Whilst formal political ties were practically non-existent, social cohesion was ensured through the performance of an elaborate array of shared rituals and ceremonies, many of which had the symbolic function of renewing the land and its resources.

Other aspects of Yurok culture, however, seriously undermine its viability as a anti-capitalist utopian ideal with which to challenge contemporary political economy. The Yuroks are, for example, generally regarded by historians to have been the most aggressively individualistic and acquisitive of North American tribes. Direct lines of comparison have been drawn between Yurok core values and the ideological foundations of nineteenth-century industrial capitalism, the Protestant Ethic. Young Yurok men were renowned for their dedicated performance of tribal rituals which involved the contemplation of material gain (typically in the form of the dentalium shells which were the primary unit of exchange), punctuated by the tearful invocation to the spirits, 'I want to be rich'. Wealth was at the centre of the Yuroks' highly differentiated system of status and prestige and there was an almost insurmountable social barrier separating wealthy families from those who were poor.

None of these facts are intended to devalue the significance of Yurok cultural history *per se*, but to challenge its appropriation in *Vineland*. Of course it needs to be remembered that the nature of Yurok life would probably have been altered dramatically as a result of initial contacts with European colonialists and that an authentic account of pre-Columbian custom is irrecoverable. In this context Pynchon may be invoking a mythic ideal of the Yurok community before they were enticed into the fur trade in the late eighteenth century and the nearby Trinidad Bay become a centre for commerce and shipping after the discovery of placer gold on

the Trinity river in 1849. Nonetheless, it is equally important to
bear in mind the sacrifices to historical actuality it is necessary for
Pynchon to make to achieve his mythic and symbolic resolution
of political conflict. A reversion to a mystical narrative register, to
a faith in *woge* and Divine Justice, may not be the most effective
means of fulfilling Benjamin's injunction to the historian of the
defeated, nor of challenging the enemy responsible for continuing
acts of dispossession and barbarism.

Such a recognition may lie behind the fact that Pynchon chooses
not to conclude *Vineland* with Brock's defeat by the ghosts of
North America's earliest victims of repression. In this tale of
geographical intersections and political betrayals, the narrative
ends with a double crossing: Brock Vond's passing over to the Land
of the Dead is followed immediately by the possibility that Prairie
may follow in her mother's footsteps, torn by her own 'Brock
fantasies', and cross over to the other side. If this should happen
it would be clear that the utopian promise of the Yurok victory, or
of Prairie's name which points to North America's mythic origins
as the Garden before the Fall into industrialisation, was undercut
by the fact that elsewhere, in Benjamin's words, the 'enemy had
not ceased to be victorious'.

The narrative structure of *Vineland*, echoing the name of *Wheeler*,
is clearly cyclical. It begins with Zoyd drifting awake and closes with
his daughter waking up in the forest after the annual
Traverses–Beckers reunion. The emphasis upon *awakening*, coupled
with the narrative circularity, numerous imagistic correspondences
and a muted transcendentalism in the concluding chapter, might
suggest an echoing of Kate Chopin's *fin de siècle* fable of a quest
for home on the part of another young heroine. But, as in *The
Awakening*, it is far from certain that Prairie Wheeler has achieved
a moment of transcendent reconciliation at the end of her quest.
As her Brock fantasies dispel, she awakes to the unconditional love
of Desmond, who has been running with the Yurok ghost dogs since
the Wheelers were dispossessed. In the narrative's opening line even
nature appeared to have imbued the neofascist political climate,
since Zoyd wakes up to the sounds of a 'squadron of blue jays
stomping around on the roof' (Pynchon 1990, p. 3). This is clearly
an omen of the imminent arrival of Vond's private taskforce, and
the fact that in the last line of the tale Desmond's face is 'full of
blue jay feathers' (*ibid.*, p. 385) may suggest another symbolic
triumph over the emblems of State oppression. However, a jay is
also a foolish or gullible person and it is difficult to shake the
suspicion that this brief pastoral idyll, with its suggestions of an end
to exile, is simply a shaggy dog story.

*Vineland* charts the betrayal of Vinland the Good. Initially in the
genocide of the indigenous population and then in the endo-

colonisation of the White Man. It portrays a culture that has turned its back on the territories of the spirit and has learned to love to watch its subjugation in the soulless eye of the Tube and the reflection in the jackboots of their leaders. Whether this exile will end is not certain. Like *Lot 49*, *Vineland* closes with the suspension of possibilities. Will the next generation of Vinlanders succumb to their 'Brock fantasies', become complicit with their repression by fascist father-figures, or will they learn to listen to the voices which speak forever out of the deep redwood forests? ...

# CHAPTER 7

# Reflections on the 'City of Glass': Paul Auster

As indicated in the previous chapter, the objective of analysing the representation of space in contemporary fiction is indebted to Jameson's call for maps of a disorientating postmodern hyperspace. The centrepiece of his thesis in the essay in which this request is made, is the assertion that, since the 1950s, aesthetic production has become integrated into commodity production generally and, as a consequence, has lost its oppositional potential. Culture in the postmodern period is depthless, ahistorical, centreless and composes the cultural dominant of late capitalism. For Jameson, postmodernism is to be understood essentially as the reflection of the deep structure of a new phase, even more penetrative, in the evolution of the capitalist mode of production.

My objections to this thesis arise from a productive dialogue with a stimulating essay, but, as a signpost in the labyrinths of discourses on the postmodern I feel it is largely misleading. Postmodern cultural artefacts, like the socioeconomic systems they are produced within, are wrought with contradictions. In my analysis of Thomas Pynchon's fictive mappings I hope to have shown that even those seemingly most paradigmatic of postmodern works often contain such contradictions. Consequently, rather than denouncing them as complicit with the (il)logic of late capital, critical energies could be devoted to drawing these out and analysing their effectivity. It might prove more fruitful to locate and address the instrumentality of counter-hegemonic spaces within the allegedly irredeemable postmodern work. In his continual movement away from specific works towards grandiose metatheories of postmodernity, Jameson suppresses the radical impulses which exist within these texts – they are erased by attractive but frequently reductive totalisations. Even if the physical landscapes of postmodern urban centres (Jameson selects Los Angeles as his example) were nothing but unambivalent capitulations to corporate finance, the landscapes of postmodern fiction seem to me to be far more ambivalent geographies, ones which simultaneously resist and reproduce the material conditions in which they are produced. It is on this point and its consequences for the oppositional potential of the postmodern art work that

Jameson is at his most reductive. Aesthetic production is just a far messier affair than his proclamations allow. A critical analysis must recognise the text less as a reflection of a developmental shift in the mode of production (culture as a fixed structure and therefore as necessarily complicit with late capitalism) and more as the site of ideological conflict, the space of discourse formation, struggle and contention (culture as a process of structuration and therefore as necessarily involved in a dialogue with the order which constitutes its material context). What follows here will be an attempt to pursue this proposition in relation to another prime example of postmodern fiction, *The New York Trilogy*, by Paul Auster (1987).

## A postmodern *protopos*?

This interpretation will focus on the opening section of the *Trilogy*, 'City of Glass'. This is a section, rather than a separate book, because the formal and typographic separation of this trilogy proves to be a hoax. In the final third of the novel, the narrator of 'The Locked Room' is revealed to be the author of the preceding stories. 'City of Glass' has been selected because, as this initial formal counterfeit intimates, it exhibits many of those technical characteristics and thematic preoccupations, in a particularly undiluted form, which Jameson and others have delineated as signatures of the postmodern. This is initially evident in the almost torturously convoluted duplication of narrative voice.

The plot concerns a character called Quinn, or rather, what we know of Quinn through Fanshawe's pursuer's account of Auster's ex-friend's interpretation of his mysterious red notebook. These convolutions reach near intractable proportions in chapter 6, where, if we were to ask Gérard Gennette's crucial question – '*who speaks*'? – the reply would be that the Old Testament parable of Adam and Eve, reworked by Milton, interpreted by Henry Dark (who is actually a creation of a character called Stillman), has been found in Quinn's notebook by Auster's ex-friend, and is narrated (and maybe perhaps invented) by Fanshawe's unnamed pursuer (see Gennette 1982). Narrative frames are folded into each other until the tale is told at some seven (or eight) removes from what might be called an original. Questions revolving around origin and authorship are of course further problematised by the presence of an author named 'Paul Auster' within the text itself.

The narrative begins with a telephone call in the night. Whether or not there is an intentional echo of Wittgenstein's rhetorical query in *On Certainty* (cited in Heller 1991, p. 87) – 'Does my telephone call to New York strengthen my conviction that the earth exists?' – there are numerous echoes of Wittgensteinean philosophy in the subsequent textual indeterminacies, word games and ontological insecurities. The phone call is received by Quinn, an ex-mystery novel writer, who wrote under the pseudonym 'William Wilson' and gets involved in a case on behalf of Peter Stillman by pretending to be a detective called Paul Auster (ontological insecurity is partly registered through the proliferation of identities). Stillman's father imprisoned his son in a dark room for twelve years, as part of a religious experiment designed to recover an original language of God. The earthly father (also called Peter Stillman) has recently been released from prison for imprisoning his son, who fears for his safety and hires Quinn, under the name of 'Auster', to protect him. Quinn tracks the elder Stillman around the streets of New York City, both writing in red notebooks, but he appears to be so involved in some eccentric experimentation that the son is not thought to be in any immediate danger. Nevertheless, Quinn stakes out in front of his client's building for several months. When he eventually ventures inside, the apartment is empty and he decides to strip off his clothes and stay. He sleeps, eats (regular meals are mysteriously provided) and continues to write in his red notebook. The story concludes with a friend of the 'real' Paul Auster, who now has the notebook, explaining that Quinn has disappeared, leaving only this document as evidence of his existence.

Within the narrative there are numerous formal and thematic signatures of the text's postmodernity: its penchant for play, particularly impersonation and puzzles; a fascination with indeterminacy and chance; its impulses towards silence, negation and exhaustion; its repetition of key words from the poststructuralist lexicon (absence, trace, erasure, difference); its persistent intertextuality, especially with nineteenth-century American fiction and the prominence of metafictional discourses; the depiction of several characters, as well as the narrative itself, as schizophrenic; the attention to surfaces. Perhaps most crucially there is the work's profound resistance to interpretation. It appears to have been constructed as an elaborate anti-narrative, built from redundant cliches from popular generic forms (the detective story), Oedipal red-herrings, Chinese box puzzles, detection which fails to detect, a mystery novel in which the mystery is tantalisingly unresolved. 'City of Glass' is a labyrinthine textual maze of interpretative culs-de-sac, dead-ends which function as a formal reproduction of its subject's experience of the city. The lines on the last page, describing another notebook, might easily be applied to the text as a whole:

All the words were familiar to me, and yet they appear to have been put together strangely, as though their final purpose was to cancel each other out. I can think of no other way to express it. Each sentence erased the sentence before it, each paragraph made the next paragraph impossible. (*ibid.*, pp. 313–14)

At the outset then, 'City of Glass' would appear to be an *Ur*-geography of poststructuralism, a *protopos* (paradigmatic place) for the Postmodern. My intention is to address the question of whether it is possible to uncover traces of a counter-hegemonic cartography within such a text. If it is objected that Auster's primary concerns are for language, it ought to be noted that as in the root meaning of 'semiotics' – which is the Greek phrase *semeion*, meaning a mark or sign in space – the discourses of this text are interwoven throughout with spatial concerns. I should like to discuss three defining features in Auster's representation of the city: first, the politics of walking and watching in the city, as it is encoded in the recurring figures of the *flâneur*, the voyeur and the detective; second, the flatness of Auster's descriptions of New York as mimetic and expressive of that placelessness of place that pervades the spatial economy of capitalism; finally, I shall return to those subjects addressed in my analysis of Pynchon and systematically erased from postindustrial cartographies – the presence of the underclass and the prominence of the anti-commodity – to address their effectivity within Auster's mapping.

## From *flânerie* to 'get lost'

On the opening page of 'City of Glass' we read of Quinn's interests outside of writing mystery stories. More than anything,

> what he liked to do was walk. Nearly every day, rain or shine, hot or cold, he would leave his apartment to walk through the city – never really going anywhere – but simply going wherever his legs happened to take him. (Auster 1987, p. 3)

In 'Postmodernism, or, the Cultural Logic of Late Capitalism', Jameson refers to Benjamin's analysis of the experience of modernity in the cities of nineteenth-century capitalism, as a precedent for attempts to map their postmodern descendants. The central figure in Benjamin's analysis is the *flâneur* who wanders aimlessly through the new, sprawling metropolitan regions and to whom these spaces reveal themselves and their secret meanings. The *flâneur*, *promeneur* or stroller was a conspicuous persona in nineteenth-century French writing. Benjamin is obviously indebted to Baudelaire's essay on Constantin Guys, but also to Appolinaire's *Le Flaneur des deux rives*, Fargue's *Le Pieton de Paris* and the prose poetry of Larbaud. In 'The Philosophy of History' Benjamin wrote that the 'true picture of the past flits by' and only the *flâneur* who idly strolls, as opposed to the hurried, purposeful activity of the crowds, is able to see this picture (Benjamin 1982, p. 257). The city gives sustenance to the *flâneur*, who in turn has the very special purpose of 'endowing the city with a soul' (*ibid.*, p. 197). At one point, around 1840, it became *de rigueur* to take turtles for a walk in the Parisian arcades – the *flâneurs* liked to have the turtles 'set the pace for them' (*ibid.*, p. 199). The pace which Benjamin refers to here extends far beyond the physical activity of walking: *flânerie* is offered as a paradigm for intellectual and aesthetic pursuits, a metaphor for ways of seeing, a style and mode of being appropriate to *la vie moderne* in the new urban spaces of Haussman and Bonaparte.

The essential point in comparing the *flânerie* of Quinn with that described by Benjamin and practised by Baudelaire, is to notice the distance, geographical and perceptual, between them. This is crystallised by the opening description of Quinn's walks:

> New York was an inexhaustible space, a labyrinth of endless steps, and no matter how far he walked, no matter how well he came to know its neighbourhoods and streets, it always left him with the feeling of being lost. Lost, not only in the city, but within himself as well. Each time he took a walk he felt as though he were leaving himself behind, and by giving himself up to the movement of the streets, by reducing himself to a seeing eye, he was able to escape the obligation to think, and this, more than anything else, brought him a measure of peace, a salutary emptiness within. The world was outside of him, and the speed with which it kept changing made it impossible for him to dwell on any one thing for very long. Motion was of the essence, the act of putting one foot in front of the other and allowing himself to follow the drift of his own body. By wandering aimlessly, all places became equal and it no longer mattered where he was. On his best walks, he was able to feel he was nowhere. And this, finally, was all he ever asked of things: to be nowhere. New York was the nowhere he had built around himself, and he realised that he had no intention of leaving it again. (Auster 1987, pp. 3–4)

This description of Quinn's walks subtly subverts a series of cartographic traditions – literary, mythological, functional – and tells us as much about the ways in which the city has been inscribed as it does about the geographical specificity of late twentieth-century New York. In nineteenth-century American literature the city was often represented as the site of a possible expansion of consciousness. The scophilia of Quinn's *flânerie* is reminiscent of the Emersonian decree – to become a 'roving transparent eyeball: I am nothing. I see all' (Emerson 1990a, p. 1504) – as Transcendentalist philosophy emerged as antidote to the initial stages in the rise of the American city. But rather than Whitman's erotic

ideal of a metropolitan *communitas* rather than the transcendentalist pinings of Hart Crane and William Carlos Williams, or the
pedagogic passage from innocence to initiation in *Sister Carrie*, *The
Ambassadors* and *Manhattan Transfer*, New York for Quinn has
become the venue for an absenting of any erotic or intellectual
identity.

At the entrance to this labyrinthine text, New York itself is
experienced as labyrinth. The conspicuousness of this figurative
analogy in modern European city writing, from Joyce to Robbe-
Grillet and Borges, has led Wendy Farris to comment that

> in many modern cities, man becomes minotaur. Old labyrinthine
> city defences were designed to keep out invaders. Modern
> inhabitants are frequently trapped inside cities described as
> labyrinths. The convolutions have moved within and are
> threatening rather than protective. (Farris 1991, p. 39)

In the 'City of Glass' this has been inverted. Once more the
labyrinth is established as a form of defence for the city dweller,
except that now it is a protection *against* the self, its convolutions
defend against the terrors within. Quinn's relation to his urban
environment is also a precise inversion of the dynamics of the
maze factor explored by Peter Smith in *The Syntax of Cities*:

> inscrutable urban space holds a fascination for people ... when
> the key to the labyrinth has been discovered, or, in psychological
> terms, a cognitive map or model has been constructed, the
> relationship between the individual and the environment aspires
> to a new level. Once a place has yielded its secrets it facilitates
> empathy between mind and artefact. Man and buildings become
> symbolically bound together. (Smith 1977, p. 171)

Quinn's walking overturns dominant romantic and modern
cartographic traditions and establishes the extent of his departure
from Baudelairean *flânerie*. The *flâneur* described by Benjamin was
an aristocratic Bohemian, assured of an income without having to
work, one who could afford to devote his time to philosophical
inquiry into the 'true picture of the past' and aesthetic appreciation
of the Parisian boulevards. His imperative was to relate to the
ordinary objects of everyday life, to understand their fleeting
qualities and yet extract eternal significances from urban
ephemerality. In stark contrast, for Quinn in the postmodern City
of Glass, walking is simply a mode of motion, a means of escaping
the obligation to think and to feel. The crowds are conspicuously
absent from the streets of Auster's labyrinthine and illegible New
York and Quinn's aim is simply to be lost in the city and to himself.

## Watching the detective

To walk through the city in this way, Auster suggests, to follow the drift of one's own body, is to lack a place. Implicitly the postmodern urban landscape is defined as an immense social experience of lacking a place. Although 'City of Glass' opens with a description of the postmodern *flâneur*, this persona is subsequently replaced by another, a more classically modernist variant of *flânerie*, that entails the highest degree of participation in plotting movements in the urban landscape – the detective.

Quinn tracks Peter Stillman around the streets of New York for several days. On impulse he begins to map each day's journey in his notebook. Eerily, they seem to form the shape of letters: 'O,W,E,R,O,F,B,A,B,E'. Having missed the first four days and with, he assumes, another day to come, he surmises that his suspect's movements have spelt out a message: 'THE TOWER OF BABEL'. This literalises the notion of one's movement through a landscape as a narrative – one explored in depth in a work published in the same year as *The New York Trilogy* and to which it bears a number of similarities: Michel De Certeau's *The Practice of Everyday Life*. De Certeau also begins his study of New York at ground level, with the practice of walking, which, he suggests, leaves a trace in the city, a graphic trail or 'spatial story' composing a 'pedestrian rhetoric' of trajectories across the urban landscape (De Certeau 1984, p. 116).

Quinn's map/plotting of Stillman's footsteps make the city, in Lynch's terms, more 'legible' (Lynch specifically suggests that grid systems like that of New York promote the effect of illegibility most intensely) even if the final message points to an anarchy of meaning. This spatial story, Quinn notes, is punctuated by traffic lights, signs and bricks which act like full stops. We might see emerging here a grammatology of the urban landscape, the beginnings of a syntax of the city-as-narrative, the street-as-sentence. This would not simply be a geographical conceit, but a means of articulating the experience of the city and in particular the omnipresence of material forms of State and corporate authority, less as abstract entities than as an everyday felt presence: 'Don't Walk', 'No Entry', 'No Trespassing', 'No Litter'. Passing through the urban text, these are the punctuation marks to the billboards and shop windows' continual enticements to consumption.

Plotting the paths of Stillman (the irony being that he rarely is), Quinn recalls Poe's Arthur Gordon Pym, who similarly discovered strange hieroglyphics on the inner walls of a chasm. The hieroglyphics on the inner walls of New York's skyscraper chasms seem to be a metaphor for the modern Babel, the global village as a 'field of stylistic and discursive heterogeneity without a norm' (Jameson 1984a,

p. 62). But, as in Poe's tale, it is never clear whether these signs actually exist, or have been written on to the landscape by the observer. Quinn's situation here is reminiscent of that confronted by Oedipa. In *The Crying of Lot 49* it is a phone call late at night that propels the protagonist into detective duties. Quinn agonises in Oedipa-like wonderings on Stillman's wanderings: was his suspect plotting against his son? Was he plotting his course each day? Were the hieroglyphic graphic trails he had found a hoax? an hallucination? a revelation?!

In *The Practice of Everyday Life*, De Certeau categorises the occupants of urban space as either walkers (*Wandersmaner, flâneur*) or as voyeurs. Both of these activities are fused in the role of the detective (the pursuing Private Eye) as the lives of scopophilic characters are dominated by the activity of watching other people. In 'Ghosts', the second section of the *Trilogy*, Blue watches Black (who turns out to be White) from an apartment across the street for almost the entire narrative in a minimalist reworking of Hitchcock's *Rear Window*. The prominence of voyeuristic activities could be interpreted as an implicit observation on the centrality of forms of surveillance to the practice of everyday life. As Soja has suggested, using the Foucauldian model of the Panoptican, the city has always served as a 'key surveillant node of the state':

> It is not production, or consumption or exchange themselves which specifies the urban, but rather their collective surveillance, supervision and anticipated control within the panoptican city. (Soja 1989, p. 119)

Surveillance exists in the information systems available to bureaucratic and police organisations. It is also a key feature of the environment with the increasing prominence of the electronic eye of the security camera. One urban space in which this technological observation can be seen is the shopping arcade and surveillance is even more pervasive if we extend our interpretative lens here to include Haug's assertion about our continual bombardment by the 'flirtatious glances' of the commodity: the way in which (without lapsing into Pynchonesque paranoia) the shop window, or television, subjects the viewer/voyeur to its own intense gaze (Haug 1984, p. 55).

## The placelessness of place

In a *New York Times* review of the state of the contemporary American novel, Charles Newman memorably defined postmodern prose fiction as 'the flattest possible characters, in the flattest possible landscapes, rendered in the flattest possible diction' (cited in Harvey 1989). Jameson is similarly critical of this flatness, or depthlessness, which he suggests is 'perhaps the supreme formal characteristic of all postmodernisms' (Jameson 1984a, p. 62). Landscape in the 'City of Glass' certainly is flat. Auster assiduously avoids urban pastoral and picturesque. At one point the reader is presented with a description of a journey which amounts to little more than a page of street names. As with Auster's representation of the activities of walking and watching in the city, however, such sequences might be seen to contain traces of a counter-hegemonic cartography, rather than being automatic capitulations to the logic of late capital.

Functionalism, featurelessness and uniformity, the systematic erosion of difference in accordance with the drive for hyperefficiency, are actual formal features of the straight-space canyons of the postmodern American city. This flatness is not only a feature of the physical environment, but of the existential textures of urban character, of that pervasive sense of what Edward Relph (1976) has evocatively phrased the *placelessness of place* across the postmodern landscape. Relph has examined the components of this placeless geography and diagnosed the main contributory factors in the weakening of the identity of regions until they not only look alike, but also feel alike. The development of mass communications infrastructure, contrary to McLuhan's panegyric, has initiated an homogenisation by electric media, a reduction in the significance of place-based styles by encouraging standardised (and standardising) environments. In conjunction with this process, Relph traces the effects of the development of 'other-directed landscapes' in many regions – places designed for passers-by, consumers, spectators. The generation of ubiquitous touristscapes is compounded by the ascendancy of international styles in design and architecture and the fact that large bureaucracies and centralised authorities consistently seek to provide universal solutions to local problems. Consequently, uniformity is promoted through the instigation of instant new towns and homogenised suburban housing developments, identical shopping complexes, highways and airports. The standardisation attributable to 'coca-colonialism' in the cultural landscapes of the world at the points of production, administration and consumption, promotes a sense of placelessness, which is exacerbated by the tendency towards continuous redevelopment, the incessant putting up and tearing down, the creative destruction which valorises impermanence and characterises the profoundly restless capitalist landscape. Quinn's anxiety at the 'speed with which it kept changing' can be seen as representative of a discomfort at the core of a culture whose spaces appear permanently destined to melt into air.

The aesthetic code of flatness then, is isomorphic with the economic code and spatial structuring of commodity capitalism. The landscapes of the 'City of Glass' exactly evoke the uniformity of the postmodern city, the erosion of heterogeneity and regional detail. Depthlessness here can be interpreted as an index of a socioeconomic system which perpetuates the establishment of placeless places and as a formal mimesis of the opacity and illegibility of its urban spaces. Jameson is critical of the attention to surfaces in recent aesthetic production, but it needs to be remembered that opacity is one of the supreme formal characteristics of the postmodern city. On any journey through the urban text it is the code of enigma which predominates – reflecting glass windows and blank concrete walls prevent the pedestrian from knowing what is taking place within most buildings, and whilst poverty is squeezed out to the margins, corporate activities take place between the lines. Visual and physical access to the cathedrals of corporate capital is everywhere restricted. The depthlessness of Auster's New York is a reproduction of the geographical specificity of the postmodern city, it carefully outlines the contours, or rather the absence of contours, across contemporary placeless flatscapes.

## A place where one could finally disappear

> the strange and transitory beauties of the urban landscape.
> Paul Auster, *Art of Hunger* (1982), p. 17

As in the fiction of Thomas Pynchon, *The New York Trilogy* can be seen not only to resist the standardisation of space, but also to plot the presence of the underclass and the anti-commodity in the postmodern city. The long sequence of street names mentioned above comes from a lengthy passage describing Quinn's movements through the city. It does not, however, occur in isolation. In fact, it is precisely counterpointed with a second account. While the first is a mundane recital of street names, the verbal equivalent of a street map, the second plotting of Quinn's journey specifically foregrounds those elements erased from official cartographies and postindustrial mappings:

> Today as never before: the tramps, the down-and-outs, the shopping-bag ladies, the drifters and the drunks. They range from the merely destitute to the wretchedly broken. Wherever you turn, they are there, in good neighbourhoods and bad ... Hulks of despair, clothed in rags, their faces bruised and bleeding, they shuffle through the streets as though in chains. Asleep in doorways, staggering insanely through traffic, collapsing on sidewalks – they seem to be everywhere the moment you look for them. Some will starve to death, others will die of exposure, still others will be beaten or burned or tortured. (Auster 1987, p. 50)

Quinn discovers his town's underclass population and the chapter closes with him sleeping rough, an activity suggesting an affinity with the poverty he confronted that day. After these experiences he stakes out across the road from Stillman's building, lives in an alley, sleeps in a trash can, learns to survive on the barest minimum of food and drink. When he catches sight of his reflection for the first time in months, in a shop window, he recognises himself as a bum, emphasising that this is as much an exercise in empathy as a part of his detective duties.

'City of Glass' recognises the anti-commodity as a crucial feature of the postmodern landscape. Stillman is an archaeologist of the city's trash. On his journeys Quinn watches him pick up 'broken things, discarded things, stray bits of junk' (*ibid.*, p. 59) – the bottom of a shattered light bulb, an umbrella shorn of its material, the severed head of a rubber doll, soggy and shredded newspapers, even a dog turd – priceless objects, each examined with reverence as though it were a prehistoric exhibit. Stillman explains to Quinn that New York, as the 'most forlorn of places', exactly suits his purpose: 'The brokenness is everywhere ... the broken people, the broken things, the broken thoughts. The whole city is a junk heap' (*ibid.*, p. 78). Fiction and historical actuality disconcertingly intersect on this point to confirm part of Stillman's assertion: currently, New York's major physical export is waste paper. If we were to follow Jameson's argument concerning the relations between late capitalism and postmodern culture, *The New York Trilogy* might be included in this. Should Auster's mapping be categorised in this manner?

To respond to this question it is necessary to move on from considerations of the oppositional *potential* of specific spaces in 'The City of Glass', to a broader investigation of the political *effectivity* of Auster's mapping. Any oppositional interpretation of a text should aim to analyse it in terms of the antagonistic dialogue between discourses, foregrounding the repressed, reintroducing the voices of those silenced and disinherited by the dominant culture. And yet it appears that it is the dominant culture itself which is absent from this text; the City of Glass is populated exclusively by the marginalised.

Such a reading would be mistaken, however, because it ignores the critical fact that none of the voices within this city-text are really understood *dialogically*, or even relationally, and certainly not as members of a specific class formation. The essence of this text's postmodernity lies in its hostility towards all didactic modernist polemics on the topic and topos of the city. Urbanism is mapped at a micropolitical level, as a series of specific everyday practices (walking and watching on the urban landscape). What prevents the potentially oppositional spaces within *The New York Trilogy* from converging as a critical cartography, however, is not the absence of any grand narrative of the urban experience, so much as the reinscription of an essentially metaphysical perspective within the city-text. There is no dominant culture present within this city, in the ordinary sense, because dominance, from Auster's primarily philosophical point of view, is itself an ideological chimera – all city dwellers are buffeted by a chaos of meaning and terminal indeterminacies of interpretation within narrativised spaces devoid of master codes.

The first stage in the development of a city without beggars is making the spaces of inequality visible. Auster's understanding of destitution, however, is only tangentially concerned with the lived experience of New York's homeless population. Destitution is in fact offered implicitly as a condition which permits access to more profound states of being. Gide's Thesus managed to plot a path to the centre of the labyrinth, but was unable to acquire Oedipus' knowledge of the divine. Quinn gravitates towards the margins of the labyrinthine postindustrial city of signs only to acquire a distinctly Baudrillardean revelation of an ontological vacuum at the heart of the American metropolis: the city and the people who inhabit it are translated into 'no more than a kind of blankness, a hole in the texture of things' (ibid., p. 146).

The tramps in the City of Glass are dropped into this textual void like so much litter. They are not situated as a historically specific underclass and their potential as a critical presence in a radical cartography of the class contours of the capitalist cityscape goes largely unrealised. The litter itself, the vast quantities of trash with which the streets are strewn, similarly remain unpoliticised spaces within Auster's mapping. 'The whole city is a junk heap' (ibid., p. 84), but these offscourings are valorised as opportunities for a philosophical contemplation of the naming process, as opposed to a politicised understanding of interpellation, environmental devastation and the detritus of commodification. To use the words of Marianne Moore, in (Auster's) New York, 'it is not the plunder, but "accessibility to experience"' that matters (Moore 1979, pp. 1180–1).

The tramp, alongside the detective and the flâneur, are each representative of alternative, rather than oppositional, cultures, to use Williams' valuable distinction. However, from the giddy Olympian heights of metaphysical absurdity there really is nothing to oppose. The New York Trilogy confirms the efficacy of Jameson's definition of narrative: 'City of Glass' offers a symbolic resolution of actual historical and geographical contradictions. From the anti-materialist perspective of its cartography, the mundane matters of class conflict and sociospatial organisation become purely secondary: for tramp, millionaire, detective and even the writer are all subject to the absurdity and absolute uninterpretability which is the essence of all geographical and historical experience. Whilst watching a tramp performer with a clarinet, Quinn expresses the wish that lies somewhere near the dead-centre of the anti-materialism within the reactionary components to postmodernism's geographical imagination: 'To be inside that music, to be drawn into the circle of its repetitions: perhaps that is a place where one could finally disappear' (Auster 1987, p. 109).

# CHAPTER 8

# Machinescapes/Dreamscapes: Jayne Anne Phillips

Jayne Anne Phillips' *Machine Dreams* (1984) chronicles two generations in the history of the Hampsons, an American family falling apart together in the small West Virginian town of Bellington. The losses, dreams and remembrances of Jean and Mitch Hampson and of their two children, Billy and Danner, constitute the moving parts of this narrative device. The two terms contained in the title unexpectedly weld that which appears antithetical. Conventionally, a machine is categorised as an object which is substantial, instrumental and explicable; conversely, dreams are felt to be intangible, unproductive and elusive. This oxymoronic construction sets in motion a series of questions about forms of technology and forms of consciousness and signals their increasing integration across physical and psychological landscapes dominated by machines. Phillips' work involves the imagination of technology in a dual sense: to dream of machines and to be the machine that dreams. This figurative fusion also anticipates the design of the narrative, for *Machine Dreams* functions through a series of intricate associative mechanisms whereby connections are continually forged between components which initially appear dislocated, relays are revealed between self and other (in its technological and familial forms), between past, present and future and a range of places and experiences. The achievement of Phillips' story of the Hampsons is that its profound recognition of conflict and discontinuity continually threatens to break down before a tapestry of interconnections and *relatedness*.

In his analysis of *Machine Dreams*, Michael Clark aims to unravel this tapestry in an essay which is representative of a problematic tendency in the criticism of postmodern narratives (Clark 1986). 'Remembering Vietnam' appears to assume that mere simultaneity of artistic and critical discourses entails their equivalence. In much the same manner as McHoul and Wills in *Writing Pynchon*, Clark proceeds from the assumption that postmodern fiction is always already the practice of poststructuralist theory (or, since the boundaries between these discourses are themselves repudiated, that the dissimilarities amount to pretty much the same *différance*).

From this position, Clark proposes that Phillips' story speaks largely about certain poststructuralist orthodoxies. *Machine Dreams* tells of the collapse of all grand narratives (with the exception, of course, of that privileged discourse which pronounces the collapse of all grand narratives), total understandings, stable egos and all the accompanying baggage of a transcendental metaphysics of presence.

One of the more perplexing features of much of this variety of criticism is that, after an initial gestural nod in the direction of indeterminacy, it tends to go on to *construct* a catalogue of all those myths which postmodern narratives are confidently deconstructing. Phillips' narrative is undoubtedly concerned with the fragmentation of memory, history and the self. However, each of the family members is also precisely engaged in an attempt to counter this dissolution, to salvage a sense of self and place (the two are intimately interwoven in Phillips' imagination), to comprehend the significance of their experiences and the value of their relations with other people. Danner, in particular, plays a central role in this allegedly decentred narrative. The daughter seeks to articulate a discontinuity which is generally only experienced by the other family members. The loss of her brother in Vietnam serves as a catalyst to her historical and political consciousness and inspires an attempt to piece together the fragments of her family's past – so that to be lost is not to have lost.

This attempt is recognised by Clark only to be hurriedly dismissed as a regrettable resurgence of nostalgia in an otherwise textbook manifesto of the postmodern (*ibid.*, p. 52). Rewriting *Machine Dreams* according to the poststructuralist paradigm, any difficulty associated with establishing a historical narrative, or making sense of identity, must of necessity be immediate confirmation of the impossibility of such tasks. No matter how tenuous and provisional, Danner's attempt to pull things together, to construct a narrative of her self, her family and her culture, it is surely far too easy to write them off as the messy emotions of 'regret and longing', contaminating the text with 'loss' as opposed to 'pure absence' (*ibid.*, p. 54). The analysis of Phillips' novel which follows will offer an alternative to Clark's reading and the philosophical model it endorses. It will propose that *Machine Dreams* is a major contribution to discourses on the relations between people, places and technological forms in postmodern culture. In particular, Phillips' fierce spatial sensitivity reveals that we cannot separate the geographies of who we are from where we are.

## Class contours in a small town

*Machine Dreams* offers a critique of traditional understandings of alienation and reification in its representation of labour and of relations with technology in specific workspaces. Alongside this critique there is a detailed re-presentation of the politics of domestic space and the private sphere – 'those networks of kinship and collectivity which we call friends and family, those experiences we group together as our private and personal lives' (Pfeil 1990, p. 100). These are examined within the context of macrosocioeconomic developments in American culture, especially since the Second World War, with particular attention to changes in class structure, the family, patterns of consumption and demographic distribution.

The personal history of Mitch Hampson can be interpreted as a microcosmic representation of aspects of his culture's geographical development between 1910 and 1970. Born on a farm in Randolph County, he moved at an early age to Raynell, an emergent railroad town. This migration underscores the contemporary intensification of urbanisation and industrial expansion. Later, in the years following the death of his foster father, Mitch loses contact with industrial production by leaving his work in construction for a job in insurance and as an automobile salesman. Mitch's reluctant exchange of clothing, from khaki overalls to white collar and tie, which accompanies a move to the suburbs, crystallises the embourgeoisement of large sections of the US working class which took place during the post-Second World War period.

The Hampson's increased sociogeographical mobility is structured within the narrative around the polarised image clusters of 'Mitch–dirt–labour' and 'Jean–cleanliness–learning'. Jean, who has started taking college classes, insists on rolling up the car windows on infrequent visits to her husband's place of work. However, as children, both Danner and Billy are excited by the mud, dirt and grime of 'MITCH CONCRETE'. They enjoy building roads in the earth, investigating a magical, musty old air hanger, or digging up the cellar floor at home in 'flashlight games' which allow them to wallow in the dirt of secret, subterranean places. Significantly, Jean discovers these games whilst dusting and is horrified, but Mitch secretly relishes the children's exploration of the house which he built himself. Subsequently, the enthusiasm which he displays for the civil defence programme, particularly for the construction of home shelters, suggests that this is a surrogate for the manual labour denied him as a white-collar professional. The illustration on the cover of the civil defence manual is of a man, covered with dust, 'shovelling dirt onto a door' (Phillips 1984, p. 163).

Billy ponders the changes in his father's work from opening up trucks to reveal the greasy engines that he repairs, to flicking through the sales brochure containing pictures of the machines which he sells. Similarly, Danner displays remorse at Mitch's switch from building roads and shelters in their home town, to selling products to its residents. The decline in esteem and job-satisfaction experienced by Mitch and sensed by his children is inseparable from the social climb that Jean urges the family towards. This signals Phillips' awareness of degrees to the condition of alienation and challenges the authority of orthodox mappings of the postindustrial workspace.

The growing distance between Mitch and Jean is most apparent in 'Machine Dreams: Billy, 1957' (*ibid.*, pp. 135–58) and is structured around a telling geographical opposition. This section epitomises Phillips' meticulously crafted, although entirely unostentatious, use of symmetry to articulate difference and undermines the suggestion by Michael Clark that the text is composed of arbitrary and accidental images (Clark 1986, p. 54). Jean works in the school, where the desks need an extra polish 'because the janitor *did things halfway*' (Phillips 1984, p. 136) and she teaches Billy the sounds of words. Mitch works at the plant, where even the office is 'dusty, slightly acrid', with a smell of 'dry, clean dust mixed with ash' (*ibid.*, p. 150) and he explains to his son the sounds of engines. From her position in the world of education, Jean witnesses the professionalisation of the knowledge industry and realises the necessity for her children to acquire marketable language skills in the face of the growing obsolescence of mechanical competence. With the rapid expansion of the tertiary sector and the corresponding redundancy of his skills, Mitch comes to play an increasingly diminished role within the Hampson home. Through the marginalisation of Mitch Hampson, Phillips invokes the partial decline in the authority of the father in American culture, with the loss of his role as sole provider of economic security.

In 'Making Flippy-Floppy: Postmodernism and the Baby Boom PMC', Fred Pfeil seeks to relate the trends towards embour-geoisement and the restructuring of patriarchy in the postwar period to the rapid and widespread suburbanisation of American society since 1950. Pfeil's remarks are relevant to the increasingly suburbanised experience of the Hampsons:

> Snapping the nuclear family out and away from wider networks of neighbourhood, kin and class ... now the attenuated family 'unit' stayed home in its own private living room and watched TV ... by breaking up those old communal networks and cultures suburbanisation thus paved the way for the commodification of daily life on a newly expanded scale. (Pfeil 1990, p. 100)

Pfeil's analysis of an upsurge in the commodification of everyday life, following the mass migration from working-class neighbourhoods to middle-class suburban homes, resonates distinctly with Phillips' portrayal of the Hampsons: the increasing isolation and cocooning of the family in a suburban residence; the domination of domestic space by television and new appliances; and Jean's decision, amidst the 1950s' qualitatively higher standards of consumption, to re-educate herself for the new labour markets and that increasingly significant second income.

*Machine Dreams* traces the *embourgeoisement* of large sections of American society since the 1950s and situates this development dialogically in relation to other classes, for, whilst there has been a significant proportionate increase in white-collar employment, as Bell and other postindustrial prophets insist, neither the rich nor the poor have disappeared. Given their relatively humble origins, however, the upper strata of society is always less visible to the Hampsons than those immediately beneath them. Often the family will encounter the signifiers of corporate capital, such as the impressive Mobil sign, and occasionally hear about those amongst whom it circulates, such as Mayor Rafferty who 'owned the Mobil Station and some real estate' (Phillips 1984, p. 186). Rafferty pays for the Pool Dance Party which Danner and Billy attend, an occasion at which he can afford to blot out the eyesore of the railroad (symbol and backbone of the older industrial America before widespread car ownership and air travel) with some strategic landscape gardening. However, Rafferty and the class he belongs to remain a largely mythical, though no less influential, presence in their lives. Danner and Billy are always drawn, both metaphorically and literally, to the other side of the tracks. The Hampson children instinctively chart the class contours to the landscapes of capital. Geographically, Phillips' narrative, like those by Pynchon and Auster, gravitates towards the spaces occupied by the marginalised.

As an observant adolescent Danner always noticed the miners, country families and scruffy children who flocked to Main Street at the weekend: 'They were dirty and smelled of dirt, despite the casks of harsh yellow soap dispensed by the county' (*ibid.*, p. 225). Despite the best efforts of suburbanised America to cleanse itself of these people, to remove them like a stubborn stain from its recently acquired white collar, they linger. The 'clean-dirt' of Danner's father's construction site could be washed off at home, but the dirt and grime of poverty which she encounters in downtown Bellington is both more persistent and more compelling. Billy encounters the same people whilst working for the Park Service, those who use the swimming area during the weekdays when the rest of Bellington was in its offices – a 'country family or two', some 'truckers between hauls', 'miners or plant workers on night shift' and the unemployed:

> Never less than five or six kids, and the parents middle-aged on wool blankets. The kids wore shorts and T-shirts, the babies went naked. They brought big rubber inner tubes instead of toys. No radios, no plastic bottles of oil. (*ibid.*, p. 253)

In his relations with Kato and Shinner's crowd at the billiards hall and with his decision to fight in Vietnam rather than dodge the draft, Billy aligns himself with a class deprived of luxuries and many of the essentials enjoyed by suburbanised, white-collar America. After Billy's disappearance the assimilation of the Hampsons into the PMC (Professional-Managerial Class) is further compromised by Danner's decision to progress beyond simply observing these people to meeting and actively helping them. In her work for Viet Nam veterans and for underprivileged children at Project Headstart, Danner displays, like her brother, a staunch resistance to their *embourgeoisement*.

According to the poststructuralist paradigm, *Machine Dreams* is a fragmentary text. Such a reading, however, fails to engage with the possibility that this is a story about living *through* fragmentation. It articulates the experience of incoherence and disjointedness under the pressure of historical change. Phillips outlines the series of changes promoting this sense of fragmentation – in domestic space and the move from farm to town and then suburb, in the workplace experience and the arrival of new technological forms, in the geographical restructuring of class and gender relations. And their impact is consistently related to the ability to retain a political consciousness and conscience.

## Second nature

Despite his initial claims about the profound indeterminacy of Phillips' work, Michael Clark ascribes a single, fixed and decidedly determinate meaning to the title of the text. *Machine Dreams* 'focuses Phillips' interest in the *depersonalised* character of individual subjectivity' (Clark 1986, p. 55). In a similar vein he goes on to interpret the ending of the narrative, 'Machine Dream: Danner', as evidence of the 'conflation of subconscious processes with the *inhuman* apparatus of commercial icons and the machine', so that 'even the realm of desire and dream disintegrates into the random clatter and drove of an *impersonal* machine' (*ibid.*, p. 54). Between the title page and ending, Clark interprets the machine dreams of the characters as substituting for 'what might ordinarily pass as the *personal unconscious* of the people [Phillips] describes' (*ibid.*, p. 56; emphasis added). This line of interpretation relies heavily upon the conventional machine/human dichotomy which predates indus-trialisation and was canonised by romanticism. However, the notion that *Machine Dreams* charts the insidious dehumanisation of the organic by the mechanical is a reduction of Phillips' actual position. The narrative in fact enacts a redefinition of the very terms of this romantic discourse, posing critical questions about the dialogue (as opposed to Clark's one-sided conversation) which takes place between the body and its technological extensions. Phillips poses the following questions: can a mechanisation of the human take place which is not, automatically, a *de*humanisation? Conversely, can there be a personalisation of technology which is not instantly a form of reification? To rely upon the romantic opposition of Nature and Machine is to risk missing the ways in which Phillips continually foregrounds their interchangeability. In *Machine Dreams* animate and inanimate partake of qualities traditionally associated with the other within an environment in which technology is pervasive. In this context, the phrase 'personal unconscious', with its intimations of some inviolate space within human psyche penetrated by a hostile mechanical force, is a particularly problematic term for Clark to use. Technology is such an integral and pervasive component of exterior physical geography, that it is only *natural*, given the constructed nature of the self, that it becomes integrated with the interior geography of those people who populate its machinescapes.

The opening pages of the novel begin the process of redefinition. Even in early twentieth-century small-town America, technology is seen to be so omnipresent across the landscape that the interweaving of machines with the collective fantasy-life of the protagonists becomes inevitable. As the stories evolve and combine, time is revealed to be inaccurately measured by the clock and space to be refigured by cars, planes and trains. The mechanically reproduced image, photograph or home movie, is shown to be a stimulus to and a key component of memory. Machines are central to many of the novel's workplaces – construction sites, mines, railroads, telephone offices – and recreation similarly revolves around the prefabricated machine dreams disseminated through television, radio and cinema. As an ominous and continual backdrop to all of this there are also the killing machines of war, the military Fordism of the Second World War and Viet Nam as experienced by Mitch and Billy. Throughout *Machine Dreams*, Phillips' sensitivity to family history is expressed through a meticulous archaeology of these technological forms. What follows here will be an attempt to trace her excavation of social relations as they are iconicised within machine-dominated spaces.

The ticking of the clock, that mechanical device for rationalising and splitting up time into discrete sequential units, is a prominent background noise throughout the narrative. When Mitch awakes from his machine dream of the death he witnessed in New Guinea, he is startled by the sight, 'very near, [of] the round white face of the alarm clock, in black numbers afloat like fragile, meaningless shapes' (Phillips 1984, p. 60). This vision crystallises the overriding sense in Phillips' work of the inapplicability of linear time when confronted by the synchronicity and slippage of past, present and future in memory and in dream. Later, Danner spends time in Billy's room when he is reported MIA. She recollects returning home after teenage dates and being confronted by the face of the St Clair clock, hung as always in its circle of blue neon from the high balcony. 'The blue ring glowed around the moonish face of the clock. The minute hand moved with a discernible jerk, accurate, later than I thought' (*ibid.*, p. 307). Billy never paid much attention to the funeral-home clock ticking constantly over Bellington (eventually 'time's winged chariot' became a 'huey' called 'Barbarella'), but Danner remembers its 'moonish face' and 'jerky hands' as though it was the boyfriend recently departed. The clock had held her hypnotised for an instant, before she went up to bed to dream in time with the ticking of 'a clock loud in the sleeping house' (*ibid.*).

Billy's own recollections of home-life during a traumatic period in his youth, the death of his Uncle Clayton, are similarly fused with the machines which dominate domestic space. He remembers the mechanical toys he played with when not permitted to watch television, the sewing machine used by his mother and, hovering at the centre of them all, a kitchen clock:

> The clock was round and yellow and it hung on the wall with its white chord snaking down. The clock always ticked but no one heard it really; only on those afternoons was the sound so loud. Billy was quiet and his mother forgot where he was; there was only the steady buzz of the sewing machine, and the clock sound: a gentle and regular knock behind the yellow face, a circle of numbers. Someone wanted in or out but they stayed in between and kept knocking, paid no mind to anything. *Your mind is full of business.* The quiet the clock made leaked into the air, and was only a hint of the quiet Clayton made. Not like ghosts; no one was scared. What was it? (*ibid.*, p. 154)

In one of the narrative's numerous imagistic slippages the 'white face' of Mitch's bedside alarm clock and the 'moonish face' of the St Clair clock are transposed with the 'yellow face' of the timepiece in the Hampsons' kitchen. This machine is inextricably fixed in Billy's imagination to his first encounter with death. In a dream the night before their ride out to his father's concrete plant, Billy has a vision of Clayton, whose 'face was strange' (*ibid.*, p. 147), within the rotating circle of a cement mixer. This premonition of his Uncle's impending heart attack continues the sense of the asynchronicity of mechanical time and its subjective experience. Clayton is felt to be *inside* time in a more generic sense, as a vital component in Billy's understanding of what makes his family tick. Like the gentle noise of the kitchen clock, Clayton speaks in the dream 'almost in a whisper' (*ibid.*), and despite Billy's attempt to dispel any suggestion of the supernatural in the sounds (and their absence) which he hears, there are ghosts in the machine. Clocks, Clayton, cement mixer and corpse disconcertingly elide in Billy's remembrances and within the narrative – so that, for example, the father's death at his desk is itself a premonition of his son's (Mitch) figurative demise in a desk job. Confusion over the time of death and Father/Time leaks into the narrative as machines become part of an iconic programme. In this way people come to intimate and initiate the stories which construct them. Throughout *Machine Dreams* Phillips encourages this discrete density of intratextual resonance, not purely as an aesthetic exercise, but as a means of re-creating exactly what people do with and through those technological forms which dominate their physical environment.

## Real to reel

'It's strange what you don't forget' (*ibid.*, p. 3). The opening line of Jean's 'Reminiscence To A Daughter' signals the text's interest in the mechanisms of memory. Throughout the work, the tech-nologically reproduced image, the photograph signifying the presence of absence, is central to these images, to the experience and the memory of space, as remembrance is filtered through the camera's mechanical eye. Jean's knowledge of the war is largely restricted to 'Kodak snapshots' (*ibid.*, p. 8), and memories of Tom, her first love, are tied up with pictures from the family album (*ibid.*, p. 10). Mitch similarly relies on an 'old home-made album Bess must have pasted together' (*ibid.*, p. 29) for access to his past and specifically for memories of his father. Both Mitch and Billy send pictures from basic training and postcards during their military service, whilst relying on photos for views of the family back home. Danner, in particular, is fascinated by photographs – from the image of her father as a baby, to the 'before-and-after' snapshots of her brother (working for the Park Service at the river in the summer of '69 and in uniform at a going-away party), which she photocopies and distributes to various government bureaucracies in her attempt to obtain information once he is reported MIA. In one of her dreams about Billy she can

> still see his face, usually his young face more real than any photograph or memory. My sense of him is so strong I think he must be coming through from some completely foreign zone, a zone free of interference and boundaries. A zone that is out of this world. (*ibid.*, p. 326)

'Interference' is a key word for Phillips' own narrative strategy. It captures the way in which the boundaries between images, objects and memories, machinescapes and dreamscapes, continually diffuse and problematise each other. In Danner's dream this interference is concurrent with a profound ontological instability, signalled by the phrase 'more real than any photograph or memory'. Photographs, memory, dream and social reality melt into one another as the realism of remembrance is aligned with its mechanical reproduction.

Film constitutes another area of interference in the text. Danner's memories are occasionally framed by the home movie camera, and the moving cinematic image is depicted as a potent form of mechanical dreaming. The slippage between a sequence of ontological frames is particularly evident in 'Machine Dreams: Mitch, 1946' (*ibid.*, pp. 59–92), which centres upon Mitch and Katie's trip to the cinema. A warm, dark space of comfort and escape, the movie theatre is one in a series of mechanical wombs in which characters are seen to seek refuge. Katie's illness prevents her from participating in many of the rigorous outdoor pursuits enjoyed by other children and consequently her fantasy-life is fulfilled by the movies. The film which they go to see is Disney's *Peter and the Wolf*. The sights and sounds suddenly provoke war memories for Mitch and he begins to inhabit two locations simultaneously:

> in the comforting crowded dark he shut his eyes and listened. Wind blew on the sound track, realistic wind billowing; sounded like they'd recorded it in New Guinea, the most deserted place in the world, where no one ever recorded anything. Now he wished someone had, even movie people; he wished he could hear again exactly how things sounded. (*ibid.*, pp. 83–4)

This soundscape takes Mitch back to memories of his confrontation with a wounded Japanese soldier. Immediacy is generated at this point in the narrative by a switch to the present tense and the entire episode is relayed through the metaphorical frame of the camera's mechanical eye, with close-ups, aerial and slow-panning shots:

> he looked at the field with a feeling of total detachment, as though he saw the grass and the swell of the land from a low-flying plane ... As he stood, his whole frame of vision rotated once, smooth and circular, the figure of Warrenholtz turning around like the long straight khaki hand of the clock. (*ibid.*, p. 86)

Disturbed by his recollections, Mitch decides to step outside. From the lobby he can still see the corner of the screen and he watches as, suddenly, the edges 'went silent and flashed, eaten into mottled holes by a racing black edge' (*ibid.*, p. 87). Despite the fact, recognised by Mitch, that it is only the celluloid in the projector and not the cinema screen itself which has caught fire, a panic ensues as the audience struggle to escape. In these passages, which pay such close attention to elisions between real and reel, we might discern resonances with another text proposing a classic distinction between the epistemological and the ontological. As the firing of the gun becomes a fire in the cinema, the Bellington movie-house becomes a palimpsest of Plato's cave: a dark shelter in which one observes shadows on a wall, generated by a light to the rear, shadows which must never be mistaken for the real thing since they are merely reflections of a world of 'pure forms' that will always remain unattainable to the spectator.

That the profound influence of our contemporary realm of pure forms, largely manufactured in the dream-factories of Hollywood, is registered in the next generation, can be illustrated by selected quotations from Billy's war letters. In his correspondence, the experience of Viet Nam (the first televised war) is screened by the popular mythology of war movie and western:

> It's nothing like John Wayne or that show we used to watch after school – what was that? '12 O'Clock High'. Used to love that show and the bomber jackets ... [It's] like cowboys and Indians, except the Indians are ghosts and they can't lose because nothing really kills them ... I don't know why I never asked you [Mitch] about the war you went to, I guess I thought I saw it in the movies. They'll never show this one there, pictures don't say how it is. (*ibid.*, pp. 286; 290; 292)

In the final reel of the novel Billy is 'making war-movie sounds', imitating a plane which falls 'year after year to earth', like autumn leaves in the 'deep, dark forest' of Danner's final machine dream (*ibid.*, p. 331). His remarks about 'cowboys and Indians' and the persistent appropriation of the western genre in postwar American cinema – particularly in its representation of Viet Nam – might suggest that another text is being referenced here, in one of the narrative's more intriguing instances of imagistic slippage. Billy is the 'Kid' on board the Barbarella (a more overt reference to a contemporary cult movie), but it is another western that is echoed in *Machine Dreams*: *Butch Cassidy and the Sundance Kid*. As Billy and the leader of his outfit, Luke, jump from their helicopter (perhaps) to be gunned down in a foreign land, they are frozen in the still-frame final shot of a terminal western, reminiscent of the ending of George Roy Hill's film. This would make Billy the *Sundance* kid – remembered by Danner as the 'golden' boy – and with his obsession for flight, the downfall of this draftee Icarus is not flying too close to the sun, but into anti-aircraft fire. This may appear too freely correlative, but then the narrative interlocks precisely through the associative logic of memory and dream, thus producing an unsettling ontological instability between the real and its technological reproduction. People's perception and recollection of different spaces – from the local cinema to distant lands – is consistently shown to be filtered through the camera's transparent roving eye.

## The garden in the machine

*Machine Dreams* incorporates a vast range of technologies – from the military to the medical, the mythological to the most mundane and domestic – but never succumbs to the temptation to reify it as an autonomous force dictating human destiny (as do McLuhan and Baudrillard in their postindustrial cartographies). Instead, it is understood as a landscape of forms which are enmeshed in and inseparable from social relations. Phillips' narrative articulates a critical component of postmodernity: the absolute omnipresence, which renders it practically invisible, of the various mechanical extensions of the body in a postindustrial society. *Machine Dreams* was published in the same year that Jameson's seminal essay on postmodernism appeared. Both texts suggest that the saturation of both physical and psychological landscapes by technology has reached such a level that the other in contemporary society might no longer be Nature at all, but the Machine (Jameson 1984a, p. 62).

The rare pastoral moments in *Machine Dreams* always witness the intervention of a second nature of technological forms. As children, Jean and Peggy visited the Blue Hole, an expanse of 'clear water circled with massive flat boulders, like a shore beach' and inhabited by a 'colony of butterflies' (Phillips 1984, p. 9). Peggy's pre-bathing ritual, however, the gesture of hanging a wristwatch on a bush, signifies the superimposition of mechanical rhythms on natural cycles (an augury of the fact that this site is soon to be devastated by mine drainage). Similarly, Danner's bucolic interlude, whilst picking honeysuckle with one of the children at Project Headstart, is interrupted by a telephone call that tells her that Billy is MIA. Later, when she returns to the house where they spent their childhood, it is, appropriately, overrun not by nature, but by dilapidated machinery: 'a bunch of junk cars parked in the backyard, down near the field. Parts of motors sitting around ...' (*ibid.*, p. 303).

Animate and inanimate become interchangeable. Nature is referred to through the metaphoric stencil of the machine. In her youth Jean always felt that the cows in the fields near her home were 'big, stupid machines' (*ibid.*, p. 5) and she recalls that in her job as a telephone switchboard operator the supervisor 'called us her chickens, as if the clickings and scratchings of the board were *our* sound' (*ibid.*, p. 11). Nature and technology continue to merge for the next generation. In the house at night Danner and Billy listen to the sounds of the kitchen clock and the electric fan, which are accompanied by the crickets' musical engine. Outside, birds swoop down through the darkness like planes on night patrol. When the children sneak out to spy on real planes at a hangar, they discover that natural and mechanical flight co-exist, as swallows have nested in the rafters.

That this interchangeability is not exclusive to American society is evidenced by the reaction of the New Guinean natives to US Army vehicles, which seems to intimate fundamental continuities between pre- and highly industrialised cultures:

> They'd taken them out to the open beach to teach them to drive the dozers and trucks, and the black men had touched the machines hand-over-hand, seeming to measure them as horses are measured, they touched all the gears and pedals, saying Papuan words for the parts. (*ibid.*, pp. 61–2)

The (flying) machines and horses (Pegasus) which fascinate Danner, Billy, Katie and the Papuan natives are one of the text's critical imagistic clusters. This subtle intratextual fusion of manufactured, mythological and natural, is at the heart of Phillips' representation of the relationship between the second nature of technological forms and human consciousness. Individuals enter into symbiotic interdependence with and through each other and the mechanical extensions of the body which, largely through subliminal mechanisms, are invested with symbolic value and woven into a communal dream-life. For the Hampsons, images, experiences and dreams of machines become metaphors, or impacted plots, stories which interfere with the literal surfaces of the spaces they inhabit. *Machine Dreams* thus achieves an archaeology of the subliminal depths of (post)industrial America, excavating memories from its machinescapes and recovering the genealogy of technological artefacts as felt experience.

Within this technological second nature the body's spaces are sometimes treated by Phillips as a species of machine (although this is not articulated, as in Pynchon, as a falling away from what is human). For Billy, his father is always seen and felt to be fused with the machine. Standing beside the men who smell of engine oil, '[Mitch] was lost to the waist in dark gears' (*ibid.*, p. 152). In a continuation of the mythological subtext (the recurring Pegasus motif) the centaur of classical nature mythology is supplanted in a machine age by the father whose lower body is mechanical. The point here is not a dehumanisation, or a mechanisation of sexuality; instead, 'the whole point of machine dreams is that the myths we attach to machines are ancient myths that we may have forgotten about ... the machines carry the myths now' (Stanton 1986, p. 42).

From a traditional Marxist perspective, Mitch's fondness for his Pontiac and the trucks he refers to as 'she' would be interpreted as classical instances of reification. Similarly, the responses of children to commercial signs (Billy's fascination with the words 'MITCH CONCRETE' and Katie's hypnotic attraction to the Mobil gas station emblem) would be diagnosed as instances of the penetration of the unconscious by capital as it iconicised within a commercial logo. These are entirely reasonable readings, but they do not seem to be the ones that Phillips is interested in offering.

In *Machine Dreams* each of the characters invests the objects that dominate personal and public space with a magical, mythological potential. They pursue relations with technology of an intensity which occasionally rivals their relationships with each other: Mitch's affection for cars; Billy's obsession with planes; Danner's attachment to her transistor radio. As personal machine mythologies evolve, merging in collective fantasy and dream-life, a question begins to take shape: is there a relation to technology that is not, *automatically*, an instance of reification? As with the redefinition of alienation implied in Mitch's awkward embourgeoisement, we appear to be offered a recognition of *degrees* to this condition and of the possibilities for personalisation and even a *re*humanisation of and through the mechanical. To assume that all the spaces of a second nature are immediately and equally alienating is to squeeze out that which Phillips is interested in – the potential for strategies of accommodation and disalienation. Such strategies are implicit in all the human relations with technology present within the text, and one example will now be pursued in more detail.

## Autoscapes and affective archaeology

Of all the machines which populate the landscapes of Phillips' novel, perhaps the most central – that with which each of the characters, and Mitch in particular, develop a symbiotic interdependence – is the automobile. The primacy of this particular technological form to *Machine Dreams* is entirely appropriate. It would be difficult to imagine a machine than has had more of an impact upon the American landscape than the automobile. The car has made over space in its own image. Some 130 million registered vehicles, a number which has increased at a near exponential rate since the Second World War, currently drive over the 4 million miles of road which form a latticework of macadam ribbons across North America. However, the centrality of the car to landscape extends far beyond the roads themselves. A whole series of vernacular spaces have been designed and constructed to service the needs of a car-owning population. These are the sites which dominate the geography of *Machine Dreams*: gas stations and car washes, drive-in movie theatres and eat-out diners, garages and driveways, shopping malls and entertainment complexes, motels and parking lots. At the same time, the cultural significance of the car must be understood in relation to America's mythic origins as a frontier culture. The term given to the roads, the *freeway*, testifies to the car's iconic potential as the vehicle which sustains the equation in the American imagination between liberty and geographical mobility.

Initially the physical and cultural impact of the automobile is registered in *Machine Dreams* through sheer weight of reference: Reb's Pierce Arrow Coupé, the Packard, the Nash, the black '59 Ford and the big white Chevrolet, the Mercury, the Camaro, the Pontiac, the Mustang and the jeep, the trucks, cranes and bulldozers of 'MITCH CONCRETE'. The first point to make about this catalogue of vehicles is the diversity and ambiguity of response which they elicit. This is crystallised in the opening pages of 'Machine Dreams: Mitch, 1946'. In Mitch's recurring nightmare of the digging of mass graves in New Guinea, the bulldozer is a part of the dream, but it also acts as a buffer against the horrors of the experience. His actions are largely unconscious; he achieves his task by becoming an extension of the machine:

> hot metal seat of the dozer against his hips, vibration of motor thrumming ... shift of the dozer still in his hands ... the dozer was already down, when had he lowered it? (Phillips 1984, p. 60)

Mitch's self-address, in the second person, is an indication of the extent of his tactile interdependence with the machine and his corresponding dissociation from his own body. Within the dream the heated, pulsating chamber of the bulldozer is a mechanical womb which partially insulates him from the horrific sensory assault outside: the sight of mangled corpses, the sound of a child crying and worst of all the smell, as he returns bodies to (mother) earth, a gruesome inversion of birth imagery:

> bad, terrible and full of death ... like a deadness of shit and live things rotted, some gigantic fetid woman sick to death between her legs had bled out her limitless guts. (*ibid.*, p. 59)

In his waking hours, another vehicle – his prize possession, a Pontiac Eight Sedan – performs a similar function in shielding him from his memories of war:

> For a moment he thought of leaving the Philippines on the ship, seeing with a last glance the dirty women sitting on the docks, the packs they roped to their back made of hemp net, showing their paltry possessions. The moment passed, the look of their faces receded, and he saw instead the rich dark blue of the car, felt again the shock of its newness as he leaned inside at the salesman's invitation: the dash, the steering-wheel, the silver gray

> upholstered seats, even the floors – absolutely clean, shining and
> quiet like the interior of a big jewel. (*ibid.*, pp. 67–8)

A *dream car* – clean, quiet, private, unspoilt. This exemplifies the
seduction of the commodity whose promissory second skin – or
perhaps, within the context of its recurrence within *Machine Dreams*,
whose promissory second *womb* – can literally be climbed into. The
commodity which appears to stand outside time and thus will not
die (unlike lives wrecked by conflict and illness), is figured as a
bumper against the nightmare of the war-machine. The product
of near-militarised working conditions on the factory's assembly
line deflects from Mitch's remembrance of the military assembly
line (whose human scrap heap he had to bury) and from the
poverty he witnessed overseas (which his children will see at home).
Mitch is thus seen to be confined to a classic and contradictory
patriarchal defence mechanism: his experience of war is articulated
largely through gynophobic images (the 'fetid' and 'dirty' women)
and is dispelled by a foetal flight, at the salesman's invitation, to
the mechanical womb of his Pontiac Eight Sedan. The interior of
the car becomes a refuge from the horrors of war, refugees and the
symbolic spaces of the mother's body. Vehicles thus insulate the
soldier from the horrors of war and enable the veteran to live
through the experience without ever fully comprehending it. This,
however, is only one aspect of Mitch's machine dream. Phillips'
representation of the relationship between the body's spaces and
places in which technology is pervasive is never static. In the second
half of 'Machine Dreams: Mitch, 1946' the spatial conceit of
car/mother's body/mechanical womb is reworked from a different
perspective.

Mitch waxes the 'solid roof of the car' (in contradistinction to
the intangible dreams which haunt him):

> Automatic, this work, rubbing onto the long car a substance like
> cold butter, filming the hard shine of the metal. Methodically,
> he did the car in sections, beginning with the long front hood,
> the broad snout of the machine. (*ibid.*, pp. 69–70)

Mitch's relation to his car during this automatised rubbing ritual
has distinctly erotic overtones. Mitch's response here is comparable
to his close friend Reb's passion for his beloved Pierce Arrow
Coupé: 'Reb tended that car like it was living, and thought of it
every minute. His father said he was love-struck' (*ibid.*, p. 36).
Ostensibly then, Phillips' understanding here does not appear to
be radically dissimilar to that of Norman Mailer, who explored the
subject of Americans' relationship to their cars in 'A Note on
Comparative Pornography':

Talk of pornography ought to begin at the modern root: *advertising*. Ten years ago the advertisements sold the girl with the car – the not altogether unfair connection of the unconscious mind was that the owner of a new convertible was on the way to getting a new girl. Today the girl means less than the machine. A car is sold not because it will help one to get a girl, but because it already is a girl. The leather of its seats is worked to a near-skin, the colour is lipstick-pink, or a blonde's pale green, the tail-lights are cloacal, the rear is split like the cheeks of a drum majorette. (Mailer 1968, pp. 350–1)

In America an estimated five billion dollars are spent on automobile advertising each year, a sum which exceeds the total budget for public transport. The word *auto*, translated from the Greek, means 'self' and it is clearly the objective of the hidden persuaders to fuse the car with the consumer's sense of self. The automobile as a sign in the spatial economy of consumer culture, as Roland Barthes observed in *Mythologies*, is both privileged and polysemic (Barthes 1972, p. 71). It is a mode of transport (functional), a symbol of status, prestige and class membership (social), a machine associated with freedom through geographical mobility (mythological) and a fetish (sexual). The commercial association between automobile and sexuality is well established – the earliest poster advertisements displayed cars adorned with voluptuous classical figures. The construction of the car as a metal mistress in subsequent advertising campaigns has been facilitated by the fact that, as Mailer intimates, bodywork design and contouring frequently seek to evoke subliminal connections with the ideal feminine figure of the day. In the postwar period there has been an intensification in the efforts to integrate the auto and the erotic. Cars are packaged as signifiers of the phallus, commodities which carry with them the promise of power, control, potency and thrust. More typically it is offered, both in its design and through the use of self-conscious innuendo by the advertisers, as a girl-machine – broken down into various desirable components in an identical fashion to the fragmentation inflicted on the female body in advertising discourses. In either instance the overriding aim of the commercial is to promote a fetishisation which responds to the car as object, experienced exclusively from the perspective of the purchaser, and forgets that it is a product manufactured through the martial regime of the assembly line.

In the light of Mailer's analysis, Mitch's choice of imagery for the interior of his 'girl' takes on a new significance: the 'big jewel' becomes a troth of fidelity in his dream of blissful union with a mechanical bride. The salesman who invites the groom-to-be to lean inside, to pursue Mailer's metaphors, might be the invisible salesman of sex – the fuel for the economic machine in a commodity culture in which 'the happy and faithful fetish' fuck seems increasingly preferred to that 'punishing trip to a flesh outside us' (Mailer 1968, p. 351). It would be misleading to assume, however, that Phillips is engaged primarily in a Mailerean critique of reification. *Machine Dreams* suggests that there might be positive aspects to the sensuous personalisation of the body's mechanical extensions and implies the necessity for a redefinition of the concept of reification itself, in the context of a second nature of technological commodities in which the boundaries between corporeal and mechanical spaces are confused.

*Machine Dreams* recognises those auto-erotic pleasures, the psychological and sociological relations of dependency apparent in a car culture, which are denounced in the Mailer critique and celebrated within Futurist aesthetics. Similarly, Phillips suggests the contribution of the car to the technologies of war and violence and the mechanisms of reification. *Machine Dreams* identifies the automobile as a vital cog in the wheels of postmodern machine mythology, but it does not possess a totalising theory that would permit the leap to a generic Car. Phillips' representations of machinescapes lack epic pretensions; consequently, technological forms are neither demonised or deified. Instead the automobile remains firmly tied to its roots in social relations and is figured, first and foremost, as a *cultural* form.

One of the means by which Phillips focuses attention on the positioning of technological forms within social relations, whilst eschewing the cliches of apocalypse and futurism, is by depicting the car as a primary location for the American family and the mating rituals of its adolescents. Reb cruises, dates and 'makes out' in his Pierce Arrow Coupé (Cupid's piercing arrow) and the suicide pact that he enters into with Marthella involves their driving over a cliff together. Sitting side by side in their car before a party, Mitch's discomfort is transferred to Jean through the seat and when she touches his shoulder the engine trembles for a brief moment. This symbiotic interdependence of corporeal and mechanical spaces continues on into the scene in which Jean visits her mother's grave. Falling asleep in the secure mechanical womb of the Nash, whilst snow falls peacefully to the earth, she tilts the seat back, 'pulling her knees up nearly to her chest' (Phillips 1984, p. 99) and appropriately adopts the posture of uterine flight.

Danner's final moments with her brother take place in the Camaro. They are parked outside Shinner's billiard hall and the rhythms of their conversation are subtly dictated by the engine and windshield wipers. The moment that they are switched off the view of the world outside is dramatically altered: 'Rain immediately runneled on the windshield, distorting the street to colours on a black shine' (*ibid.*, p. 266). Landscapes seen from within the car are framed in a fashion analogous to the material and metaphorical framing of the human and of nature by technology. In the descriptions of Billy and Kato's love-making, in the 'heated interior of the car, like a capsule with steamed windows, drifting in space' (*ibid.*, p. 275), pressed between door, seats and steering wheel (as Danner's brother will soon be 'clicked in' to Barbarella), the body itself is redefined as a desiring machine. Kato's post-coital reactions are 'automatic'. 'Somehow his getting a car had started them off', Billy later claims, and when they are not seeing each other, 'his car reminded him of her' (*ibid.*, pp. 254–5).

The courtship rituals of teenagers revolve around cars almost as much as the boys who drive them, and the locations that couples frequent tend to be mechanised environments. At the drive-in, Danner, like her father before her, experiences a fusion at the interface of the real and the reel between car, film and lover: 'then she was sliding down on the seat under him and it was like the soundtrack at the drive-in – a surface closed over her' (*ibid.*, p. 214). Teenagers socialise at Nedelson's 'automotised' Luncheonette, between the cars endlessly arriving and leaving to the backdrop of chart-show radio, but when they wish to be alone together they visit the derelict MITCH CONCRETE plant. On one of these occasions, and in one of the text's most evocative instances of a romantic technopastoral, the site is buried in snow, with its abandoned trucks transformed into white mounds, and the couples watch the city lights and cars below for hours. MITCH CONCRETE is felt to be a place so beautiful as to 'require hymns', a 'moonscape', which, in another of those imagistic slippages which form a continual challenge to the literal surfaces of Bellington's landscape, becomes actualised in the subsequent references to the Apollo mission (and which simultaneously sustains the mythological subtext).

In each instance of the relationship teenagers and their parents have with and in their cars and with the places they take them to, there is no suggestion that reification, as it is conventionally understood, is not taking place. However, *Machine Dreams* does appear to be inquiring whether the mechanisms of fetishisation are adequately grasped by conventional understanding. Does the concept of reification itself not repress elements in the dialogue taking place between the body and the technological forms which compose the second nature of postindustrial cultures? When Billy does not return from Viet Nam, Mitch places Billy's Camaro in Bess's wooden garage and 'takes good care of it'. On her visits Danner notes that it looks 'bright and cherished' and watches as her father leans on the hood 'affectionately' (*ibid.*, p. 323). The wedding to a mechanical bride is replaced by another ceremony, a laying on of hands on a family relic as part of a ritual of remembrance (as previously Mitch had watched the New Guinea natives laying their hands on the US Army jeeps). Reification, contrary to Adorno's definition (cited in Jameson 1990, p. 96), is not *always* a form of forgetting. The Camaro is de-eroticised. It becomes person-specific for Mitch, and perhaps for Danner and the reader it also becomes class-specific (the car is part of what is left over from Billy's decision, as a child of the middle classes, not to dodge the draft but to align himself with the oppressed and his family's class origins by going to war). In *Machine Dreams* different technological forms might mean different things in different times and places. The social practice of reification is implicitly defined as essentially diachronic and not wholly irredeemable. The moral dimensions to this redefinition are not avoided but problematised, since what is reified is specifically the human residues located across machinescapes through memory and dream.

# CHAPTER 9

# Burning Down the House: Toni Morrison

An acute sensitivity to the politics and poetics of space, especially at boundaries and frontiers, is often an integral component in the efforts of canonical white writers to secure a sense of self. So pronounced is this tendency that it has become something of a critical truism to insist upon the centrality of geographical concerns within their work. Such sensitivity is often even more accentuated in African-American writing. Given the historical experience of the black community this is hardly surprising. The dislocations of the diaspora were followed by centuries of formal sociospatial apartheid under slavery. In the wake of slavery's abolition the community was then subjected to generations of informal apartheid. Discrimination, fuelled by the interlocking orders of white racism and urban-industrial capitalism, produced segregation, ghettoisation and incarceration. Whilst an understanding of the intersections between the geographies of *who* we are and *where* we are has typically appeared in the work of white writers as part of an existential quest, it has been nothing less than a condition for survival within African-American literary culture. From the poetry of Phillis Wheatley and the earliest slave narratives, through the Harlem Renaissance, to the contemporary upsurge in black cultural activities, the issues of race and space have been close to the core of African-American art.

Nowhere in contemporary African-American writing are these issues being explored with more forceful eloquence than in the novels of Toni Morrison. Each of her six prose works to date has charted specific passages in the history of her race: the decades enclosing the Civil War in *Beloved*; from the Great Migration through to the 1920s in *Jazz*; the interwar years in *Sula* and *The Bluest Eye*; from the Depression to the early 1960s in *The Song of Solomon;* and up to the late 1970s in *Tar Baby*. As well as a telling historical record, the Morrison *oeuvre* also constitutes a counter-hegemonic cartography of colour, one that charts key spaces within the geographical experience of African-Americans. The geographical imagination articulated in Morrison's writing shares certain affinities with that examined previously in relation to writing by white

American authors: the search for sacred spaces (Pynchon); the destructive imprint of capital on the landscape (Auster); the persistence of place in individual and collective memory (Phillips). However, the elements in Morrison's work that I should like to focus upon here are those that distinguish her writing from her Caucasian contemporaries.

Morrison's cartographies, like the 'circles and circles of sorrow' that ripple through *Sula* (Morrison 1973, p. 174), are arranged around a series of concentric spatial spheres that share the body as a common centre. For a considerable period in African-American history the body, that most intimate of spaces, was objectified and brutalised as fixed capital. Morrison's work frequently dramatises the attempt to reclaim this territory from white oppression, to overcome self-alienation and feel at home in one's own body. Corporeal spaces become a cynosure that signify the impact of race across the American landscape, from the country to the city, in the South and the North, their interiors and exteriors.

These attempts at reclamation rarely result in unequivocal success, but where progress is made it is usually as a result of an integration between the individual and the community. In interviews and essays Morrison has repeatedly drawn attention to the tendency in white American writing to privilege the individual over the collective. In 'City Limits, Village Values' she argues that '[white critics] tend not to trust or respect a hero who prefers the village and its tribal values to heroic loneliness and alienation' (Morrison 1981a, p. 38). One might challenge this thesis by pointing towards African-American fiction that has focused upon a heroic search for a space by an alienated individual (Bigger Thomas and the Invisible Man, for example). Nevertheless, it is irrefutable that Morrison's own work is centrally concerned with the dialectical tension between individuals and various collectives and that typically it valorises communal spaces over the atomised enclaves of white bourgeois individualism. This concern is informed both by a recognition of the conditions of mass disempowerment and a keen sense of

> this life-giving, very, very strong sustenance that people got from the neighbourhood. One lives, really, not so much in your house as you do outside of it, within the 'compounds', within the village, or whatever it is. (Morrison, cited in Stepto 1977, p. 474)

What follows here will be an attempt to trace some of the broad brush strokes in Morrison's mappings. I shall examine each of her novels, with specific attention to the concentric arrangement of corporeal, domestic and communal spaces and the effort to establish a sense of place within a largely hostile landscape of white racism and destructive capitalism.

# No place to go

Morrison's first novel, *The Bluest Eye*, is a bifurcated *Bildungsroman* charting the stories of two young black girls: Claudia McTeer, who achieves assimilation into the adult social order, and Pecola Breedlove, who becomes increasingly alienated from the community and from herself. Spatial concerns are at the forefront of this cleft narrative. Pecola is described as 'a girl with no place to go', for whom all spaces, from the family home to her own body, come to be experienced as increasingly alien (Morrison 1970, p. 11).

Pecola's tale is prefaced by a quotation from a children's primer that underlines the root causes of self-estrangement:

> Here is the house. It is green and white. It has a red door. It is very pretty. Here is the family. Mother, Father, Dick, Jane live in the green-and-white house. They are very happy. (*ibid.*, p. 1)

*The Bluest Eye* scans a transition in the dynamics of oppression confronted by the African-American community. Pecola's predicament is representative of that faced by her people, since the overt exploitation of the plantation economy has been displaced by the covert internalisation of slavery's manacles. The superficially benign tableau introduced in the children's text in fact signifies an imperialism of the image, its colonisation of public and private spaces. The green-and-white house occupies the epicentre of white American normality, an inviolable nucleus that the black community are simultaneously encouraged and forbidden to enter. The coercive dissemination of white bourgeois values occurs through a range of media and its valorisation of Caucasian ideals of beauty, iconicised in the luminous blue eyes of a Shirley Temple doll, involves a secondary castigation of black skin and selfhood. In this social order racist ideology saturates space and enforces African-American self-alienation. The internalisation of hegemonic norms is administered through commodified lifestyles and Aryan ideals of physical perfection that they encounter 'leaning at them from every billboard, every movie, every glance', in shops, window signs, magazines and newspapers (*ibid.*, p. 28). The coercive gaze of this specular apparatus delivers the white master's judgement – 'You are an ugly people' – and this process is crystallised in Pecola's yearning for clear blue eyes (*ibid.*).

*The Bluest Eye* is concerned then with the colour filter deployed within a society of the image. Morrison offers a close-up of the role played by the culture industry in the structuration of racist ideology and sociospatial apartheid. The cumulative effect of the messages encoded in these images is seen to depend upon the extent to which the black self is able to conform to or elude these proscriptive norms, but typically it fosters a self-negating violence within the family, community and the self.

The key geographical counterpoint in the text centres on dissonant domestic spaces. The motif of the family home pictured in the children's primer embodies a coercive ideal which both disrupts and throws into relief the actual living spaces occupied by Claudia and Pecola. The McTeer home is 'old, cold, and green', but occasionally love, 'thick and dark as Alaga syrup', can still be tasted there (*ibid.*, pp. 6–7). Conversely, the home of the ironically-named Breedloves, 'an abandoned store on the southeast corner of Broadway and Thirty-fifth Street', is dominated by emotional impoverishment (*ibid.*, p. 24):

> The furniture had aged without ever having become familiar. People had owned it, but never known it. No one had lost a penny or a broach under the cushions of either sofa and remembered the place and time of the loss or the finding ... No one had given birth in one of the beds – or remembered with fondness the peeled paint places ... There were no memories among those pieces. Certainly no memories to be cherished. (*ibid.*, pp. 25–6)

Significantly, Pecola comes closest to the bliss promised by the 'very pretty' house when she leaves the abandoned store and enters the home of the group who have moved furthest away from the conventional family unit. Her secret refuge is the apartment above the Breedloves occupied by three whores – China, Poland and Miss Marie – where she can listen to cherished memories in their bawdy tales.

Morrison's mappings of space in *The Bluest Eye* move outwards from the black body politic, to the domestic sphere and on to the community surrounding both. In each phase of this concentric cartography there is a disheartening insistence on a drive towards the displacement of authentically African core values and traditions. The black child longs for blue eyes. The black home has become a hollow mimicry of the white middle-class domicile, 'those soft houses with porch swings and pots of bleeding heart' (*ibid.*, p. 75). Understanding that homelessness, being left outdoors

> was the real terror of life ... bred in us a hunger for property. The firm possession of a yard, a porch, a grape arbor. Propertied black people spent all their energies, all their love, on their nests. (*ibid.*, pp. 11–12)

Consequently, many black northern neighbourhoods offer themselves as a pastiche of the white suburbs, scrubbed clean and sanitised of that vibrancy of soul that Morrison calls 'Funk':

The dreadful funkiness of nature, the funkiness of the wide range of human emotions. Wherever it erupts, this Funk, they wipe it away; where it crusts, they dissolve it; wherever it drips, flowers, or clings, they find it and fight it until it dies. (*ibid.*, p. 64)

The erosion of black Funk in the body, home and neighbourhood, results in an atrophy of self and space. Pecola's story becomes a salutary Sisyphean fable of the dissipation of Funk and the subsequent struggle to plot a path between nature and the commodified spaces of white racism, 'between the tire rims and the sunflowers, between the coke bottles and milkweed, among all the waste and beauty of the world – which is what she herself was' (*ibid.*, p. 162).

Claudia also fails to plot a path successfully. In her closing words, inspired by the image of her dead friend 'searching the garbage', she returns to a correlation suggested in her opening lines, between Pecola and the unyielding earth (*ibid.*, p. 163):

I even think now that the land of the entire country was hostile to marigolds that year. This soil is bad for certain kinds of flowers. Certain seeds it will not nurture, certain fruit it will not bear, and when the land kills of its own volition, we acquiesce and say the victim had no right to live. We are wrong, of course, but it doesn't matter. It's too late. At least on the edge of my town, among the garbage and the sunflowers of my town, it's much, much too late. (*ibid.*, p. 164)

Claudia realises the inadequacy of reverting to a geographical mysticism that pins Pecola's fate on the land itself. However, she is unable to deliver a more authoritative judgement, since, at the time of narration, she too has succumbed to that which caused her friend to fall. Her assimilation into the adult world has been 'adjustment without improvement'; she has learnt to worship Shirley Temple and 'delight in cleanliness' (*ibid.*, p. 16). Claudia knows that the 'best hiding place [is] love' (*ibid.*). But when love is scrubbed clean of Funk it is too late for Claudia as well and something of herself has been buried alongside the girl with no place to go.

## An experimental life

Morrison's second novel, *Sula*, is similarly structured around the divergent life-stories of two black women. Whilst Nel Wright remains dutifully within the folds of the social fabric, Sula Peace chooses to live an 'experimental life' (Morrison 1973, p. 118). Her ten-year departure from the Bottom in the hills above the valley town of Medallion, Ohio, is a geographical testament to a willingness to cross boundaries that the community venerates. The outsider often plays a critical role in Morrison's account of the sociospatial organisation of African-American lives. Sula, like Pecola, assumes the position of scapegoat, a functional folk devil that enables the community to define itself whilst nurturing social cohesion. There are two specific ironies attendant on this process. First, the pariah becomes pivotal – the core and periphery are inverted as the marginalised element develops into a centrifugal nub for the emotional and symbolic life of the community. Second, the alienated African-American is used by her people in a manner that mimes their own mistreatment at the hands of the dominant white culture. As in *The Bluest Eye*, these social concerns are seen to be inseparable from and articulated through a dynamic interaction between communal, corporeal and domestic spaces.

The story of Sula and Nel is framed by the story of the place in which they lived. *Sula* opens elegiacally by mourning the destruction of the landscape. The occupants of the Bottom had enjoyed a greater degree of insulation from the dominant white culture so omnipresent in *The Bluest Eye* and thus greater possibilities for the preservation of their African heritage and identity. At the time of the narration, however, in the mid-1960s, a standardising white culture has encroached:

> In that place where they tore the nightshade and blackberry patches from their roots to make room for the Medallion City Golf Course, there was once a neighbourhood. (*ibid.*, p. 2)

Initially the Bottom is referred to as a 'place', then as a 'neighborhood' and towards the close the narrative voice asks the critical question of whether it had ever been a 'community'. To answer this *Sula* investigates relationships between friends and family, men and women, black and white. The narrative takes its name from the character who issues the most provocative challenge to the community's sense of coherence and its moral codes. At the time that Sula's tale is told 'there weren't any places left, just separate houses with separate televisions and separate telephones and less and less dropping by' (*ibid.*, p. 166). Whilst surveying the devastation wrought by a suburbanised placelessness, Morrison does not indulge in a nostalgic idealisation of Sula's hometown. The Bottom is shown to be the location of excessive violence and want, but it is also a potential communal space containing far greater opportunities for contact and communication, for the flourishing of Funk, prior to its decimation by homogenising white 'developments'.

In *Sula* the black body is subjected to exclusion and seen as the site of a semiotic struggle over meaning and self-possession. Nel and her mother encounter Jim Crow laws on a train journey to New

Orleans, whilst African-American men in the community are the victims of racist employment practices that forbid access to the valorised locations of white labour. Like Bigger Thomas in *Native Son*, Ajax is left standing at the fenced perimeters of an airfield watching the planes, knowing that he will never fly. Similarly, Nel's husband, Jude, along with the rest of the men in Bottom, seethes with resentment at not being permitted to work on the transport infrastructure that offers a geographical link between their community and the surrounding white world. Towards the end of the narrative the unfinished tunnel near to the Bottom becomes the scene of a collective symbolic return to the mother's body (one of several in the text), as an angry crowd seek to claim and instead are claimed themselves by the landmark they were forbidden to build. They are led to their watery grave within the collapsed tunnel by Shadrack, a traumatised war veteran seeking to overcome his anxieties about death and the fragility of the human form with the annual ritual of a 'National Suicide Day', 'making a place for fear as a way of controlling it' (*ibid.*, p. 14). After witnessing battlefield scenes of horrific dismemberment in the First World War, Shadrack loses control over his own body and wakes to the defamiliarised sights and sounds of an army hospital:

> Before him on a tray was a large tin plate divided into three triangles. In one triangle was rice, in another meat, and in the third stewed tomatoes. A small round depression held a cup of whitish liquid. Shadrack stared at the soft colors that filled these triangles: the lumpy whiteness of the rice, the quivering blood tomatoes, the grayish-brown meat. All their repugnance was contained in the neat balance of the triangles – a balance that soothed him, transferred some of its equilibrium to him. Thus reassured that the white, the red and the brown would stay where they were – would not explode or burst forth from their restricted zones – he suddenly felt hungry and looked around for his hands. (*ibid.*, p. 8)

The colour symbolism of this sequence carries a dual significance: the red, brown and white are both representative of the key colours of the body and of US demographics, with the major racial groups segregated into their respective restricted zones. Shadrack's post-traumatic stress disorder manifests itself in a fear of and inability to control his hands. Whilst this disorder contains distinct intertextual echoes (of 'Hands' in Sherwood Anderson's *Winesberg, Ohio* and Homer Simpson in Nathaniel West's *The Day of the Locust*), its primary significance, given the date of *Sula*'s publication, is clearly the plight of the disproportionately high numbers of black Americans drafted to fight in another white imperialist war then taking place in Southeast Asia.

Observing the features of his face reflected in toilet bowl water, Shadrack achieves a degree of self-possession through the cathartic recognition of his own physical integrity. As a child Nel Wright manages to attain a comparable sense of self-awareness whilst examining her face in a mirror after her last and first journey beyond the borders of the Bottom:

> There was her face, plain brown eyes, three braids and the nose her mother hated. She looked for a long time and suddenly a shiver ran through her. 'I'm me', she whispered. 'Me'. (*ibid.*, p. 28)

Helene Wright seeks to transfer her own sense of racial inferiority to her daughter, straightening her hair and encouraging her to pull her nose incessantly in the hope of achieving a different profile. But Nel's relationship with a young girl with a distinctive birthmark that alternately resembles a rose, a tadpole and a snake, enables her to resist her mother's hypnotic attraction to the bluest eyes. Sula and Nel lay claim to themselves through their relationship with each other and the social tensions at the heart of their community are both acted out upon their bodies and embodied in the juxtaposition of their respective homes.

The Wright household, like Shadrack's cabin on the outskirts of the community, is a domestic space of 'oppressive neatness' and order (*ibid.*, p. 29). Helene's aspirations to assimilation are expressed in a denial of her black folk heritage and a Puritanical dread of sexuality. Morrison's fondness for the ironic misnomer is apparent throughout *Sula* in the interweaving of Christian and classical traditions (characters called Hannah, Eva, Judas, Shadrack, Ajax, Helene) and whilst there is clearly a lot wrong at the Wright household, like the barren Breedlove residence, the Peace household is home to an incessant cacophony. Sula's home is a labyrinth of sex, secrets and stories that throbs with a funky freneticism.

The polarisation of the two homes is extensive without being ostentatious: one is compulsively tidy, isolated, modelled on the white bourgeois dwelling and dominated by a sombre Puritanical repression; its antipode is messy, collectivist, in touch with folk origins and vibrant with 'manlove'. The Peace household appears to consist largely of bedrooms and is open to the community. Eva presides over a matrifocal colony, adopting a succession of orphaned children and alcoholic bachelors whilst entertaining a procession of gentleman callers. Outsiders are welcomed and at any time the house will include 'cousins who [are] passing through, stray folks, and the many, many newly married couples', thus undermining the bourgeois model of home as a monadic cell for the nuclear family unit (*ibid.*, p. 37). In Morrison's mapping the Peace household occupies an alternative epicentre for a community marginalised by the dominant white culture. At the same time this paradigmatic space is feared by many of the neighbourhood women for its lack of discipline and inhibition. Morrison consistently resists the temptation to idealise, revealing it to be home to violent emotions, possessiveness, self-destruction and murder, but still, like the Bottom itself, replete with a potential absent from the white world beyond its borders.

## Listening to the storied earth

> Goddam, Milk, I do believe my whole life's geography.
> Toni Morrison, *Song of Solomon* (1978), p. 114

In *Song of Solomon* Morrison continues to embody social logics in polarised spaces, alongside a more conspicuous utilisation of African-American folk traditions. This mythopoeic fable of flight and fall is structured around a series of geographical oppositions: a capitalist city and an enchanted countryside; commodified and communal living spaces; the stasis of the earth counterpointed with the fluidity of water and flight. The narrative follows the paths plotted between these realms by Milkman Dead. Milkman is born at what the black community have dubbed 'No Mercy Hospital', on 'Not Doctor Street', in an unspecified Michigan city bordering on Lake Superior. These place names signify the African-American neighbourhood's symbolic function as Other to the dominant culture and also its determination to claim the space it inhabits through rhetorical subversion.

Growing up in the city Milkman is poised, like Pecola and Nel, between two houses that trace the trajectory his life might take. On one side there is the house of his father, Macon Dead II, a space of acquisitive soullessness. Macon has thoroughly imbued the city's capitalist ethics and sees place only in terms of real estate. The message he seeks to pass on to his son suggests that an erstwhile victim of reification has become its willing disciple. 'Own things', he tells Milkman. 'And let the things you own own other things too. Then you'll own yourself and other people too' (*ibid.*, p. 55). The house of Macon Dead is built upon the same architectonic principles as the house of the white master: here space is standardised as it is strained through the sterile materialism of the cash nexus. Macon's real estate business is a corruption of the philosophy behind his father's establishment of 'one of the best farms in Montour County' (*ibid.*, p. 235):

> We live here. On this planet, in this nation, in this country right here. *No*where else. We got a home in this rock, don't you see!..
> Grab it. Grab this land. Take it, hold it, my brothers, make it

my brothers, shake it ... and pass it on – can you hear me? Pass it on! (*ibid.*)

Macon's version of this philosophy is devoid of his father's sensuous pragmatism and owning land, rather than a means to an end (securing a home), becomes purely an end in itself.

Macon's acquisitiveness and his desire for assimilation into the dominant socioeconomic order is traced back to the trauma of childhood experiences. Much of his early life with his sister, Pilate, had been rooted in the comparative security of his father's farm in Pennsylvania. *Song of Solomon* contains echoes of the Bottom's history, as Macon's father is murdered as part of a plan by a white family to dispossess them of their land. Whilst Macon's response to this is to learn the language of the oppressor, Pilate moves in the opposite direction. As a child, like Sula, she develops a passionate interest in geography and a radically different relation to place than that pursued by her brother. Milkman finds himself increasingly attracted to the house of his father's estranged sister. Aunt Pilate lives in a 'notorious wine house' (*ibid.*, p. 47) with relatively few material comforts, but 'peace was there, energy, singing' (*ibid.*, p. 301). Like the Peace household, this is a matrifocal and communal space that, whilst relatively impoverished in material terms, is rich with a folky funkiness. Here, Milkman begins to discover an alternative system of values, listening to the singing and story-telling that encourages contact with their shared tribal and rural past – a system founded not upon owning, but 'a deep concern for and about human relationships' (*ibid.*, p. 149).

The spatial parallelism of Macon and Pilate's homes is mirrored on a macro level by the oppositions between the lacustrine city and the small village of Shalimar. Shalimar is an enchanted region of woods, wilderness and secret caves, a territory of tribal spirits in which Morrison interweaves classical (Ulysses and Icarus), European (Hansel and Gretel) and African-American legend. Milkman journeys to the rural South in search of a fabled horde of buried treasure, 'Pilate's Gold'. His quest is partially motivated by the materialistic cravings fostered by his father, but in Shalimar he discovers the secrets of his family and folk history that align him with his aunt's antithetical value system. Milkman uncovers the hidden meaning of the Song of Solomon, the myth that tells of his great-grandfather's escape and flight across the sea to the African homeland.

At the same time Milkman experiences a contact with his surroundings not permissible in the city. Setting out on his journey he sees the country as a rather tedious picturesque:

> For a few minutes he tried to enjoy the scenery running past
> his window, then the city man's boredom with nature's repetition
> overtook him. Some places had lots of trees, some did not; some
> fields were green, some were not, and the hills in the distance
> were like the hills in every distance. (*ibid.*, p. 226)

Subsequently, this perspective is severely challenged during a night
time hunting expedition. Alone in darkness in the Shalimar woods,
stripped of material possessions, Milkman begins to perceive the
possibility of a relationship between self and space beyond the
proprietary calculus of his father:

> he sank his fingers into the grass. He tried to listen with his
> fingertips, to hear what, if anything, the earth had to say. (*ibid.*,
> p. 279)

Following Guitar's attempt on his life Milkman finds himself

> exhilarated by simply walking the earth. Walking it like he
> belonged to it; like his legs were stalks, tree trunks, a part of his
> body that extended down down down into the rock and soil,
> and were comfortable there – on the earth and on the place where
> he walked. (*ibid.*, p. 281)

The site of this awakening for Milkman is significant and recalls
the fact that since childhood Pilate had always smelled of the forest
(*ibid.*, p. 27). The description of his experience also echoes that of
Pilate's home, which 'seemed to be rising from rather than settling
into the ground' (*ibid.*). And as his journey continues something
about Shalimar reminds Milkman 'of how he used to feel in Pilate's
house' (*ibid.*, p. 293). He begins to sense connections between
himself, the land and his people, 'as though there was some cord
or pulse or information they shared. Back home he had never felt
that way, as though he belonged to anyplace or anybody' (*ibid.*).
   Milkman returns to the city with a tremendously aroused interest
in the historical intersections between and the stories behind
people, place and language:

> He read the road signs with interest now, wondering what lay
> beneath the names. The Algonquins had named the territory
> he lived in Great Water, *michi gami*. How many dead lives and
> fading memories were buried in and beneath the names of the
> places in this country. Under the recorded names were other
> names, just as 'Macon Dead', recorded for all time in some dusty
> file, hid from view the real names of people, places, and things.
> Names that had meaning. (*ibid.*, p. 329)

## Not from anywhere

This place dislocates everything
        Toni Morrison, *Tar Baby* (1981b), p. 286

Much of the action in Morrison's fourth novel, *Tar Baby*, takes place on the exotic Caribbean *Isle des Chevaliers*, but despite the atypicality of the setting, the core geographical concerns remain largely constant. At the heart of the narrative lies a luxuriant and loveless mansion, *L'Arbe de la Croix*, owned by a white retired confectionery manufacturer, the wealthy Valerian Street. Whilst Valerian refers to his wife Margaret as his 'Principal Beauty' (*ibid.*, p. 9), her function in the home is largely ornamental and most of his attention is devoted to an opulent greenhouse, 'a place of controlled ever-flowering life to greet death in' (*ibid.*, p. 51). Valerian's temporal and emotional investment in his greenhouse in the tropics is a reflection of the obsessional ethos that governs his life: 'I can't be responsible for things outside of my control' (*ibid.*, p. 70). The symbolic design of the narrative is reminiscent in parts of Pynchon's 'Entropy': the fecund hothouse is actually a space of sterility and death. The Streets live alone together in a sumptuous sepulchre, insulated from the island, its people and the past. The atmosphere of excessive affluence breeds an emotional poverty and rootlessness that suppresses any eruptions of Funk in the lives of the white couple.

The nature that Valerian struggles to contain and conquer often plays an important role in Morrison's fictive cartographies: *The Bluest Eye* opens with the absence of marigolds in the fall of 1941; Sula's return to the Bottom is accompanied by siroccos and a plague of robins; the woods near Shalimar have a profound effect on Milkman Dead. Morrison's representation of an empathy between people and the natural world owes something both to the pathetic fallacy of romantic pantheism and to African-American folk lore. In *Tar Baby* this indebtedness manifests itself in a lush tropical paganism and the personification of the island. *Isle des Chevaliers* seems disgruntled at the intrusion of real estate. Its rivers are diverted to facilitate the construction of grand winter mansions for wealthy visitors. Subsequently, the monsoons fail to arrive on time and the trees appear to mutter amongst themselves.

Sharing the Street's disconnection from the island and its black community are Sydney and Ondine Childs. They live and work at *L'Arbe de la Croix*, enthusiastically miming their white masters' culture and proudly proclaiming their status as 'Philadelphia Negroes' (*ibid.*, p. 59). Unlike the Childs, Gideon and Thérèse are representative of the islanders who are less than hungry for assimilation. Thérèse, Ondine's kitchen helper, displays an openness to relationships and connectivity with the island's history that is far from at home in the Street mansion. Like Pilate, Thérèse is a source of myth and legend – such as the fable of the blind black horsemen, spectral emblems of a muted colonial history, who roam the island and give it its name.

Alongside Valerian and Margaret, Sydney and Ondine, Gideon and Thérèse, the most important dyadic relationship in the text involves Jadine and the mysterious Son. This pairing represents something of a departure for Morrison in that many of the social and symbolic antipodes she explores in earlier works appear here distilled into forms so pure they verge on the schematic. Jadine and Son occasionally threaten to collapse into caricatures of the cultural myths surrounding nature, nurture and racial difference. Jadine, the Childs' niece, has grown up amidst wealth and privilege, been educated in the Northern States, travelled to Europe and integrated wholly with bourgeois white culture. Son, as his name suggests, has experienced a rudimentary socialisation, growing up in the impoverished backwaters of the American South, formally uneducated and unregulated by middle-class mores. Elements of the African-American past and a possible future for a minority are brought together under the roof of the white master and stick like tar babies in the mucilage of sexual magnetism.

It is Son's entry into Valerian's house that acts as a catalyst to the action of the story. The 'riverbed darkness of his face' (*ibid.*, p. 114) brings to light the secrets, power struggles and abuse buried beneath the bourgeois pleasantries in this 'demoralised house' (*ibid.*, p. 218). Son's disruptive presence is articulated through imagistic associations with nature, the elements and the wild: 'Spaces, mountains, savannas – all those were in his forehead and eyes' (*ibid.*, p. 159). Valerian's atomised cocoon of luxury begins to crack up and the funkiness of messy passions seeps in. In particular the suppressed family secret of Margaret's sexual abuse of her son comes to the surface and Valerian, forced to confront the guilty fact of his innocence, allows his greenhouse to fall apart: 'Things grew or died where and how they pleased. *Isle des Chevaliers* filled in the spaces that had been the island's to begin with' (*ibid.*, p. 244).

In certain respects Son's impact upon Jadine is equally corrosive. He issues a direct challenge to her cosmopolitan rootlessness: 'Anybody ask you where you from, you give them five towns. You're not from anywhere. I'm from Eloe' (*ibid.*, p. 268). In the later stages of the novel two journeys allow the couple an unwanted glimpse into the other's world. Jadine takes Son with her to New York, her favourite place, where the past appears to have no hold and she perceives only endless possibilities for the protean pleasures of self-reinvention. Son, however, sees only façade and banal commercialism. On television, he watches in horror as 'black people in whiteface [play] black people in blackface' (*ibid.*, p. 217). His earthy anti-materialism goes against the grain of the city's rampant consumerism. The built environment itself appears to conspire in an oppressive pantomime: 'pre-stressed concrete and steel contained anger, folded it back in on itself to become a craving for things rather than vengeance' (*ibid.*, p. 222).

This metropolitan expedition is mirrored by a journey to Eloe, Son's hometown in the South which, predictably, Jadine finds equally abhorrent: 'A burnt-out place ... [And] all that Southern small-town country romanticism a lie, a joke, kept secret by people who could not function elsewhere' (*ibid.*, p. 262). Like the characters with which they are associated, these places occasionally hover on the brink of Manichean antipodes without falling in. At least for the affluent minority, New York does seem to enable an escape from traditionally oppressive race and gender roles, if only into a consumerist masquerade. Eloe retains traces of a communal connectivity to the land, people and history erased within the city, but is also the site of extreme poverty, patriarchal prohibitions and conservative rigidity.

Torn between these two worlds the tar babies come unstuck. Jadine retreats from the past by fleeing to Paris. She will continue to worship that culture of images that destroyed Pecola, whilst being haunted by another image that unsettles her racial and sexual identity. The sight of 'mother/sister/she; that unphotographable beauty', seen appropriately enough whilst looking out from within a supermarket, will always travel with Jadine (*ibid.*, p. 43). Son's fate is less certain. He returns to *Isle des Chevaliers* and is left running through the fog with the blind horsemen – possibly in pursuit of Jadine, or possibly away from her and towards those things her city life denies: collectivism, myth, nature and the past. In between the broad brush strokes in Morrison's mapping of colonialism, the city and the country, there are more than enough details to *Tar Baby*'s picture of blackness in the First and Third Worlds to make this a significant addition to her contemplation of the crossings between people and place.

## Ghosts might enter here

Each of Morrison's first four novels underscores the critical import of remembrance and the maintenance of an organic union with the past. *Beloved* dramatises the plight of those who cannot afford to remember; it insists vehemently upon the necessity of forgetfulness as a prerequisite for survival in unbearable historical circumstances. The narrative is based upon records of Margaret Garner, a runaway slave mother who, when confronted by the possibility of recapture, took the life of one of her children to rescue it from enslavement. In *Beloved*, Sethe's life is consumed by the incessant demands of 'beating pack the past' in the wake of infanticide and her experiences of slave life on a plantation with the savagely ironic appellation of 'Sweet Home' (Morrison 1987, pp. 35–6). One of the most remarkable facets of this truly remarkable historical novel is the way in which it effects a spatialisation of time. Morrison explores the geography of 're-memory' and charts a decentred and mystical prospect of the symbiotic interdependence of people and place across time. Landscape is not figured in this story as merely a catalyst to remembrance, rather it is offered as the repository of semi-autonomous human traces. The past has a place of its own, one that impinges on the present incessantly, both in tribal and individual memory. As Sethe instructs her daughter, Denver:

> I was talking about time. It's so hard for me to believe in it. Some things go. Pass on. Some things just stay. I used to think it was my rememory ... But it's not. Places, places are still there. If a house burns down, it's gone, but the place – the picture of it – stays, and not just in my rememory, but out there, in the world ... Where I was before I came here, that place is real. It's never going away. Even if the whole farm – every tree and grass blade of it dies. The picture is still there and what's more, if you go there – you who never was there – if you go there and stand in the place where it was, it will happen again; it will be there for you, waiting for you. (*ibid.*)

Sethe's philosophy is dramatised in the text in relation, once more, to the intrinsic bonds between corporeal, communal and domestic spaces, ceaselessly broken and forged.

'124 was spiteful' (*ibid.*, p. 3). Our entry to *Beloved* begins with the malign disposition of a haunted house on Bluestone Road, the 'outrageous behaviour of that place' (*ibid.*, p. 4) on the outskirts of Cincinnati, Ohio. One of the distinctive features to Morrison's representation of domestic space in *Beloved* is the discreet presence of literary ghosts, textual traces of works by white writers from the time of the narrative's historical setting. Two works contemporaneous with Sethe's time at Sweet Home are of particular significance: *The Scarlet Letter* and *Uncle Tom's Cabin*. Hawthorne's romance dramatises the collision between desire and law in Puritan New England. It focuses upon a woman who, like Sethe, is alienated by an act of love, left alone with her child and spectres from the past, in a house on the border between the community and the wild. One of the most significant geographical parallelisms between these two works comes in their representation of the forest. Whilst Morrison does not share Hawthorne's muted Puritanical anxiety about the symbolic status of the woods as a 'wild, unredeemed, unchristianized, lawless region' (Hawthorne 1990b, p. 2240) she does mirror the leitmotif he weaves between the trees, children, water and the fantastic. Sethe's children, like Hester's Pearl, are often associated with the glades, rivers and spirits at the heart of a magical forest: Denver is born on the banks of the Ohio River and builds a secret shelter for herself in the woods; her sister, Beloved, experiences a naiadic resurrection from the water before she begins her spectral seduction of the occupants at 124.

Before the story of Hester Prynne begins, in a famous passage from the prefatory 'Custom-House' essay, Hawthorne describes a domestic scene in terms that anticipate both the narrative and the aesthetic design of *Beloved*:

> Thus, therefore, the floor of our familiar room has become a neutral territory, somewhere between the real world and fairy-land, where the Actual and the Imaginary may meet, and each imbue itself with the nature of the other. Ghosts might enter here, without affrighting us. It would be too much in keeping with the scene to excite suprize, were we to look about us and discover a form, beloved, but gone hence, now sitting quietly in a streak of this magic moonshine, with an aspect that would make us doubt whether it had returned from afar, or had never once stirred from our fireside. (Hawthorne 1990a, p. 2197)

The second major source of intertextual reference in *Beloved* is the book that Lincoln once credited with starting the Civil War: *Uncle Tom's Cabin*. Stowe's book typifies the preoccupation of many women writers of the day with the cult of domesticity and the action is structured around a succession of disparate dwellings. Alongside the place that gives the narrative its name there is the Shelby plantation upon which the story begins and concludes, the St Clare residence and Senator Bird's abode. Each house occupies a different point on the spectrum of attitudes towards slavery and at each end there is a location that encapsulates the utopian and dystopian extremes of the cult of domesticity: the matrifocal, egalitarian and God-fearing Quaker Home finds its antipode in the patriarchal, oppressive and godless Legree plantation. In *Beloved* Morrison self-consciously reworks this cartography of domestic space from an African-American perspective that challenges the racist and sexist stereotypes underlining much of Stowe's attempted assault upon the twin towers of slavery and patriarchy. The Quaker Home, Uncle Tom's Cabin and the various plantations function as a palimpsest beneath Sweet Home and 124 Bluestone Road, but one in which Stowe's confident dualisms are discarded. Sethe is afflicted by re-memories of the plantation as a sublime *mélange* of heaven *and* hell:

and suddenly there was Sweet Home rolling, rolling, rolling out
before her eyes, and although there was not a leaf on that farm
that did not make her want to scream, it rolled itself out before
her in shameless beauty. It never looked as terrible as it was and
it made her wonder if hell was a pretty place too. Fire and
brimstone all right, but hidden in lacy groves. Boys hanging from
the most beautiful sycamores in the world. It shamed her –
remembering the wonderful soughing trees rather than the
boys. Try as she might to make it otherwise, the sycamores beat
out the children every time and she could not forgive her
memory for that. (Morrison 1987, p. 6)

Part of the source of Sethe's anguish is the segregation of 124
from the rest of the community: 'When 124 was alive – she had
women friends, men friends from all around to share grief with',
but for twelve years after the death of Beloved 'no visitors of any
sort and certainly no friends' have entered this house (*ibid.*, pp. 95–6).
The root cause of this division is twofold: partly it is the result of
the community's inability to comprehend Sethe's infanticide, and
partly it is a collective sense of guilty complicity in her actions. When
Schoolteacher arrived to reclaim Sethe, in accordance with the
Fugitive Slave Law, the neighbourhood women, suspicious of the
funkiness at 124, fail to let her know. For Morrison, however, the
source of this breach is ultimately of less significance than its being
bridged, so that Sethe can rediscover a 'joy and protection in the
clan' (Morrison 1981a, p. 38). As Patrick Bjork has argued:

> the community, for better or worse, has the power to become
> the site of renewal for its members. Morrison's novels
> demonstrate that the community is a multiple, refractory space
> within each self which, as it dispossesses and nurtures, deceives
> and instructs, assails and comforts, serves as the ultimate
> touchstone in the search for self and space. (Bjork 1992, p. 164)

The reintegration of 124 into this communal space is initiated by
Denver and culminates with the second exorcism of Beloved. It is
Sethe's daughter who takes the courageous decision to 'step off the
edge of the world ... and go ask somebody for help' (Morrison 1987,
p. 243). Gradually, the community begins to accept its responsibility
for the hurting at 124 and its members recolonise a space being
consumed by the insatiable need embodied in Beloved:

> Now she is running into the faces of the people out there,
> joining them and leaving Beloved behind. Alone. Again. Then
> Denver, running too. Away from her to the pile of people out
> there. They make a hill. A hill of black people, falling. (*ibid.*,
> p. 262)

Geographical and aural tropes dominate the imagery during this epiphanic moment in the narrative. As the women gather outside her home Sethe feels as though

> the Clearing had come to her with all its heat and simmering leaves, where the voices of women searched for the right combination, the key, the code, the sound that broke the back of words. Building voice upon voice until they found it, and when they did it was a wave of sound wide enough to sound deep water and knock the pods of chestnut trees. It broke over Sethe and she trembled like the baptized in its wash. (*ibid.*, p. 261)

This is a dense and evocative passage that approaches the heart of *Beloved*. The voices that break over Sethe, allowing her to be born again from the imprisoning womb of unbearable memory, might be identified with the *ecriture féminine* posited by the new French feminism. In *La Révolution du Langage poétique* Julia Kristeva applies the Platonic concept of the *chora* (from the Greek sign for a womb or enclosing space) to the possibility of a pre-Oedipal language linked to the mother's body, a discourse that 'only admits analogy with vocal or kinetic rhythm' (Kristeva, cited in Moi 1985, p. 161). Hélène Cixous has described the semiotic *chora* in terms that are even more obviously applicable to the chorus outside 124:

> There is almost nothing left of the sea but a word without water: for we have translated the words, we have emptied them of their speech, dried, reduced and embalmed them ... But a clarice voice only has to say: the sea, the sea, for my keel to split open, the sea is calling me, sea! calling me, waters! (Cixous, cited in Moi 1985, p. 115)

It is the Voice of the Mother, a 'song before the Law, before the breath was split by the symbolic ... inexhaustible milk', that washes over Sethe and saves her from the desiccating desire of her dead infant, from Beloved's rapacious need for her mother and a past she has never had (Cixous, cited in *ibid.*, p. 114).

The use of the term 'code' in relation to this voice is a cipher for another language, pre-diaspora rather than pre-Oedipal, that stands outside the symbolic order of the white master. Discussing her own childhood with Denver, 'picking meaning out of a code she no longer understood' (Morrison 1987, p. 62), Sethe has vague recollections of the women close to her speaking in a mother tongue: '[Nan] used different words ... The same language ma'am spoke, and which would never come back. But the message – that was and had been there all along' (*ibid.*). The voices that save Sethe are associated with the key locations in Morrison's mapping of the geography of African-American life: communal spaces, the mother's body and the motherland.

These spaces converge in *Beloved* at the Clearing where Baby Suggs, Sethe's mother-in-law, preaches a sensual spiritualism that offers the possibility of a non-reified relation to the black body:

'Here', she said, 'in this here place, we flesh; flesh that weeps, laughs; flesh that dances on bare feet in grass. Love it. Love it hard. Yonder they do not love your flesh. They despise it'. (*ibid.*, p. 88)

*Beloved* is a fable of possession. In this work the struggle to control and define the black body apparent in all Morrison's writing has an added urgency. Daughters, mothers and lovers are locked in a struggle for self-ownership of the most intimate of spaces. Baby's inspirational sermon is founded upon the doctrine of pleasurable self-possession and in this it echoes those delivered in the 1840s by female religious orators such as Julia Foote and the teachings of the African Methodist Episcopal Church. Her visionary valorisation of the parts of the black body, as the site of love and life, stands in opposition to the instrumental itemisation practised by Schoolteacher – the exercise in scientific racism that he sets his nephews, to list the slave's 'human' and their 'animal' characteristics side by side, is a clear expression of the master's voice, that threatens to drown out all others.

Schoolteacher silences Paul D. by making him wear a bit and beats Sixo, 'to show him that definitions belonged to the definers – not the defined' (*ibid.*, p. 190). Excluded from the dominant discourse, during his years on a Georgia chain gang, Paul D. and his fellow prisoners come close to discovering a penal correlative to the semiotic *chora*. Enclosed inside boxes dug into trenches, stuck in muddy water, the prisoners learn to communicate through the umbilical cord of the chains that confine them. And subsequently the poignancy of the moment at which Paul D.'s relationship with Sethe breaks down lies in the fact that in challenging her decision to take Beloved's life, he speaks with his master's voice, recalling Schoolteacher's tables: '"You got two feet, Sethe, not four", he said, and right then a forest sprang up between them; trackless and quiet'(*ibid.*, p. 165). This metaphor sustains the motif introduced by the sight of the scars on Sethe's back, that become the site of a semiotic struggle over meaning reminiscent of Sula's distinctive birthmark, or Pecola's eyes. Schoolteacher seeks to define Sethe as fixed capital and subhuman by leaving his mark on her back. When a 'whitegirl' helps her during her escape from Sweet Home, she begins the process of encouraging Sethe to reclaim her body by telling her the scars resemble a 'chokecherry tree. Trunk, branches, and even leaves' (*ibid.*, p. 16). Initially Paul D. sees it as a 'wrought-iron maze' he could explore 'like a gold miner pawing through pay dirt', although post-coital dissatisfaction reveals to him nothing more than 'a revolting clump of scars', not like the trees he trusted and spoke to at Sweet Home (*ibid.*, p. 19). And of course the struggle for corporeal possession at the core of the narrative concerns Beloved herself who suffers an Orphic dismemberment at the point of Sethe's reintegration into the community. Her physical disintegration at the end serves as an allegorical reminder, both of the grisly punishments inflicted upon the black body and the threat of the falling apart of the landscapes of memory if not kept alive by story-telling.

The closing section contains the thrice-repeated refrain: 'This is not a story to pass on' (*ibid.*, pp. 274–5). Initially this may appear to confirm the hesitancy of the penultimate chapter. Sethe's reintegration into the community is far from an end to her problems. The white owner of 124 decides to sell the house and Sethe withdraws to her bedroom like Baby Suggs before her and the contemplation of colour (a far from insignificant activity) in a quilt. Paul D. returns and now it is Baby Suggs, rather than Schoolteacher, who seems to ventriloquise through him: 'You your own best thing, Sethe. You are' (*ibid.*, p. 273). Sethe's reply intimates that she is still marooned in uncertainty and unable to respond to this call of affirmative selfhood: 'Me? Me?' (*ibid.*). Read in sequence, 'This is not a story to pass on', seems to accentuate the tragic impulses in the denouement, insisting upon the necessity of forgetfulness. But this message has only a restricted applicability, to those, like Sethe, burdened with an unbearable history. For others the message is that this is not a story whose questions can be left unanswered, a history that cannot be *passed over* without remembrance and censure. As the dedication to the 'Sixty Million and more' who failed to survive the Middle Passage suggests, the story of Beloved is the story of all of the abandoned and dis(re)membered daughters of the diaspora, a story that ought never to be forgotten.

## City lights, country blues

*Jazz* (Morrison 1992b) concerns another vital chapter in African-American history: the Great Migration that witnessed a mass exodus by the black community, in the wake of Emancipation, from small rural communities in the South to the urban North. Against this backdrop *Jazz* focuses upon the lives, loves and losses of Joe and Violet Trace and the effect upon them of a young woman called Dorcas Manfred. This triad becomes increasingly dissonant, as Joe murders his young lover and both he and Violet continue to be haunted by her memory. In the Book of Acts, Dorcas was brought back from the dead by Saint Peter and in her investigation of the difficulties of killing the dead Morrison returns to familiar territory.

As Morrison explained in an interview with Salman Rushdie, *Jazz* crosses over with the canonical white prose tradition of the 'Great American City Novel' (Morrison 1992a). New York is not mentioned here by name, but the location is clear. The urban landscape is capitalised as an archetypal 'City', a major player in the cacophony of the Roaring Twenties:

> And the City, in its own way, gets down for you, cooperates, smoothing its sidewalks, correcting its curbstones, offering you melons and green apples on the corner ... The City is smart at this: smelling and good and looking raunchy; sending secret messages disguised as public signs: this was, open here, danger to let colored only single men on sale woman wanted private room stop dog on premises absolutely no money down fresh chicken free delivery fast. And good at opening locks, dimming stairways. Covering your moans with its own. (Morrison 1992b, pp. 63–4)

The syntax of state authority and capital encountered on the New York streets by Auster's *flâneur* is appropriated here as a lyrical cryptograph. The anonymous narrative voice repeatedly indulges in these improvisatory urban pastorals, describing the City as a space of concupiscent possibility. However, as in her earlier works, Morrison also recognises the City as a space of disconnection between black people and their past. The site of the Jazz Age has a seductive allure, but it is also the stage of race riots, segregation and discrimination, the Red Menace, violence, need and oppression. And as in *The Song of Solomon*, this oppression is seen to stretch back across time: when the narrative voice drifts from wistful descriptions of the empyrean scenes above the City back down to earth with the phrase 'Iroquois sky' (*ibid.*, p. 34), there is a recognition that this is the same sheltering sky that looked down on the original Other to the White Man in the New World.

As the narrative tempo picks up, attention shifts with increasing frequency from the urban present to the Southern rural past shared by most of the older members of the Harlem community. Beneath the syncopated jazz rhythms of improvised city lives one can still detect the pulsating backbeat of country blues riffs. The Traces left Virginia in the later stages of the Great Migration. This mass movement was inspired by the promise of new opportunities, new beginnings, but also threatened a break with folk roots and an assimilation into the standardising market system which structures space in the city. The determinants behind this migration involved both push and pull factors. There was clearly a push away from the South, with its social and political inequalities (Jim Crow legislation, disenfranchisement, racial violence) and environmental difficulties (a spate of severe flooding and share-cropping devastated by a boll weevil infestation). Morrison hints at these factors, but foregrounds the pull factors exerted by the City, the centrifugal force perceived by the migrants, the tune that sang:

> Here comes the new. Look out. There goes the sad stuff. The bad stuff. The things-nobody-could-help stuff. The way everybody was then and there. Forget that. History is over, you all, and everything's ahead at last. (*ibid.*, p. 7)

During the 1850s, in the wake of the Fugitive Slave Law, escapees to the North were often returned forcibly to their owners in the South. In *Jazz* Morrison shows how the City's promise of an end to the past is broken by the psychological manacles that tether many first-generation migrants to the South in memory. Joe Trace, in particular, has brought considerable emotional baggage with him on his journey towards the north star. Like Sethe, he is haunted by the suppressed memories of an unresolved relationship with an unknown mother that spills over into his life in the City with Violet and Dorcas. His hunt through the City for his young lover is spliced together with his childhood search for a cave beyond the fields, a protective maternal space housing a wild woman who might or might not have been his estranged parent. At the end of his search Joe kills Dorcas because, in terms of his emotional needs, she is the mother he could not find and could not bear to be abandoned by for a second time.

The profound sense of an entanglement with the rural past in the urban present is sustained by the unnamed narrator observing Joe, Violet and Dorcas from the safety of the window in her Harlem flat. At one point this jazzy voice, in love with its own tone and timbre, departs on a lengthy improvisatory digression concerning the tale of Golden Gray in a semi-mystical South of dark forests and darker secrets. The South in this tale and throughout *Jazz*, like Shalimar in *Song of Solomon*, possesses an air of magic realism and unlike the monolithic City it has an abundance of place names that are ironic, lyrical, romantic and religious: Rome, Vienna, Palestine, Wordsworth and Vesper.

In the denouement, as in the musical form that lends this narrative performance its name, there is a return to the opening motif but with a difference: the strident tones of the opening bars are replaced by a muted, intimate cry that recognises the need for stepping out by the isolated narrator; progressing to an active involvement in the life of the community she has been observing from afar, moving beyond the protective shield of imaginative (non-)involvement. The narrator even intimates subtly that the wild woman, Joe's mother and herself may be one and the same person. In her voice and in the memories of Joe and Violet, the urban present of the black community is shown to be haunted by the refrain of their shared rural past of miscegenation, violence and need.

## Praying for a breeze

In his 'Definition of a Revolution' Malcolm X elaborated upon his infamous distinction between branches in the black political activist movement in the 1960s:

> There were two kinds of slaves, the house Negro and the field Negro. The house Negroes –they lived in the house with the master, they dressed pretty good, they ate good because they ate his food – what he left. They lived in the attic or the basement, but still they lived near the master; and they loved the master more than the master loved himself. They would give their life to save the master's house ... On that same plantation, there was the field Negro. The field Negroes – those were the masses. There were always more Negroes in the field than there were Negroes in the house. The Negro in the field caught hell ... he hated his master ... When the house caught fire, he didn't try to put it out; that field Negro prayed for a wind, for a breeze. (Malcolm X 1990, pp. 276–8)

In certain respects this is an opposition that reappears in the geographical imagination of Toni Morrison. The central spatial division in her writing is between those who seek to live inside the house of the master and those praying for a breeze. In each of her novels there is a loveless house (the Breedloves, the Wrights, Macon Dead, the Streets, Sweet Home, the Traces) in which black people have isolated themselves from the tribe. These spaces are diametrically opposed to those which witness eruptions of Funk and a vital connectivity between the members of the community and their past (parts of the Bottom, Eloe, *Isle des Chevaliers*, the Clearing and Vesper County). Morrison's mappings always belie the apparent manichean simplicity of this summary: the City in *Tar Baby* and *Jazz* has its possibilities and there is no casual sentimentalisation of nature and the rural South. The aim is always to distinguish between those places that manage and fail to resist homogenising capitalism and white racism. In the process place is both cherished and problematised in her writing. And in the search for her mothers' gardens, Morrison continually foregrounds the richness of its narrative content, valorising the storied earth.

# Part Three

# Landscapes on the Screen:
# Space and Film

# CHAPTER 10

# Mapping the City of the Future:
## *Blade Runner*

Assessments of the political effectivity of fantasy are characterised by a compelling ambivalence: it is invoked simultaneously as the most radical and the most reactionary of aesthetic categories. It has been celebrated as a subversive discourse at the margins of cultural production, an *écriture* which engages with the taboo, addresses the thematics of the Other and illuminates the dynamics of political and libidinal economies from angles not normally accessible within a naturalistic idiom. Alternatively, it is charged with the fabrication of diversionary dream-worlds, escapist reveries which cloak and naturalise relations of power in that place it defines itself in relation to – the real world. Strategically, in various guises, fantasy both transgresses and consolidates boundaries.

Science fiction shelters beneath the generic umbrella of the Fantastic and in the postmodern period has become one of its most conspicuous and contentious forms. Critical attention has tended, in line with fantasy's typically Janus-faced duality, to produce wildly antithetical assessments. Fredric Jameson, amongst others, has been hostile to this burgeoning subgenre, interpreting it as the designer apocalypse of a dying class – 'the cancelled future of a vanished colonial destiny' (Jameson 1984b). On the opposite edge of the critical spectrum a number of critics have challenged the Jameson thesis of a fashionable and reactionary dystopianism. Fred Pfeil (1990), for example, has suggested that New Age science fiction constitutes nothing less than a form of counter-Enlightenment cultural terrorism.

To determine the political effectivity of the genre I intend to offer an examination of the cutting edge of the genre, beginning with one of its most celebrated cinematic examples, *Blade Runner* (1982). This reading will pay particular attention to the film's fabular construction of the future of the postindustrial city. With its regular appearances in more-or-less avant-garde film and popular cultural studies' journals and on the circuits of late-night cinema shows in western metropolitan centres whose physical and existential textures it so vividly reproduces, *Blade Runner*, as one of the PMC's most fashionable and cherished aesthetic artefacts, ought to provide an opportunity to determine the political effectivity of postmodern science fiction fantasy's vision of the future of place.

Amongst mass audiences and mainstream cinema critics, the initial reception of *Blade Runner* was far from enthusiastic. In the same year that *E. T., the Extra-Terrestrial* (1982) was breaking records for box-office receipts, a film about a rather less cuddly breed of alien was establishing a reputation as dark and difficult. Robin Wood begins his stimulating analysis of Ridley Scott's film with this fact . and interprets Spielberg's comparative fiscal success as encoding a choice made by American audiences. This choice expresses 'a preference for the reassuring over the disturbing, the reactionary over the progressive, the safe over the challenging, the childish over the adult' (Wood 1986, p. 182). Wood goes on to concede that *Blade Runner* is not without its flaws, but suggests that these may stem from the fact that it is simply 'too revolutionary to be permissible'(*ibid.*, p. 187). At a time of conservative hegemony *Blade Runner* is figured as a rogue text roaming the margins of Reaganite America, although in an era of 'militancy, protest, rage, disturbance and radical questioning ... [it would] appear quite at home' (*ibid.*, p. 188).

*Blade Runner*, however, is far less distinct than Wood contends. It is in fact all-too acutely representative of a range of postmodern science fiction films which bear the traces of Reaganism in their profound dualism and disorientation. This genre is characterised by terminally ambivalent relations to the patriarchal authority inscribed in spatial relations, by a problematic convergence between aesthetics and politics in its city images and by a recurring scenario in which a *de rigueur* cynicism about the shape of landscapes to come is dispelled by the seductive and saccharine sentimentalism of nostalgia.

## The *noir* charisma of placelessness

Generically *Blade Runner* is a hybrid which, within the framework of science fiction fantasy, incorporates strands of horror, romance and an unmistakably *noir* narrative and visual design which echoes the Hollywood Private Investigator thrillers of the 1940s and early 1950s. The plot involves dramatic chase sequences, roof-top confrontations and cryptic clues. Its central character is an isolated, hard-boiled cop, who, in the long overcoat uniform of the PI, delivers a droll and sardonic voice-over, makes a habit of hard drinking and getting beaten up – physically and psychologically – by glamorous *femmes fatales* and charismatic villains.

Los Angeles in the twenty-first century is heavily indebted to the cinematic tradition of *noir* city images. The permanently nocturnal streets of this futuristic LA are partially illuminated by neon signs and a chiaroscuro lighting, whilst its gloomy interiors are cloaked by the shadows that fall from drawn blinds and rotating fans. From the writings of James M. Cain and Raymond Chandler to, more recently, the novels of James Ellroy, Los Angeles has enjoyed an intimate relation with the narrative of detection. As in the film and fiction whose idiom it flaunts, the urban landscape in *Blade Runner* is not merely a setting or backdrop to the actions of the characters. The built environment exudes an aura of social collapse and the city becomes a protagonist in its own right.

Regardless of the steadily increasing economic ascendancy of some Japanese cities, Los Angeles retains its status as the capital of Capital. If Los Angeles were to secede from the United States it would be the seventh most wealthy economy in the world. The phenomenal, though highly unevenly distributed financial prosperity of this region is founded largely upon the design and manufacture of military hardware. In *City of Quartz*, Mike Davis undertakes a neo-Foucauldian mapping of the relations of power which make this a key site for the late capitalist order, attempting to excavate the future through a critical archaeology of this representative geocultural entity (Davis 1990). The number of poignant co-occurrences which occur between the urban landscape envisaged in *Blade Runner* and the central components of Davis' thesis in *City of Quartz* might suggest that rather than an apocalyptic aberration, Scott's vision manages to map out the actuality of late *twentieth*-century LA. If the capital of Capital is an exemplary place, anticipating the future of the postmodern city, then *Blade Runner* projects a dystopian vision of the future of that future. To determine the precise effects produced by this vision, however, it is necessary to trace the various co-occurrences in detail.

Davis suggests that, in the rigorous cordoning-off of high-price property districts and financial zones from the poor regions of the city, one can detect a 'siege mentality' underlying the sociospatial organisation of contemporary Los Angeles (*ibid.*, p. 84). The Pleasure Dome is also a Fortress: the cathedrals of corporate capital are laid siege by a burgeoning city of working-class blacks and Third World immigrants. The wave of ghetto insurrections which swept across America's cities during the mid-1960s and again in the summer of 1992, is the historical context for the adoption of this strategy by urban planners. The strict race and class segmentation which typifies the postmodern city must be interpreted as a response to the threat posed by urban counter-insurgency.

Each of the authority figures in *Blade Runner* – Tyrell, Bryant, Deckard, Holden – are male, white and occidental. Race and class lines here are inscribed vertically in space, as these men reside in the clouds, whilst Third World low-lifes are confined to the streets

below. In the film's opening sequences, as the camera descends
from the vertiginous heights of the Tyrell building interrogation
rooms to street level, we are introduced to Deckard, the character
who both literally and metaphorically manoeuvres between both
camps on this urban battlefield. With its stark oppositions between
the imposing Tyrell corporation building and the overcrowded
city streets populated predominantly by Chinese and Asiatics,
Davis' depiction of the postmodern urban landscape could easily
be applied to the ethnogeographic organisation of Scott's
futuristic LA:

> Since the ghetto rebellions of the 1960s a racist, as well as
> class, imperative of spatial separation has been paramount in
> urban development. No wonder, then, that the contemporary
> American inner city resembles nothing so much as the classical
> colonial city, with the towers of the white rulers set off militarily
> from the casbah or indigenous population. (Davis 1985, p. 85)

Los Angeles, 2019 AD, with its dilated Chinatown, is even more
pre-eminently a besieged World City. 'Cityspeak', the dialect of
the casbah, is described by Deckard as 'a mish-mash of Japanese,
German, Spanish, what have you' – a combination which accurately
condenses elements of both the economic and racial anxieties of
late imperial America. In terms of its visual design, with its dissonant
clash of architectural styles, the city itself is something of a mish-
mash. Elements of the Futurist aesthetic, Mayan, Wrightian and
art deco styles collide with Greek statues and roman columns. The
acid-rain drenched streets of the shopping mall and market place
are illuminated by neon ideograms and figures from popular
Oriental mythology. The Egyptian pyramid of the Tyrell building
evokes connotations of empires built on trade and of slaves, like
the replicants, forced to die with their masters. One of the
consequences of this bricolage (which resonates distinctly with
the playful pastiche of contemporary architectural design) is that
the World City loses much of its vernacular particularity. In the
process of relinquishing a distinctive regional identity this place
becomes instantly interchangeable with other metropolitan centres:
this might easily be New York, Hong Kong or Taiwan, circa 2019
AD, only the opening credits clearly establish its location. As it steals
its styles from everywhere, regardless of time and place, the
postmodern city begins to look and feel like nowhere. It is precisely
the anonymity of the urban landscape in *Blade Runner* which is
authentic and instantly recognisable as that distinctive placelessness
of place which presides in the late twentieth-century capitalist
cityscape.

The opening frames of *Blade Runner* alternate between Leon's
eye as it reflects the city and that which seeks to keep it and him

under surveillance: the huge panoptican eye of the Tyrell building. Echoing Mike Davis' departure from Fredric Jameson's interpretation of the Bonaventure, a building which currently dominates part of the skyline of downtown Los Angeles, it might be argued that the primary significance of the Tyrell building is not so much the playfulness of its architectural design, as the 'savagery of its insertion' into this crumbling metropolis (*ibid.*, p. 86). The Tyrell building, as an air-conditioned cocoon of luxury, sealed off from over-population and pollution, testifies to the force of Benjamin's classic equation between the artefacts of civilisation and acts of barbarism.

This savage insertion is enforced by a powerful security apparatus. The area is permanently patrolled by police transporters, physical access is restricted to roof-top landing docks, or to voiceprint-activated elevators. Visual access is also severely limited and there are a number of on-site interrogation rooms in which Tyrell employees are regularly screened in spaces protected by video cameras and electric fields. In the city outside a pervasive police presence is poised just above street level, ready to descend at the first sign of any transgression. In spite of this presence there are signs that street crime is rife.

In its images of the militarisation and segregation of public space, *Blade Runner* once again registers Davis' sense of a besieged city, reproducing key visual icons of the archisemiotics of the class and race war being waged across Fortress LA (Davis 1990; see especially chapter 4). Increasingly the strategies of anxious urban planners are being consolidated by the operations of private security apparatuses, which aim to guarantee individual safety within heavily fortified and regularly patrolled locales. And as Davis emphasises, security at home, in the workplace and at the mall, is not simply a corollary of a particular level of income and lifestyle – rather, it comprises the material and the symbolic representation of the middle-class imagination, a high-tech barricade beyond which the fears and phobias of the PMC are projected.

In a similar vein to the studies produced by David Harvey (1989) and Edward Soja (1988), Davis' interrogation of the postmodern urban landscape frequently returns to the prevalence of forms of *contrary*. This inescapable signature of the postindustrial scene is also inscribed within the *mise-en-scène* of *Blade Runner*. Side by side with the gargantuan Tyrell corporation, the existence of a large pool of cheap immigrant labour appears to have brought with it Third World labour practices and organisation: ranging from Eyeworld and the back-street merchandisers of animal simulacra, to frenetic outdoor markets, small stores and sweatshops. The co-existence of vastly disparate levels of technological development in *Blade Runner*'s nocturnal metropolis is echoed in a range of Reagan era science fiction fantasy films fixated on the prospect of a New Bad Future (in, for example, Scott's *Alien* (1979), *Brazil* (1985), *Back to the Future II* (1986), and *Total Recall* (1990)). The structural overlay of different means of production is evident in the juxtaposition of hovercars and bicycles and in the glaring inappropriateness of clumsy 'Voight-Kampf' equipment as a screening device for the Nexus-6 replicants which are 'more human than human'. Similarly, the luxury and extravagance of Tyrell's interiors clash violently with the garbage-strewn streets of the city outside. The 'Medusala Syndrome', from which J.F. Sebastian suffers, appears to be a highly contagious disease that has spread to the built environment itself. Much like parts of late twentieth-century Los Angeles, 'Ridleyville' is inflicted with accelerated decrepitude, cluttered with anti-commodities and the detritus of planned obsolescence, crumbling under the corrosive effects of pollution. The geographical disparities which result from the capitalist dynamic of uneven development are extended in *Blade Runner* to an interplanetary scale with the advertisements for Off-World. These colonies are specifically packaged as the New Frontier Los Angeles once was itself – a place seeming to offer 'the chance to begin again in a golden land of opportunity and adventure' – and represent a logical extrapolation of the core/periphery model which dominates contemporary economic geography.

It needs to be emphasised that the series of contraries that dominate space in *Blade Runner* – between scales of organisation, labour practices, levels of technological development, core and periphery – are not contradictions; rather they are the same functionally interdependent juxtapositions, in a cityscape whose contours are carved by capital, as are unearthed in the writings of Pynchon, Auster and Phillips. However, to the same extent that the simple act of noting the existence of postmodern tendencies in the work of these authors does not automatically confirm the absolute complicity of these texts with the cultural logic of late capital, to itemise the features of the city in *Blade Runner* in this way, tracing its proximity to contemporary conditions of class and race conflict, does not answer so much as beg the crucial question of to what extent these aspects of the film can be said to coalesce into a *critique*. The vision of the future of Los Angeles in Scott's film undoubtedly constitutes a distension of current conditions, with even greater concentrations of wealth and power, but such a compilation of details does not guarantee the text's status as a *critical* dystopia, to employ Constance Penley's (1990) useful term. In fact, by offering selective details within a work as evidence of a radical political effectivity, one can obscure the mechanisms by which counter-hegemony is often contained.

Any claim that the vision of the future of LA in *Blade Runner* constitutes a critical dystopia has first to negotiate the fact that the city is perhaps the film's most celebrated creation. As part of the pre-Oscar ceremony publicity in the year of its release, the team responsible for art direction on the film received Academy Award nominations. Mainstream critical assessment, whilst hostile to narrative structure (or its alleged absence), were unanimously enthusiastic about the 'look' of the film: the 'rich detail' of its 'impressive sets', the 'sensory assault' and 'atmospheric design'.[1] These accolades from the film industry establishment are indicative of the way in which the progressive content of *Blade Runner*'s fantasy of twenty-first-century LA can be diluted by the sable allure of its exquisite visual design. The aesthetic experience of slick and vertiginous FX shots, the continual visual bombardment by neon signifiers and an immaculately stylised urban landscape, work to undermine any recognition of this place as a critical commentary upon current conditions. The hard lines of the city, its violence and decay, are softened by a soothing Vangelis soundtrack and dissolve into *noir* charisma. Distinctions between the oppositional imagery of a critical dystopia and the glossy surfaces of a designer apocalypse blur disconcertingly.

The presence of aestheticised elements of *actual* sociospatial crises in works of dystopian fantasy can do more to mask than foreground their urgent reality. This is a problematic which *noir* has always had to confront. In his history of this cultural practice and its relations with Los Angeles Mike Davis has sought to specify the nature of its dilemma (see Davis 1990; especially chapter 1). In America the genre emerged during the Depression years of the 1930s, partly as a critical corrective to the hegemonic fable of California as the Sunshine State. It constituted a transformational grammar which substituted for each aspect of the booster's arcadia its sinister and shadowy counterpart: as the Garden of Plenty was seen through a glass darkly, images of prosperity were distorted into reflections on moral and social disintegration, a culture of leisure usurped by an underworld of violence, self-reliance displaced by surveillance. The Sunshine was eclipsed. One of the more devastating ironies of this inversion was that the dream-factories of Hollywood managed to generate vast profits by capitalising on the urban nightmare being acted out on its own back lot. Once the studios had appropriated the *noir* geography of mean streets and scenic sewers the fact, the brute fact, that the streets of LA *really were mean*, for many of its poorer inhabitants, tended to get obscured.

1. These phrases are selected from articles in *The Sunday Times*, *Daily Mail* and *Sight and Sound* and are listed in Haliwell (1989, p. 117).

The physical construction of Los Angeles has been fuelled by lucrative real estate deals and defence contracts *and* by five generations of fervent propaganda by the boosters. Davis' lament for the possibilities for today's 'de-bunker' echo Jamesonian pessimism concerning the oppositional potential of aesthetic practices such as *noir* and is certainly applicable to the visual design of the city in *Blade Runner*. Los Angeles appears to possess an uncanny ability to convert its critiques into glamorously sleazy commercials, whereby even the most disturbing of nightmares becomes a form of 'perverse boosterism' (Davis 1991). *Noir* science fiction films exemplify the difficulties inherent in the process of representing the geographical specificity of urban crisis. Los Angeles in *Blade Runner* and *Predator II* (1990), Chicago in *Robocop* (1987), 'Biffsville' in *Back to the Future II*, the Martian geodesic dome in *Total Recall* and other images of the city of the future, fail to offer an antidote to the 'sunshine and oranges' propaganda which underwent a resurgence during the Reagan era. Collectively these fabular projections of the prospects for urban landscapes ravaged by corporate capital only offer a fashionably cynical and complimentary twilight mythology. Science fiction cinema, in its postmodern phase, tends to distract from frighteningly real urban crises by manufacturing an exhilaratingly pessimistic celluloid fantasy of the New Bad Future from them.

## *Logos* and logos

> a being intermediate between God and the world. The *Logos* is diffused through the world of the senses ... The *Logos* does not exist from eternity like God, and yet its genesis is not like our own and that of all other created beings; it is the first-begotten Son of God, and is for us, who are imperfect, a god.
>
> Judaeus Philo, *Uberweg* (1907), p. 475

Unearthing oppositional elements within the urban landscape of *Blade Runner* one is confronted by the aporia (literally, a series of paths or passages leading in confusing directions) of its *noir* charisma. Similarly, obstacles arise within the film's use of and intersection with the discourses of advertising. Los Angeles, 2019 AD, is a city saturated by screens, simulacra, competing signs and significations. The aesthetic of strip development has extended high above street level and the site of the Dream Factory is even more pre-eminently a society of image and spectacle. The gaze of the masses on the city streets tends to be downcast, but that of the cinema audience for *Blade Runner* is captured by a number of advertising images for fictional and actual corporate empires. There are over twenty separate instances in the course of the film of product placement for Coca-Cola, Pan-Am, Atari, TDK, Budweiser and RCA. This is becoming an increasingly common practice in Hollywood cinema as it collaborates with capitalism's official art form, the advertisement. In the second instalment of Robert Zemeckis' *Back to the Future* trilogy, for example, over fifty mini-commercials were incorporated for, amongst others, Pepsi, DeLorean, Nike and Texaco. There is, however, a distinction to be drawn here. In the Michael J. Fox movie, audiences witness the positive usage of actual products – soft drinks, leisure wear and sports cars – whilst in *Blade Runner* the advertisements are disengaged from the commodities which they promote (no cans of Coke or Bud, Pan-Am jets or Atari hardware appear in the course of the film).

In the political economy of the sign the signifiers and signifieds of corporate capital have floated free from one another. Quotidian and relentless, detached from any material referent, corporate icons compose the extravagantly textualised surface of the postindustrial city. On the streets, in mid-air, at Deckard's apartment, or within the crumbling Bradbury building, this visual bombardment forms a prominent part of the dystopian critique of the future of place which may be detected in *Blade Runner*. However, the distance from the practice of product placement in *Back to the Future II* and the impact of the explicit association of social injustice and eco-catastrophe with the operations of corporate finance should not be overestimated. To a certain extent the mere inclusion of easily recognisable logos in a futuristic fantasy which is screened internationally helps to maintain high profile and provides a graphic testimony to the stamina of organisations whose overriding goal, after all, is survival at any cost.

As Robin Wood has persuasively argued, the advertisement involving an immaculately made-up Oriental woman, seen from various angles and on huge aerial video screens, is one of *Blade Runner*'s most intriguing spatial motifs. It constitutes a Brechtian exercise in *clarification*, the compression of a complex idea into a single image which is 'connected in the film (directly or indirectly), with emigration, Coca-Cola, and pill-popping, various forms of consumption, pacification and flight' (Wood 1986, p. 183). This image intimates the prospective legitimation of currently illicit drug economies – the regulation, for the pacification of a large urban proletariat, of activities defined as a social ill only so long as they remain beyond the auspices of state authority. The imagistic linkage with that ubiquitous icon of western cultural imperialism, Coca-Cola, might be interpreted as suggesting a return to its original cocaine-based ingredients (soma for the Brave New World Order). In both cases, the non-specificity of the advertisement is of itself significant. As with the film's corporate logos, this image has floated free (literally) from any particular product and seems engaged in an unceasing battle for the gaze of the consumer within a political economy of the sign. It vividly testifies to Marx's celebrated critique of capitalism's titanic potentiality as a dematerialising force, under which the very spaces of the city itself seem incessantly to melt into air.

A comparable degree of imagistic density in an advertising sign can be uncovered at a point in *Blade Runner*'s penultimate scene. The carnivalesque hide-and-seek chase sequence involves some rather transparent religious symbolism. Since his opening Blakean (mis)quotation, the renegade replicants' leader has been associated with the figure of the Devil-Angel.[2] Roy's self-crucifixion imparts a specifically Christian dimension to his characterisation, one which is pursued in a valedictory speech which brackets him with the heavens, thus completing his apotheosis. The god or *Logos*, in a similar manner to the monster, has been used to help locate and define the limits of the human as it is conventionally defined in the western imagination. With the repetition, as his final words, of the phrase 'time to die', a conversion is signalled from monster (Leon, the avenging robot), to god (Roy, whose eleventh-hour redemption positions him as a symbol of Christian brotherliness and stoic dignity in earthly suffering). Philo's description of the *Logos*, a principle traditionally associated with Christ, might be applied to Roy at the moment of his death: with his tale of unique sensory experiences in the heavens, he is a being whose genesis is 'not like our own', who possesses Olympian strength, intelligence and beauty as the 'first-begotten son' of Tyrell, the 'god' of biomechanics.

These are the sorts of interpretative trajectory implied by the narrative at this epiphanic moment. However, close attention to the representation of space suggest a different direction, pointing towards a more quotidian manifestation of logos. Whilst he delivers his valedictory speech, Christian iconography is eschewed as Roy is illuminated not by a shaft of heavenly light, but by the nimbus from a neon sign bearing the logo of the TDK corporation. (The selection of a company which specialises in the manufacture of electronic devices for *replication* is surely not accidental). Tracing the etymology of the Greek word *Logos* back from Philo and the Stoics to its origin in the work of Heraclitus, it was initially defined as a law of nature, objective in the world, giving order and regularity to the movement of things. It is this earlier pre-Christian usage which is most pertinent for the logos of corporate capital – the governing

2. Appropriately, the quotation comes from Blake's 'America: A Prophecy' (lines 115–16): 'Fiery the angels fell; thunder rolled / Around their shores, burning with the fires / of Orc'. Wood offers the ingenious interpretation that this is an esoteric, coded reference to the failure of the New Jerusalem. It might also be read as a reference to the 'fiery fall' of Los Angeles – the City *of Angels* become Hades.

principle throughout the second nature of urban-technological landscapes, that which controls and regulates the movement of commodities across capitalist spaces. Jameson's bleak prognosis upon the omnipresence of this law, whereby culture has collapsed into commerce and the resultant postmodern productions may hereafter be decoded as simply the discourses of shopping, seems discouragingly apposite for an interpretation of this moment in *Blade Runner*.

Roy, the property of the Tyrell corporation and linked imagistically with TDK, is portrayed by Rutger Hauer – an actor subsequently used by and associated with the Guinness Group in a series of commercials where, in a monochrome costume reminiscent of the uniform worn by Roy (black overcoat topped by a shock of white hair), he is tailored to impersonate the commodity being promoted. Off-camera, the director of this scene, Ridley Scott, went on to make a series of commercials for Barclays Bank, in a campaign which utilised and specifically echoed the spatial design and thematics of *Blade Runner*. At the moment of maximum frustration in the advertisement, a dystopian city simply melted away into the dazzling light, spaciousness and comforting intimacy apparently associated with a bank interview room. This transition reproduced exactly the detail and effect of *Blade Runner*'s closing scene, in which a gloomy, claustrophobic dystopia miraculously dissolves into a pastoral wilderness. It becomes difficult to placate Jamesonian pessimism with regard to this disquieting disjunction between art and advertising in a denouement which seems almost mischievously to mimic a car commercial (as, to the accompaniment of a mellow jazz saxophone, Deckard drives away from the city of signs into the sun on the open road, with a glamorous and totally impassive model in tow on the passenger seat). *Blade Runner* is then both *about* the usurpation of public spaces by corporate logos and an example of the extent to which place in postmodern cinema is increasingly traced through the metaphoric stencil of the advertising image.

## The (non)sense of an ending

The key textual spaces in *Blade Runner*, in terms of its critical representation of the capitalist city, are the ending and Roy's confrontations with the corporate executive and the cop. After Roy battles his way through to the inner sanctum of corporate power, his execution of Tyrell is the major act of resistance within the film against the social injustice and economic inequality which can be seen as endemic to the landscapes of twenty-first-century capitalism. Yet, crucially, the scene is carefully structured so as *not* to be recognised as such. Tyrell's fall *ought* to be presented as legitimate and even liberatory vengeance, instead it is cast as the narrative's central horrific act – one which is consolidated by the motiveless off-screen slaughter of the puny J.F. Sebastian. This mutation is achieved primarily through a subtle strategic shift in ideological frames of reference, a decoding of justifiable sociopolitical revolt into the transgression of a sacred transhistorical covenant. During this decisive encounter, the critique of the effects of corporate power upon the city and the objective class lines which have been spatially inscribed become enmeshed in an oedipal dragnet. The revenge of the representative of alienated slave labour upon the head (literally) of capital is made suitably appalling by cloaking the protagonists in the familiar costume of Son and Father. Roy identifies Tyrell not as master, but as 'fucker'. Moments before his demise Tyrell affectionately strokes the prodigal son's hair to arouse previously unfelt and patently undeserved sympathy. As the subsequent act is translated from valid nemesis to taboo, the object of rebellion is displaced from Capital to the Oedipal Father.

Critical assessment of *Blade Runner* has tended to note both the critique of the capitalist city and the film's Oedipal narrative, with the assumption that they are somehow complementary. However, at its pivotal moment, the latter interferes with the former to suppress the relations between capital and patriarchal authority. The pyramidal Tyrell building loses its hard edges as an architectural metaphor for class structure in the city and instead becomes home to an Oedipal triangle. As he gouges out Los Angeles' panoptican and Tiresian eye (Tyrell is both father and mother to the replicants) Roy's vengeance is depoliticised through the shift from the geopolitical reality of the postindustrial city to the timeless stage of psychoanalytical drama, since the act of militant transgression is traced through an Oedipal stencil.

The impulse towards the containment of a potentially oppositional portrayal of the future of space in *Blade Runner* becomes increasingly conspicuous in the closing shots. Romance veils the radical and as the sole units of resistance are removed or conveniently run down, the smooth and continuing functioning of the circuitry of the capitalist city is ensured. Darkness, urban decay and claustrophobic confinement in the city spontaneously dissolve into brilliant sunshine and expansive pastoral spaces – an appropriate vista for what promises to be the lover's perpetual honeymoon. But the holiday is cut short by a pressing question: '*Exactly where is this*!?' Preceding events have clearly established that the wealthy have left for the Off-World colonies in their droves due to over-population, pollution and social collapse – the presence of arcadia just beyond the city limits makes any such mass migration inexplicable. In its sheer implausibility and stark incongruity this place becomes a palimpsest for the crumbling second nature of technological forms which comprise the recently departed LA. Pastoral romance in the Garden becomes a rather anxious cryptogram for suffering in the postindustrial city. Adorno's commentary upon the self-erasing pastoral interlude in Chaplin's *Hard Times* might be applied to the dramatic re-emergence of the booster's arcadia at the conclusion of *Blade Runner*, for if nature is viewed solely as a salutary contrast to society it is systematically *denatured*: 'Pictures showing green trees, a blue sky and moving clouds make those aspects of nature into so many cryptograms for factory chimneys and service stations' (Adorno 1990, p. 277). In its anxious and diversionary longing for unsullied, natural landscapes, this futuristic fantasy's (non)sense of an ending inescapably constitutes a nostalgic retreat.

CHAPTER 11

# Mapping the Body (I): *Alien*, Gynophobia and the Corporeal Cartography of Consumerism

In *Alien* (1979), Ridley Scott's previous excursion into science fiction fantasy, there are comparable problematics embedded in its representation of place. As Douglas Kellner and Michael Ryan suggest, the very camera rhetoric of this film suggests the significance of space:

> [it] travels through the ship, establishing a sense of material context, setting, and environment; it shows a world not defined by an individual subject's experience but by material place, social setting. (Ryan and Kellner 1988, p. 184)

As with Scott's projection of the likely trajectory of the postindustrial city, there are unmistakable traces of a neo-Marxist critique of contemporary capitalist spaces within *Alien*'s futuristic vision of the nature of work and power relations in the twenty-third century.

The Nostromo, the space in which most of the film's action occurs, is a corporate space vessel transporting some twenty million tonnes of mineral ore. This suggests the continuation of primary and secondary economic activities (against the prophecies of automation technology enthusiasts) well into the postindustrial future. In marked contrast to the ultra-hygienic and hyperefficient workplaces imagined in numerous science fiction fantasies before the 1980s (the USS Enterprise in *Star Trek* would be a prime example of this) the Nostromo, in places, is dark, dirty and dangerously unreliable. This is part of a general suspicion about the technological forms that dominate space in the film, a wariness about the Company's machines, be they industrial (engines which break down, failing flame throwers) or postindustrial (a deceitful computer and a homicidal android). The crew on board the Nostromo wear drab clothes, smoke cigarettes, drink coffee and struggle with barely digestible food. Their living quarters are cluttered with the kinds of objects one might expect to find inside the cab of a long-distance lorry driver (styrofoam cups, little mementoes, baseball caps, pornographic and family pictures side by side). Cumulatively, these details suggest that the workplace of the future, like the city of tomorrow imagined in *Blade*

*Runner*, will not look dramatically different from today's. Mining the moons of Saturn (*Outland* (1981)), Mars (*Total Recall*), or deep space (*Alien*), enforcing the law (*Robocop* and *Predator II*), or working for the civil service (*Brazil*), there are no miraculous improvements in the conditions of the workplace experienced by labour in science fiction's New Bad Future.

This pessimistic vision of the nature of work/place in a capitalist future is corroborated by the symbolism of the alien creature that disrupts it. The alien is defined by one of the characters as 'a survivor, unclouded by conscience, remorse or delusions of morality'. Within the narrative design the creature is thus configured as the double of the Company which seeks to appropriate it – both are intent upon their own survival at any cost, ready to sacrifice anyone who stands in the way of their violent self-reproduction. The creature embodies the monstrous energies of capitalist *alien*ation, of an economic geography founded on the principles of ruthless efficiency and the survival of the fittest in the marketplace. Both the alien and the landscapes of capital are aggressive, parasitic and predatory, engaged in a relentless process of creative destruction. In the context of its literal and metaphorical anti-capitalism, the denouement of *Alien* can be interpreted as a Marxist fantasy about destroying the monstrous vitality of capital. Jameson's contention, that narratives often fulfil the social function of providing imaginary resolutions to actual historical problems, seems entirely appropriate at the point when Ripley, in rapid succession, destroys both her workplace and the creature that symbolised its internal dynamic.

*Alien*, like *Blade Runner*, thus not only constructs a critique of capital, but also struggles in its conclusion to transcend historical problems by providing an imaginary resolution to the violence and inequality associated with the spaces it represents. The status of *Alien* as a critical dystopia, however, is consistently compromised by its corporeal cartographies, by its mapping of the body. Traditionally, cartographic discourses have been heavily inscribed with the heritage of Enlightenment rationality, which, in its definition of the self, focuses upon the intellectual rather than the physical and upon the relative autonomy of body and space. These two, however, have always enjoyed a dialectical relation. As Lefebvre has argued:

> Before *producing* effects in the material realm (tools and objects), before *producing itself* by drawing nourishment from that realm, and before *reproducing itself* by generating other bodies, each body *is* space and *has* its space: it produces itself in space and it also produces that space ... The whole of (social) space proceeds from the body, even though it so metamorphoses the body that it may forget it altogether – even though it may

separate itself so radically from the body as to kill it. (Lefebvre 1991, pp. 170; 405)

A critical dimension of the spatial vogue which has emerged since the late 1960s in the academy has been the breaking down of a disciplinary apartheid whereby the human form has been excluded from the activity of mapping. This is apparent in work from a variety of sources. Undoubtedly, Lefebvre's *The Production of Space* is at the forefront in radical social theory. From a different angle, Foucault has been instrumental in developing the critical notion of the significance of space, the body and their unceasing exchanges. Place and physique are both seen to be bound in a matrix of power relations and disciplinary technologies. To understand the spatial politics of the asylum, the prison, the clinic, it is essential to consider the body of the madman, the convict, the patient and how it interacts with the institution in which it is placed. Throughout his writings Baudrillard returns repeatedly to the spatial significance of the body: 'The entire contemporary history of the body is the history of its demarcation, the network of marks and signs that have covered it, divided it up' (Baudrillard 1988b, p. 92). And an increasing number of feminist critics, typified by the contributors to Nancy Duncan's *Bodyspace* (1996) collection, have focused on the extent to which, particularly in a society of spectacle, women's bodies have become the site of a social and semiotic struggle, a space of pain, pleasure and conflict over cultural definition.

The body cannot and should not be separated from the spaces within which it moves. Given that the body too is a place, what follows will aim to decode the place of the body in the postmodern cartographies of contemporary science fiction cinema. Unrestricted by the mimetic prohibitions of the naturalist code, this branch of fantasy is both a reflection of and a contribution to cultural anxieties associated with the most intimate of spaces.

## In the belly of the beast

The sexual symbolism of *Alien*, a symbolism which defines reproductive sexuality and particularly *female* reproductive sexuality, as loathsome and horrific, has been so frequently commented upon and is so conspicuous, that critics, conditioned in a hermeneutic of suspicion which trains them to hunt for the hidden, seem to lose sight of the possibility that this is an integral part of the text's *primary*, as opposed to *subtextual* meaning. The body of the mother was entirely absent from *Blade Runner* (no human females were apparently present and men had devised their own elaborate reproductive technologies), but in *Alien* it is so omnipresent that the Macherean notion of the *absent* centre seems wholly inappropriate. The maternal body dominates the *mise-en-scène* in the repeated iconography of birth, wombs and vaginal entrances. The ship is called the Nostromo, but, in one of the many confusions over sexual difference, 'our man' (*nostro homo*) contains and is controlled by a computer referred to as 'Mother'. The crew live inside and are dependent upon Mother for their survival. In the film's opening shots the camera explores the inner space of the mother-ship in a lengthy tracking shot down a corridor, to a chamber where the crew are awakened from their sleep in womb-like containers, a space which nurtures and protects them for months at a time. They rise from these technological wombs in a rebirthing scene as fully developed adults. In the context of a culture experiencing rapid advances in the technologies of reproduction this opening constitutes part of a fascinating and disturbing imagistic opposition around which the film will revolve: between the bloodless births facilitated, as in *Blade Runner*, by an implicitly male science and the horrors of conventional biological and explicitly female parturition. In the course of the film smaller crafts or bodies are occasionally ejected from the inner space of the mother-ship into outer space – although in one instance the ejected vessel remains attached to Mother by a long lifeline referred to as the 'umbilicus' – and in the final showdown the alien is forcibly evacuated from the escape craft, as it had previously pushed itself from the inside of Kane.

Similarly, the scene in which a landing party from the Nostromo approach the alien mother-ship is entirely dominated by the imagery of conception. Three clumsy, vaguely child-like, or even spermatic figures stumble clumsily towards the mother-ship and enter through a narrow opening at the apex of its upstretched limbs. They pass through dark, sticky passages in this foreign vessel's intrauterine interior, but only one manages to make it all the way to a huge womb-like enclosure replete with eggs. The tropical heat of this fecund maternal cavity, as opposed to the surgical sterility of the 'freezers', is represented as a dark and sinister space. Following a grisly conception the film's most notorious birth scene takes place, as the alien bursts through Kane's stomach and he is forced, symbolically, to assume the role of mother at the dining table. As Barbara Creed has suggested, in '*Alien* and the Monstrous-Feminine' (Creed 1990, p. 130), the details in this scene recall Freud's observations on the misconceptions of young children about pregnancy and birth. Freud recorded that many youngsters believed that their mother was impregnated through the mouth, perhaps by eating a special food (the birth scene in *Alien* occurs at the dinner table whilst Kane is eating) and that babies grow in the stomach, from which they are also born.

Perhaps the most significant manifestation of an aversion to reproductive sexuality in the film appears in the form of the monster itself. The alien creature was intentionally designed as a bundle of terrifying sexual fantasies by the Swiss artist H.R. Giger. Giger's expressed intention was to combine two types of classic Freudian sexual phobia in one nightmare creation. First, as the creature erupts from Kane's stomach, it appears like a monstrous cartoon phallus equipped with chrome teeth. Subsequently, in the few glimpses permitted of the creature, there are repeated shots of a sleek, erectile head. At the same time, Giger intended the alien to be a visual correlative of the sexual phobia, *vagina dentata*. Much of the horror in *Alien* focuses upon orifices (the images of the mouths of the female replicants in *Blade Runner* continue this motif) – Kane's oral rape by the creature and Ash's violation of Ripley with a rolled-up magazine – and this culminates in the gaping, salivating mouth of the alien itself, a black hole which opens up to reveal a layering of razor sharp teeth. The monstrous phallus and *vagina dentata*: the alien represents a composite image of classic patriarchal sexual phobias.

*Alien* is fairly untypical of commercial cinema in its complete omission of love scenes or sexual relations between the characters. However, there is a spectacular return of the repressed in the *mise-en-scène*. Structurally, the narrative design of *Alien* is cyclical: it opens and closes with sleep. The final image is of Ripley resting in peace (RIP), with, as Robin Wood notes, her 'safely domesticated pussy' (Wood 1984, p. 199), having returned to her high-tech womb (a classic response to trauma according to psychoanalysis). *Alien* begins and ends with sleep, but the nightmare, the return of the repressed occurs in between and is condensed into a demonisation of the mother's body: in the voice of spiteful computers, in the rows of hatching eggs, in fallopian tube corridors and uterine passages, in the womb-like interiors and birth scenes. Whilst it is highly problematic to assert, as branches of feminist film theory has done, that the horror genre is *exclusively* devoted to the expression of patriarchal phobias concerning female sexuality, it is certain that there are many instances of the bodies of women being depicted as uncanny vessels, objects of dread and fascination. In *Alien* certain concessions are made to feminism at the level of narrative structure (woman-as-heroine), but in its symbolic design, it clearly belongs to this gynophobic tradition: the Mother becomes Other, her biology is equated with that which is different and disturbing. From this perspective it is the bodies of women like Ripley which are being symbolically defined in the film as that which is truly alien.

A similar dichotomy can be discerned in the 1986 sequel, *Aliens* (1986). At the level of narrative structure there is a valorisation of particular notions of the feminine – as career woman, as mother, as fighter. However, the symbolic design continues to equate female physicality with that which is loathsome and fearful – the new woman is only the handmaiden of the old monstrous feminine. There is also a worrying new inflexion to this dualism in *Aliens* which coincides with an intensification in forms of racial conflict in America during the 1980s. Structurally this film is founded upon a juxtaposition between a rather saccharine and sentimental portrayal of *white* middle-class motherhood (Ripley and Newt) and the monstrous feminine which is embodied in an explicitly *black* alien mother. Amy Taubin's suggestion, that the monstrous matriarch in the Cameron/Hurd film might covertly represent the black welfare mother might appear rather over-ingenious, but it does tally with a range of subtextual possibilities (Taubin 1992). Whilst *Aliens* (like the Arnold Schwarzenegger vehicle *Predator* (1987)) is quite clearly a Hawkish science fiction rewriting of the American experience of Viet Nam, it might also be read as a text concerned with ghettoisation. The unmistakably WASPish LV426 colony, crammed with nice white nuclear families, is overrun by hordes of black aliens. The neighbourhood is torn to shreds rapidly and at the centre of it all, unable to control her reproductive sexuality and secretly signifying one of the folk devils of Reaganomics, is the monstrously productive black (welfare) mamma.

## Body culture/body horror

An alternative reading of the symbolism of the *Alien* films is possible, but it similarly reveals the containment of their counter-hegemonic potential as critical dystopia. This alternative reading involves displacing attention from a patriarchal social order to the economic system of consumer capitalism. It also necessitates a return to the question of genre.

Like *Blade Runner*, *Alien* must first and foremost be classified as a work of fantasy – that is, as a text whose representations fail to intersect with that ideologically produced space termed the 'real world'. Under the general rubric of the Fantastic, *Alien* is a combination of the science fiction and horror genres. It is possible and indeed necessary for current purposes however to be even more specific about the classification of *Alien*, since it belongs to a special subgenre in postmodern cinema referred to as 'body horror': the pronounced tendency in a number of films produced over the past two decades towards making the corporeal the locus of terror.

As Robin Wood contends in his analysis of horror, the genre has witnessed a geographical migration during the twentieth century (Wood 1984, p. 183). The monster used to live overseas, in foreign lands, occupying Gothic castles in deepest Transylvannia. Gradually, however, the horror has edged closer to home. In the 1950s a sequence of alien invasion films appeared which coincided with the manufacture of Cold War paranoia, and during the 1960s a spate of haunted houses or isolated motels began to appear at the edge of town. By the 1970s monsters had reached suburbia: they were at the shopping mall in Romero's *Dawn of the Dead* (1979) and in *The Stepford Wives* (1974), the High School Dance in *Carrie* (1976), they were sighted roaming the leafy suburban boulevards in *Halloween* (1978) and *Friday the Thirteenth* (1980). More recently, in the *Stepfather* (1986–1991) series and Wes Craven's *The People Under the Stairs* (1991), the monsters have infiltrated the inner sanctum of normality, the bourgeois home. However, in a number of contemporary horror films, and *Alien/s* clearly belongs amongst these, this journey has continued on inwards towards the body itself. In *The Howling* (1980) and *An American Werewolf in London* (1981), the remakes of *The Fly* (1986), *The Thing* (1982) and *Invasion of the Body Snatchers* (1978), in the *Hellraiser* (1987–1991) and *Nightmare on Elm Street* (1984–1987) series, there has been a spectacular intensification in the terrors associated with the flesh, a foregrounding of the fears associated with the processes of bodily transformation, mutation and disintegration, or, as in *The Silence of the Lambs* (1991), with the body being reduced to mere meat.

The earliest examples of this special subgenre were made by the Canadian director David Cronenberg, whose *oeuvre* is perhaps incomparable in terms of the fascinated disgust it continually expresses for the human body. The subgenre of body horror in general and the films of David Cronenberg in particular have received often hostile response from academic critics, usually on two major counts. First, they have been accused of a deeply conservative and puritanical dread of the body, especially the female body. Cronenberg's *Videodrome* (1982), *The Fly* and *Dead Ringers* (1988) in particular have been singled out for an even more excessive display of womb envy/aversion than is apparent in *Alien*. Body horror, in this context, is often decoded as a gynophobic reaction to the sexual revolution and the rise of feminism – a cultural practice which responds to dramatic changes in the body politic and the politics of the body with visions of horrific mutation and the disintegration of a recognisable human form. From this perspective the symbolic design of *Alien* might be interpreted as a form of fearful *cross-dressing*: the sexual revolution results in an inversion of traditional gender identities to the extent that audiences are presented with anxious images of women stomping around with flame-throwers and men being forced to give birth.

A second recurrent criticism of body horror is that it represents both a response and a contribution to the manufacturing of AIDS hysteria within a deeply homophobic culture. *The Thing*, directed by John Carpenter, could be read as a classic example of this practice. The film concerns an all-male community at a polar ice station who are killed off, one by one, by a mysterious and apparently unstoppable virus. The disease is deadly, but there is no way to tell who has it and it can only be transmitted in private through contact with a carrier. At one point in the film the characters even resort to organising a blood test to enable them to identify the enemy within.

These criticisms have an undoubted validity in certain instances. Body horror often does respond and contribute to cultural anxieties associated with the sexual revolution, to patriarchal phobias and AIDS hysteria. There are problems, however, associated with the assertion that these are the only, or even the primary impulses within the genre. First, the criticism that body horror is gynophobic fails to contend with the fact that it focuses upon men's bodies far more than it does upon those of women. Second, there is the fact that some of the most significant contributions to the subgenre predate the panic associated with the HIV virus. (This point has been made by Jancovich 1992, p. 116.) Cronenberg's *Rabid* (1974) and *Shivers* (1976) *are* all about rapidly spreading plagues and the sexual transmission of viral infections, but they were made in the mid-1970s. Body horror may in fact be a response to a far more widespread and contagious malady – the social disease designated *consumerism*.

Superficially, in a consumer culture, the body is defined as a private space, but in practice it is subject to and the object of a variety of forms of regulation. The development of medical technologies such as genetics and prosthetic surgery, which play such an important part in science-fiction fantasy, is a significant part of this process, one which increases the dependence of the individual upon machines and a range of experts. At the same time, individuals in a consumer culture are incessantly bombarded by images of the commercialised means of re-creating and idealising themselves. As desire is channelled into consumerism and the fetishism of commodities, reification intensifies and the consuming self becomes perhaps capitalism's most valuable product. In this culture the institutions of advertising perform the critical function of encouraging self-obsession with the body – its surfaces and its depths, what it absorbs and how it is adorned. Advertising appears to promote affirmative messages about the self, but its primary purpose is to produce feelings of inadequacy which are the essential preconditions for purchase. To this end the body is remorselessly objectified – in televisual images, in magazines and on billboards – with the covert intention of convincing the consumer that they are in some way deficient. A culture of narcissism, to use Christopher Lasch's phrase, is a culture of anxiety and insecurity about the body and its image (Lasch 1979).

The terrors and pleasures of body horror cannot be dissociated from the terrors and pleasures of a body culture. In this sense it can be argued that films such as *Alien*, with their visions of bodily mutation and disintegration, are simply the underbelly of advertising discourses. Norman Mailer's analysis of advertising in the 1960s, as a form of comparative pornography which encouraged the consumer to substitute the 'happy and faithful fetish' for that 'punishing trip to a flesh outside us', has become obsolete (Mailer 1968, p. 351). The promissory second skin of the commodity and the flesh of the body of the consumer are becoming increasingly interchangeable. The punishing trip is now to a body which the consuming self likes to think of as its own, but which has been colonised by the imperatives of consumption to such an extent that it may no longer even be recognisable. Its distortions are simply writ large in the cinema of body horror. Ultimately, images of exploding stomachs form a direct line of continuity with the whispering voices of the hidden persuaders who ask insidiously: 'Can you pinch more than an inch?'

# CHAPTER 12

# Mapping the Body (II): *The Terminator*, *T2* and Testosterone Topography

The tensions between critique and the containment of counter-hegemony in postmodern science-fiction cinema is exemplified by *Blade Runner* and apparent in *Alien*, with its mappings of the body of the mother and the consumer, but is in no sense exclusive to the films of Ridley Scott. In fact, precisely the same dynamic can be seen in operation within the film for which Constance Penley (1990) originally developed the term 'critical dystopia'. Throughout *The Terminator* (1984) it is made clear that the origins of an imminent nuclear armageddon can be traced to contemporary decision-making within the military-industrial complex. *The Terminator* can be read as a text which expresses and explores general cultural anxieties associated with the New Cold War and to the mechanisation of place and subjectivity within a consumer culture saturated by technological commodities.

The man-machine in *The Terminator* represents the physical embodiment of the logic of scientific rationalism taken to its limit. Its actions proclaim the superior efficiency of the mechanical and the programmed over the organic and spontaneous. It is an appropriate folk hero/devil for a capitalist culture which relentlessly pursues the mechanisation of space at the points of production and consumption and which, during the early 1980s, witnessed numerous advances in prosthetic surgery and the rise to mass appeal of various health and fitness regimes. (This was articulated partly through the iconographic appeal of one-time Mr Universe Arnold Schwarzenegger.) As well as responding to cultural fears about reification and the programming of subjectivity, the Terminator is also simply a paradigmatic form for the intractability and occasional hostility of the more mundane technological forms which comprise the landscape through which the characters in the film move: a process that begins with answering machines and personal hi-fis, it is suggested, builds to global transportation and communication systems and culminates with the 'Skynet'/Star Wars computer network, which will eventually design the perfect fusion of human and machine. Individuals are presented as becomingly increasingly identified with and through a second nature of technological forms:

Sarah Connor routinely clocks in for work and her flatmate is permanently plugged in to her Sony Walkman; she is reduced to a voice on a tape recording, or a number in a telephone book and is heavily reliant upon machines in her flight from the Terminator. Other characters in the film exhibit mechanised behaviour patterns, ranging from compulsive chain-smoking to the delivery of seemingly pre-programmed telephone seduction techniques. The freedom fighter from the future, Kyle Reese, has a bar code stamped on to his flesh and aims to triumph over his mechanical adversary by mimicking his unimpassioned focus and ability to disconnect pain. Whilst the human is being encased within a second skin of technologies, the technological, in the guise of the Terminator, has acquired a living tissue to flesh out its robot skeleton.

## Daddy and Destroyer

In the sequel to *The Terminator*, *Terminator 2: Judgment Day* (1991), there is a dramatic shift in the characterisation of the monstrous and a significant new inflexion to its technoparanoia. The original villain becomes a saviour and hostility is now directed at the 'T2000', the latest breed of technological assassin which is manufactured from liquid metal. Whilst the original Terminator is now associated with the vernacular, blue-collar poetry of biker subculture, rock'n'roll and industrial production, the T*2000* (a millenial marker) embodies a series of characteristics – advanced chemical technology, simulation, informational systems and a terrifying adaptability – which David Harvey has described as the economic signifiers of a flexible Fordist regime of accumulation (Harvey 1989). The original Terminator now adopts the role of father to John Connor (who would himself become the father-figure of the resistance in the future war against the machines) and is programmed to protect him from his patricidal nemesis. Therefore, at a symbolic level, the narrative enacts the triumph (which significantly takes place in an iron foundry, as does the denouement of *Alien*[3]) of a romanticised paternalism, associated with an ageing but vibrant industrialism, over a postindustrial bureaucratic facelessness, associated with an imminent future.

*Terminator 2*, like its predecessor, traces the possibility of a future nuclear apocalypse to contemporary social practices and relations with a second nature of technological forms. However, as was argued in relation to Scott's *Blade Runner* and *Alien*, apparently radical political messages can often be undermined at the level of sexual politics. In this instance the gender preoccupations and the scopophilic drive have less to do with the maternal body (unless we accept Constance Penley's ingenious suggestion that time travel narratives are covert primal scene fantasies) than it does with the physique of the all-action male hero (Penley 1990, p. 120). For the *Terminator* films are at least as concerned with masculinity as they are with machinery. Arnold Schwarzenegger, the star of both films, is the point at which they traverse generic boundaries and cross over with the spate of extremely lucrative action films produced during the 1980s. In this subgenre which paraded a series of sinewy icons such as Sylvester Stallone, Chuck Norris, Christopher Reeve and Jean-Claude Van Damme,

> the male body – principally the white male body became increasingly a vehicle of display – of musculature, of beauty, of physical feats, and of a gritty toughness. (Jeffords 1993, p. 245)

The argument sometimes forwarded by critics of this genre is that these testosterone topographies construct masculinity as a variety of denaturalised performance, as a self-conscious and parodic masquerade. According to this reading, the instantly recognisable formulae of this genre – the ritualised death and destruction, the innumerable aestheticised explosions and rounds of ammunition – are not the *real* subject of these texts. Rather than being violent, sadomasochistic fantasies, films such as *The Terminator* are actually *about* violence, sadomasochism, power and display in a patriarchal culture.

It is of course possible that this is the form of address encoded in these mappings of the male body. However, it is often difficult to determine in what ways the self-reflexive miming of masculine aggression in film differs from its off-screen practice. The images of masculinity produced in Hollywood circulate in fields larger than the discursive practices of film theory. When Ronald Reagan declares, in a public address, that he knows what foreign policy decisions to take in relation to Latin America after watching the exploits of Rambo, it is highly unlikely that his militaristic fervour was inspired by that film's parodic subtext. The distinctions between a postmodern 'performing the masculine' and old-style macho aggression may be too fine to be recognised outside of the academy.

*The Terminator* and other contemporary action films are not primarily engaged in performing the masculine, at least not in the sense that it is currently defined. In part the display of the white male body permits a surreptitious homoeroticism which would otherwise be taboo in a culture which enforces a compulsive heterosexuality. But to uncover the primary ideological imperative behind these muscular mappings it is necessary to trace the genre to its specific sociohistorical context: the postmodern period in America from the late 1960s.

During this period the women's movement and the Civil Rights lobby launched a dual assault upon white male privilege. The concomitant withering of gender polarities (especially within the workplace) was exacerbated by the shattering of a sense of economic self-sufficiency in the wake of the oil crisis-inspired slump. Meanwhile, in the international political arena, national pride was severely wounded by a spate of hostage crises, Third World revolutions and embarrassing military failures in Viet Nam. In the wake of these events, in certain quarters, masculinity could no longer be accepted as the given against which the feminine might be defined and displayed. It needed to be *made visible*, to be reinscribed in the symbolic interstices of an anxious patriarchal order. The dramatic resurgence of the action genre from the mid-1970s onwards, a resurgence greatly consolidated under the Reagan presidency, might then be interpreted as a semiotic salve, a means of sublimating anxieties associated with a series of historical changes understood in terms of an insidious *feminisation* of the nation (inevitably, the loss of political, economic and military muscle would be articulated in this way within a culture which symbolically equates the feminine with weakness and with lack). Collectively these texts constitute a clarion-call for a remasculinisation of America, rather puerilely imagined here and in the wave of comic book heroes who appeared in Hollywood cinema at this time (*Superman* (1978), *Batman* (1990), *Indiana Jones* (1984) *et al.*) as a *remuscularisation*. This represents, in terms of the mapping of the male body in popular culture, a recuperation of the most archaic formulation of masculinity as brute physical presence and an ability to withstand and mete out unbelievable excesses of violence. The muscles themselves are a significant component in the contours of this corporeal cartography – not as a parodic costume, but as signifiers of power and of the traditional forms of manual labour which has gone into their production. These signifiers might appear particularly pleasurable to both the disempowered and to a largely white-collar male labour force sharing its office space and authority in some instances with women and deprived of its traditional role in the family as the sole source of economic security. As Yvonne Tasker has suggested:

> A reorientation of the relationship between men, masculinity and consumption in the West necessarily affects those definitions of male identity achieved through production. (Tasker 1993a, p. 232)

*Terminator 2* offers a different relation to technology to its predecessor and its representation of gender is similarly rewritten. Whilst in the first film Sarah Connor performed the more conventional feminine role of the victim needing to be rescued endlessly by the hero, in *T2* she adopts a role similar in certain respects to that performed by Ripley in *Aliens* – of woman as an

Amazonian warrior pathologically devoted to the protection of her young. Transformed into a humourless and hysterical guerrilla fighter, Sarah Connor's duties as a caring parent are fulfilled by the Terminator who acts as a surrogate father.

Between the two instalments of this diptych there occurs a significant (although largely superficial) alteration in the implicit definition of the functioning of the male body. In the early 1980s the Terminator was entirely ruthless, determined and goal-oriented – in other words he was a perfect role model for those battling for the futures in the money markets of Reagan's America. In the early 1990s, during a time of increased unemployment, he retains this single-mindedness, but now it is channelled into the more socially responsible goals of conservation and parenting. In *T2* masculinity is attained by men (or machines achieving humanity) who are willing to sacrifice their careers for their sons: the Terminator is lowered into the melting pot and the black American scientist, Miles Dyson, when he realises that devotion to his work may hasten armageddon, is similarly willing to destroy his workplace and give up his life so that the future is safe for his son. The choice is seductively simple: nuclear family or nuclear apocalypse.

Once again the generic boundaries of science fiction fantasy blur and *T2* crosses over with a chain of Hollywood films produced during the late 1980s and early 1990s which offered an implicit definition of masculinity as fathering. In *Three Men and a Baby* (1991), *Three Men and a Little Lady* (1993), *Look Who's Talking* (1991) and *Look Who's Talking II* (1992), *Parenthood* (1992), *Regarding Henry* (1991), *Father of the Bride* (1992) and *Boyz in the Hood* (1991), it is clear that father knows best. This *oeuvre* does not indicate a full-scale realignment in patriarchal ideology; rather it suggests the marketability of the myth of the New Man and perhaps a strategic dissolution in the classical gender apartheid whereby place is classified according to sex (that is, the assumption that the public sphere should be a predominantly male preserve and the private, domestic sphere is the appropriate female domain). In *T2* the superficiality of this development is evidenced by the patently ironic (re)construction of Arnold Schwarzenegger as an icon for the aspiring New Man. In several of his films since the original *Terminator* he has attempted to integrate the roles of father and fighter (*Commando* (1985), *Kindergarten Cop* (1992), *The Last Action Hero* (1993)), but it is the familiar repertoire of violence and destruction which continues to constitute his most financially successful gestures. Finally, the effort to fuse the figures of Daddy and Destroyer in one body is as problematic and unconvincing as an actor renowned for his endorsements of the Hawkish Republican Party appearing in a film about nuclear disassembly (the terrorist attack on Skynet):

I only play the Terminator in my movies. But, let me tell you, when it comes to the American future, Michael Dukakis will be the real Terminator. (Schwarzenegger 1992)

## Does the future have a future?

If these readings (Chapters 10–12) of the future of space in postmodern science fiction cinema are accurate it seriously undermines the claims made by the likes of Pfeil and Wood concerning their radical political effectivity. In *Blade Runner*, the disturbing projection of the trajectory of the late capitalist order is consistently undercut by the sheer glossiness of its urban landscape and impaired by obfuscatory oedipal and romantic subtexts. Disturbing, challenging, progressive – Robin Wood's description of *Blade Runner* has undoubted validity, but such qualities do not exist in isolation. The text, like the society in which it is produced and consumed, is riven by conflict, within the city and its signs and in the actions and inactions of its inhabitants.

Similarly, *Alien* and the *Terminator* films construct a critique of the landscapes of capital, militarism and their social technologies, whilst symbolically reinforcing the patriarchal social order with which they are integrated in their mappings of the body. These texts are characterised then by a distinct dichotomy in their representation of space: their critical, although immaculately choreographed assaults upon capitalist landscapes are undercut by a reactionary recuperation of patriarchal authority, which is initiated through a demonisation of the mother's body, or mapped on to the ultra-violent exploits of the body of the male hero.

In any attempt to chart a cartography of postmodern America from its popular artefacts, critics on the left, in their eagerness to establish an oppositional culture, need to be especially sensitive to the intricate mechanisms by which counter-hegemony, or what Lefebvre terms 'counter-spaces', can be contained (Lefebvre 1991, p. 367). Equally, however, the Jamesonian paradigm of a postmodern hyperspace which is practically unmappable, due to the irredeemable incorporation of culture and commerce, provides an interpretative frame inadequate to the intricacies of these pictures. Whilst the simple presence of critical elements does not guarantee an oppositional status in its mapping of urban and corporeal spaces, the application of a symptomatic reading which reduces a text to its 'problematic' (the *ipso facto* complicity with capital) is a strategy that relegates the contradictions within cultural productions to insignificance and thus ignores the precise means by which critiques can be compromised. That Janus-faced ambivalence associated with the Fantastic, which was noted earlier and has been uncovered in postmodern science fiction's engagement with space, is usually the first casualty of any large-scale generic renunciation or valorisation. This caution is not intended as a casual fetishisation of the indeterminate, but as a means to foregrounding that confusion and insecurity which is itself a significant factor through its prominence in postmodern cultural practices.

# CHAPTER 13

# Cherry-Pie Heaven: David Lynch

> Two clichés make us laugh but a hundred clichés move us ...
> the extreme of banality allows us to catch a glimpse of
> the Sublime.
>> Umberto Eco, *Travels in Hyperreality* (1987), p. 209

In the year that *Alien* was released, Ridley Scott was approached
by the producer Dino de Laurentiis to direct a screen version of
Frank Herbert's *Dune* (1984). In 1975, a team including *Alien*'s
collaborators H.R. Giger and Dan O'Bannon, began drafting
storyboards and set designs for the translation of this epic science
fiction novel to the cinema. This venture, however, was beset by
severe financial difficulties and work was temporarily suspended
in 1978. With de Laurentiis' backing, Scott was briefly involved
in a reactivation of this ambitious project before leaving, once
more due to budgetary constraints, to work on *Blade Runner*.
Finally, in 1981, fresh from the critical and commercial successes
of *The Elephant Man* (1980), the young American director, David
Lynch, was guaranteed a mammoth $45 million budget by the de
Laurentiis production company to bring *Dune* to the screen.

In terms of box-office receipts and mainstream critical reception
*Dune* was one of the more memorable blockbuster catastrophes of
the 1980s. As with Scott's *Blade Runner*, the consensual opinion
was that the stunning images in Lynch's stylish adaptation could
not compensate for a Byzantine storyline. Robin Wood's suggestion
that the poor initial response to *Blade Runner* was attributable to
its subversive political content needs to be reassessed in the light
of *Dune*'s failure. Lynch's film flaunted a potent admixture of
militarism and fundamentalist messianism, alongside a reactionary
sexual politics and an explicit insistence on the necessity for strong
leaders and nuclear families within a stable society. If consonance
with the dominant ideology were the only factor determining
commercial success then *Dune* ought to have been a cinematic
flagship for Reagan's America. The fact that it failed so spectacularly
is suggestive of the nebulous mechanisms of aesthetic pleasure and
cultural instrumentality at work within the cinema of David Lynch.

With the exception of his single foray into the realm of science
fiction, Lynch's film and TV career to date has been strewn with

success. His first film, *Eraserhead* (1977), was instantly established as a cult classic, whilst the more conventional *The Elephant Man* received an Oscar nomination for best film. *Blue Velvet* (1986) similarly picked up Academy Award nominations and won the National Society of Film Critics best film award. More recently, *Wild at Heart* (1990) was awarded the *Palme d'Or* at the 1991 Cannes Film Festival and *Twin Peaks* (1989–1990) was one of the most widely watched and talked about serials in television history.

One of the few constants in the work of this celebrated *auteur* has been generic diversity. Lynch has created surrealist fantasies and historical melodramas, rites-of-passage tales and ultra-violent road-movie musicals, TV documentaries and Gothic soap operas. Underlying this generic differentiation, however, there is a distinct batch of aesthetic devices and thematic preoccupations that are instantly recognisable signatures of a 'David Lynch' production: the formal self-consciousness and intertextuality; the preoccupation with images that are alternately bizarre, absurd and surreal; the obsession with violence and sexuality; the fantastically wooden acting performances and stilted dialogue.

The political dynamic outlined in relation to the representation of space in recent science fiction cinema can also be detected in the Lynch *oeuvre*. From *Eraserhead* to the *Twin Peaks* prequel, *Fire Walk With Me* (1992), Lynch's work is characterised by immaculately stylised re-presentations of key capitalist spatialities, in which critical potential is contained by a darksome charm and an integration with the discourses of advertising. As in recent science fiction film, Lynch's cinema displays a profound anxiety about the body and its image across landscapes saturated by the technologies of production (industrial manufacturing machinery) and reproduction (postindustrial devices such as TV, radio and camera). Lynch's sexual politics combine New Age science fiction's virulent anti-feminism with the self-conscious manipulation of a pop psychoanalysis. And the narrative curve of *Blade Runner* – from *noir* cynicism to nostalgic sentimentalism – resonates distinctly with the tonal register and denouements of many of Lynch's films. Lynch has been celebrated and denounced as the doyen of postmodern cinema. What follows here will be an attempt to map the key spaces in his quintessentially postmodern cartographies – the city and the suburb, small town and the road, nature and second nature, the body and the bourgeois home – in relation to their dialogue with dominant ideology.

## Lynch's mappings and the 'dark continent'

In terms of their corporeal cartographies Lynch's films clearly intersect with the mappings of body horror. Bodies are regularly severed and split open to reveal their sticky interiors (the ear found in *Blue Velvet*, the multiple head wounds, vomiting and abortion in *Wild at Heart*, the autopsies in *Eraserhead*, *Twin Peaks* and *Fire Walk With Me*). Bodies which transgress physical 'norms' are displayed frequently (the dwarf and giant in *Twin Peaks*, disfigured infants and adults in *Eraserhead* and *The Elephant Man*, club feet and rotten teeth in *Wild at Heart*). Bodies consume other bodies (the hideously bloated cannibal, Baron Harkonnen in *Dune*), or are fused grotesquely with machinery (the First Stage Guild Navigators in *Dune* and Mr Beaumont in a hospital bed in *Blue Velvet*). Representation of bodyspace is dominated by images of mutation, dismemberment, deformity and decay.

Lynch's mapping of the corporeal, as John Alexander has suggested, is organised around a structural opposition between a 'closed' perfect body and an 'open' abject body (Alexander 1993, pp. 24–5). The Lynchian closed-body hero always displays a decidedly conservative sartorial preference – dressed formally in dark suit and tie and juxtaposed with the degeneracy of the ungroomed open body. This opposition was established in Lynch's first feature-length film, *Eraserhead*, with the imagistic counterpoint between Henry Spencer and the mutated infant he unwillingly shares his apartment with. Subsequently, it has been particularly apparent in Lynch's use of the clean-cut and boyish-looking actor Kyle MacLachan. In *Dune* MacLachan plays the smartly dressed Paul Atreides, whose absolute physical and mental control is pitted against the diseased, obese and semi-naked Baron Harkonnen, who feasts on the internal organs of young men in orgies of homosexual sadism. In *Blue Velvet* MacLachan plays Jeffrey Beaumont, who achieves the horrified recognition that the 'well dressed man' disguise hides his sociopathic alter ego, Frank Booth. And in *Twin Peaks* this opposition is sustained as Agent Dale Cooper, in regulation FBI dark suit and tie, is pitted against the slovenly, denim-clad 'Bob'. Significantly, in *The Elephant Man*, the rescue and redemption of John Merrick from the uniformly vile working-class subjects of London's East End by Sir Frederick Treves, is accompanied by a change of clothing (to the vestments of a uniformly benign Victorian bourgeoisie).

The fear that accompanies this structural opposition and haunts Lynch's corporeal cartographies is twofold: homophobia (the fear that the closed body of the hero might be 'open' to a man) and gynophobia (the fear of the feminine as the most 'open' of bodies). Lynch's (mis)understanding of homosexual desire is best described as a form of heterosexual hysteria. In *Dune* Baron Harkonnen sexually abuses young men before eating them – confirming the mythic equation in a compulsively straight patriarchal order between gay desire, violence and paedophiliac defilement. Jeffrey Beaumont's violent encounter with the camp sadist Ben is followed by a night-ride with Frank in *Blue Velvet* which was originally intended to conclude with a literal rape scene, rather than the symbolic performance that takes place at Deer Meadows. The narrative of *Twin Peaks* follows the exploits of the perverse Bob, hiding inside Leland Palmer and fuelling obscene erotic excesses. The horror of being possessed by Bob, of having him *inside you*, represents the climax of the series, when the most closed of closed-body Lynch heroes, Dale Cooper, is penetrated by this libidinal demon.

A virulent homophobia is apparent in both the literal and the symbolic co-ordinates of Lynch's corporeal cartographies. However, it takes place against the backdrop of a far more pervasive dread, a fear of the 'dark continent' that is the open body of Woman. The range of roles offered to women in Lynch's cinema is both restricted and reactionary. Women are portrayed as Bad Mothers (Mary X in *Eraserhead*; Marietta, the Wicked Witch in *Wild at Heart*; the Reverend Mother Gaius in *Dune*), or, less conspicuously, as Good Mothers (Dorothy in the closing frame of *Blue Velvet*; Irulan and Jessica in *Dune*; the absent Mrs Kendal in *The Elephant Man*). Alternately, women are portrayed as predatory *femmes fatales*, or innocent, small-town, all-American Girls. These archetypes are frequently represented as prone to psychological disorder and their madness provokes varying degrees of hilarity (the Log Lady and Nadine in *Twin Peaks*), or horror (Marietta and a disabled voodoo-practising psychotic in *Wild at Heart*). Finally, there is a cast of extras that includes wholesome secretaries and waitresses, obese prostitutes and angelic singers. Whilst they are typically central to the plot these figurines are largely passive and function primarily as a catalyst to the actions of the male hero (Jeffrey, Sailor, Cooper) who battle to rescue women, body and soul.

As with the open/closed body hero these stereotypical personae are usually paired off within each film. Thus, in a flamboyantly self-conscious appropriation of film *noir* traditions, *Blue Velvet* juxtaposes the dark, foreign *femme fatale* (Dorothy Vallens) with the redemptive, asexual blonde girl-next-door (Sandy). The absence of psychological depth to such flagrantly one-dimensional roles restricts the possibilities for character development in a conventional sense, but Lynch is consistently uninterested in such qualities. Instead he explores the landscapes of female corporeality and in particular the 'mystery' of reproductive sexuality.

Lynch's aversion to the mother's body is most striking in his first feature-length production, *Eraserhead*. The *mise-en-scène* is dominated by an iconography of grotesque female fecundity. The narrative revolves around the invasion of inviolate male domesticity (the bachelor pad) by loathsome femininity and the unwanted responsibilities of fatherhood. Mary X fills Henry Spencer's apartment with the screams of a mutant infant and his bed with writhing umbilical cords. Meanwhile, the Lady in the Radiator, a deformed 'flamenco placenta-dancer', crushes umbilical cords that ooze spermatozoa beneath her heels and the Beautiful Girl across the Hall clasps him in an erotic embrace whilst dragging him down into a filthy quagmire.[1] With its ubiquitous pipes and tubings and an incessant hum that blurs the industrial with the intrauterine (the assembly line of reproduction), even the city exists largely as an architectural trope for anxieties about the maternal body.

In Lynch's subsequent work his gynophobia is rarely expressed with the vehemence evident in *Eraserhead*, but it persists nonetheless. The sand worms of *Dune*, like Giger's *Alien*, are a surreal embodiment of the cartoon phallus and *vagina dentata*. Frank Booth's sadistic exploration of Dorothy Vallens' vagina in *Blue Velvet* is echoed in the multiple autopsies on female corpses in *Twin Peaks* and *Fire Walk With Me*. In *Wild at Heart* the interiors of the 'dark continent' are signified by its abject emissions: vomit, an aborted foetus and blood. During their night-ride across a Gothic American South, Lula Pace and Sailor Ripley encounter a young road-accident victim screaming hysterically whilst examining a sticky head wound, before collapsing with blood gushing from her mouth. This spectacle has been anticipated by an earlier scene in which Momma Marietta smeared a lurid red lipstick over her entire face. The close-up on the heavily made-up mouth is one of the most conspicuous motifs in the Lynch *mise-en-scène*, an image of desire and dread that clearly signals other lips that bleed.

Lynch's gynophobia results in a predilection for punishment and photography. The monstrous feminine is alternately confined within the comparative safety of a picture frame, or subjected to extremes of sadistic violence and ritual humiliation. The most disturbing aspect of this tendency is that, simultaneously, Lynch's films intimate that this is a pain that women secretly desire (and thus deserve). In *Blue Velvet*, Dorothy Vallens' masochistic pleasure is foregrounded during the scenes with Frank and Jeffrey and there is no psychological pre-history that might enable a contextualisation of her desire for pain in terms of an eroticisation of powerlessness, a defensive gesture to cope with situations over which she has no control. In *Wild at Heart*, Bobby Peru's sexual violence towards Lula Pace constitutes one of the most unashamedly anti-feminist scenes in American film history. Lula's submission mirrors Sailor's subsequent betrayal (his collusion with Bobby Peru for the promise of money), but it simultaneously reinforces one of the grossest of misogynistic myths: women have no control over their sexuality, they secretly desire, provoke and enjoy sexual

1. The phrase 'flamenco placenta-dancer' belongs to John Alexander (1993, p. 42).

assault. Lynch's own commentary upon the brutalisation of Dorothy Vallens does little to challenge such pernicious fictions:

> There are some women that you want to hit because you're getting a feeling from them that they want it, or they upset you in a certain way. (Lynch, cited in Borden 1986, p. 62)

Acts of violence towards women form the narrative backbone of both *Fire Walk With Me* and the *Twin Peaks* series. In his reading of the prequel, John Alexander, using Claire Douglas' study of incest trauma in *The Woman in the Mirror*, suggests that the evil spirit Bob can be understood as an apparition, devised unconsciously by Laura Palmer, to shield her from the horrific recognition that she has been sexually abused by her father:

> Laura denies the truth, choosing to live in self-manifested illusion. 'Victims of incest ... learn secrecy and subterfuge in order to conceal the extent of their pain even from themselves ... victims of incest need help in calling things by their real names'. (Alexander 1993, p. 140)

By accommodating Laura's experiences to a conventional Hollywood realist frame, Alexander is also able to make sense of her subsequent turn to prostitution and drug addiction. Such a reading, however, is problematised by the fact that the evil of Bob continues well after Laura's demise. More fundamentally, the realist explanation of sexual violence in this film is founded upon the notion of a centred subjectivity and the primacy of the real, both of which are continually challenged in Lynch's work. Character is continually cartooned and flamboyantly one-dimensional, it becomes the space on to which a montage of media and pop psychoanalytical cliches can be projected. The repeated use of a photographic image of Laura Palmer during the closing credits of each of the thirty episodes of *Twin Peaks* might seem to evoke the presence of absence, the loss of a young woman. But this distracts from the fact that there is a profound epistemological loss at the core of Lynch's work itself. The photographic image does not conceal the true Laura Palmer because there is no 'true' Laura Palmer; the realist frame, with its focus upon the notion of a coherent centred subjectivity, is shattered. Lynch's depiction of her drifts disorientatingly from innocent prom queen to teenage prostitute, from traumatised incest victim to predatory *femme fatale*, sublimely disinterested in the possibility that there might be an 'authentic' individual beneath the masks. Identity dissolves into the soft-focus *jouissance* of the endlessly reproducible Image. In *Blue Velvet*, similarly, *glissante* is visualised in Dorothy's slide from one cartooned cliche of femininity to the next: *femme fatale*, willing victim, devoted Mommy. Dorothy is the 'blue lady': an appellation which signifies her pornographic objectification, but which also anticipates her subsequent redemption as holy mother in the film's closing images (reunited with her child, showered with a kitsch suburban sunshine, as the camera pans to Mary's colour in the cloudless sky).

The foregrounding of artifice in the construction of character in Lynch's films has been applauded as a radical device. Lynda Bundtzen (1988, pp. 187–203) and Tracy Biga (1987, pp. 44–9), amongst others, have argued that Lynch's work is less an expression of the patriarchal imagination than a deconstruction of it *from the inside*. Dorothy and Sandy conform so completely to the stereotypical figures of the innocent, blonde/bland American Girl and the bad, dark, foreign Lady, that they become a self-conscious parody of these ideological constructions. The oedipal overdetermination of the relationships in a film like *Blue Velvet*, alongside its Hitchcockian attention to the mechanisms of voyeurism, have also been offered by postmodern feminists to advance the claim that Lynch's work is about misogyny, rather than being misogynistic. Critics who grant Lynch a critical distance from the anti-feminist traditions of classical Hollywood cinema rarely detail the precise differences between the two, except by referring to an apparently redemptive self-consciousness. The self-conscious play that Lynch indulges in with the archetypes of Madonna and Whore, like the self-conscious performing the masculine allegedly taking place in contemporary action adventure films, treads a line between classical sexism and the camp critique of classical sexism so fine as to be practically invisible. Dorothy Vallens wears a black wig during her performances at the Slow Club, but beneath her wig her natural hair colour is also black. Lynch foregrounds patriarchal stereotyping in the ludicrously stark oppositions of Fair Maiden and Dark Lady, but similarly intimates that these myths both conceal and are the essence of female identity. The female body is mapped as a mystery of sliding surfaces which the closed body male detective must investigate without hope of solving its enigmas.

The colonisation of identity by image in *Blue Velvet* is accentuated by Lynch's casting of Isabella Rossellini in the role of Dorothy Vallens. The director gives a series of make-overs to one of the most conspicuous faces in contemporary American popular culture, the daughter of Ingrid Bergman and figure-head for the Lancome cosmetics corporation. This is only one instance of the interface between art and advertisement that takes place in Lynch's work. During the scene at Ben's brothel in *Blue Velvet*, Frank's vehement insistence upon the excellence of Pabst Blue Ribbon beer both continues the film's central leitmotif and recycles an earlier conversation between Jeffrey and Sandy, concerning the relative virtues of Heineken and Budweiser, the 'King of Beers'. The casual and comic appropriation of the *mise-en-scène* of the commercial is one of the trademarks of a Lynch production: seen, for example, in Sailor and Lula's comments on different cigarette brands in *Wild at Heart* and the endless accolades in *Twin Peaks* to 'damn fine' cups of coffee and slices of cherry pie.

The tracing of dialogue and setting through the stencil of the commercial in Lynch's work, is one example of the way in which people and places are imagined as decentred features across a depthless mediascape. Spaces in a Lynch film always owe less to geographical reality than to its media representation – or, rather, they challenge, implicitly, the distance between the two in a hyperreal society of the spectacle. The opening frames of *Blue Velvet* are crowded with visual and audio references to the media mythologisation of the Eisenhower 1950s. Places and people are introduced through and indistinguishable from their reproducible image (the poster of Lumberton, the picture of Sandy); an image on television of a man with a gun climbing a staircase anticipates a key moment later in the film; a walk through woodland is accompanied by the sound of trees being felled as part of a radio station jingle. As media simulations colonise space in the American small town there is a distinctly Baudrillardean diminution of the distance between 'real' spaces and the mediascape. Interiors and exteriors in Lynch's work are incessantly overdetermined with regard to media intertextuality. One of the pleasures of consuming a Lynch text is the continual recognition of the recycled sets, characters and scenes from a range of media codes: film *noir*, soap opera, B-movie, musical and the work of specific auteurs. This can be seen in each of the prime locations in Lynch's cinematic cartography: the city, the suburb, the small town, the road and the wilderness.

## Lynch's mappings as a mediascape

According to Lynch's comments, *Eraserhead* may be read in part as an act of cinematic catharsis, enabling the director to articulate his own traumatic experience of rural–urban migration. Moving from the small towns of the rural Northwest to Philadelphia as a young art student, he claimed to have encountered 'the sickest, most corrupt, decaying city filled with fear I ever set foot in my life' (cited in Kaleta 1993, p. 6). Lynch's first full-length production is set in an unnamed metropolis, in which, contrary to the conditions of rustbelt economic crisis currently plaguing Philadelphia and other Northeastern cities, an industrial metastasis has effectively mechanised all aspects of urban existence, from the manufacturing of foodstuffs to the recycling of dismembered body parts (Henry's decapitation complements the headless man-made chickens).

Technophobia and gynophobia embrace in Lynch's depiction of an urban-industrial milieu in which the city – with its indefatigable assembly lines and hissing pipes – appears considerably more animated than its listless inhabitants. The incessant drone of heavy machinery, an industrial symphony, accompanies the deconstruction of organic desire by technological will in a surreal *ballet mécanique*. This particular sound effect and much of the metropolitan imagery is recuperated in *The Elephant Man*'s re-creation of Victorian London and the equation of the urban-industrial with dehumanisation and moral poverty is extended by the representation of Geidi Prime in *Dune*.

These early cinematic exorcisms of the 'city filled with fear' are heavily indebted to German Expressionism and film *noir*. Subsequently, Lynch has returned to more familiar territory and become preoccupied with America's mythological heartlands: small town, suburb, road and wilderness. Lynch chooses to ignore urban-industrial spaces and postindustrial landscapes are similarly marginalised, thus conveniently side-stepping the contemporary restructuring of American economic geography by focusing upon small-towns dependent upon primary activities, particularly forestry (Lynch's father worked for the Forestry Commission in the Pacific Northwest). The extent to which these places are located through the incestuous introversions of media intertextuality can be established by considering the opening images in *Blue Velvet*.

Following the credit sequence there is a montage shot in a brash technicolour excess. This is accompanied by the Bobby Vinton ballad that is the film's title track and is saturated with a syrupy nostalgia suggestive of an earlier phase in film-making history. The first shot is of blood-red roses beside a whiter-than-white picket fence, both transposed over a cloudless deep blue sky. Red, white and blue – clearly a significant choice of colours for the entry point into an exploration of small-town America. The white picket fence sustains the historical regression, evoking memories of archetypal Americana, Tom Sawyer and Huckleberry Finn, frozen in perpetual childhood summers. Next, the camera cuts to a Rockwellian vignette: a 1940s firetruck glides by with a an old man on the running board waving serenely towards the camera.

*Blue Velvet*'s opening images clearly conform to one of the defining features of postmodern art as outlined by Jameson: the effacement of boundaries between past and present. The juxtaposition of 1950s ballads, 1940s firetrucks and halcyon images of small-town America form a timeless rerun from the Eisenhower era, spliced together with car and clothes styles from the 1980s. History, particularly media history, is treated as a junkyard of materials for casual appropriation and place is consequently dehistoricised.

Everything in this opening montage initially appears to signify a valorisation of suburban America. But, at the same time, the way in which the images are framed threatens to undercut their authority. All the colours have a surrealistic intensity and the slow-motion tracking accentuates the dream-like ambience of the scene. The exaggerated normality of this landscape encourages incredulity and the degree to which it conforms to advertising utopias or a Norman Rockwell illustration, threatens to make these spatial signifiers self-erasing. Lynch offers an image of the suburb as simulacrum, foregrounding geographical unreality through the use of colour filter and self-reflexive camera rhetoric.

Lynch's suburbs are clearly candy-coloured, but it is less than certain that he is clowning. This is due to a series of mirrorings in Lynch's mapping of Lumberton's moral landscape. The first character encountered is the hero's father, Mr Beaumont, engaged in an archetypal suburban activity, watering the lawn. He appears to suffer a stroke and as he falls to the ground Lynch employs a rapid tracking shot beneath the green carpet to the hidden miniature jungle of the insect kingdom where nature is feeding on itself rapaciously. Beneath the apparently settled surfaces lies unexpected violence. Freud's classic analysis of the uncanny threatens to be inverted, as the line between *unheimlich* (something hidden and dangerous) and *heimlich* (homelike) is distorted.

This is an ambiguity that recurs in and is central to Lynch's geographical imagination. He offers a seriocomic pastiche of key American locations, but fails to offer anything in their place. In fact, since these sites are opposed geometrically to the 'city filled with fear', the spectator is encouraged to swallow the saccharine-coated pill of suburban sentimentalism. The suburb may be a simulacrum, but it still offers a sanctuary from Frank's place, the cities of dreadful night, iconicised in the insect kingdom lurking beneath the carpet of verdant lawns.

The return to the suburbs in the film's closing scene sustains this confusion. The denouement constitutes a mawkish pastiche of Hollywood closure and the media apotheosis of traditional family values found in an archetypal suburbia. In comparison to classical Hollywood narrative this ending might appear to be a radical subversion of convention, a Baudrillardean logic of reversal seems to be in play. But, as in Baudrillard's America, where 'the ground itself has already gone', there is no position from within the text from which to activate its oppositional potential.

Intertextuality is sustained in the scenes following the opening montage. The junior Private Eye discovers a severed ear in a vacant lot. The ear is covered with insects, recalling the B-movie horrors beneath the suburban lawn (*Them* (1954)) and other Cold War science fiction fantasies of insect invasion/atomic mutation),

Bunuel's *Un Chien Andalou* (1928) and Van Gogh's self-mutilation. The ear has been severed by a character called *Booth* whose tortured victim lives on *Lincoln* Street. Jeffrey's gradual entanglement in this case transports him from the blinding light of the Lumberton suburbs to its seedy downtown, a nightscape of sexual violence and criminal knavery. Downtown is the landscape across which the primordial forces seething beneath the surface of suburbia have erupted. This opposition, between kitsch Americana and a de Sadean cityscape, reproduces the geography of *noir*, as do the female characters associated with these antithetical zones (the most obvious intertextual signposts point towards Lang's *The Big Heat* (1953) and Tourneur's *Out of the Past* (1947)). Jeffrey's mother and aunt are watching a *noir* film on television in the opening shots, but the family name, Beaumont, also suggests the soap opera tradition from which Lynch appropriates dialogue stylistics (Mr Beaumont was one of the stars of a popular 1950s' sitcom set in the suburbs, called *Leave it to Beaver*).

Whilst his surname signifies television soap opera Jeffrey's forename, along with his equivocal voyeuristic tendencies, direct the spectator back to cinematic texts. Powell's *Peeping Tom* (1959) might be discerned, but in the light of Sandy's comment – 'I'm not sure whether you're a detective or a pervert' – the most obvious reference is to L.B. *Jefferies* in Hitchcock's wry commentary on scopophilia, *Rear Window* (1954). Jeffrey and Sandy's night-time stroll provides a reference to another James Stewart role, as George Bailey in Frank Capra's *It's A Wonderful Life* (1946). Lumberton is a geographical mosaic composed from strands of *noir* and sentimental comedy drama from the postwar years.

Intertextuality in the modernist text was typically functional, a formal device intended to denote deeper meanings and connections. Thus, Sherwood Anderson's twenty-six short story cycle of life in the mid-western American small town, *Winesberg, Ohio*, is unified by 'the notion of unspoken depths beneath its surfaces', either religious, Freudian or mythological (Bradbury 1984, p. 49). Lynch's postmodern intertextuality precisely relishes its adestinationality, its failure to go anywhere. Accordingly, cinematic space collapses in on itself in a black hole of vertiginous self-referentiality, a kenotic draining of the illusion of significance. To pursue the allusions is to miss the point. Lynch's references to surrealism, Sirk, Hitchcock, Capra and *noir*, offer only the pleasures of recognition rather than the possibility of understanding.

The same pleasures are offered to the spectator in Lynch's subsequent productions. *Wild at Heart* opens in Cape Fear and then proceeds to integrate extravagant references to road movies, Elvis musicals and *The Wizard of Oz* (1939). The rebellious Sailor Ripley declares that his distinctive snakeskin jacket 'represents my individuality and my belief in personal freedom'. But in Lynch's strange world of decentred subjectivity this costume is borrowed from an earlier screen rebel. In Sidney Lumet's road movie, *The Fugitive Kind* (1960), a young rebel clad in a snakeskin jacket and his girlfriend drive into a small-town hell comparable to Big Tuna, the place that almost proves to be the end of the road for Lula and Sailor. At the same time, Sailor's exaggerated Southern accent and his performance of 'Love Me' and 'Love Me Tender', suggest that his individuality is based upon the impersonation of a second media icon, Elvis Presley. Whilst Sailor's identity constitutes a recycling of characters from the road movie and musical, Lula similarly understands her experiences in relation to the Victor Fleming film that traversed both genres: *The Wizard of Oz*.

Conventionally, the road narrative charts a rite of passage, performing a suture between physical, moral and psychological explorations. To operate on Lynch in this way however is to go down an interpretative cul-de-sac: his journey exhibits the Derridean quality of adestinationality and the mythic value of the archetypal quest is desiccated by cinematic introversion. *Wild at Heart*'s extravagant intertextual performance undermines the efficacy of the quest motif. It is less a road movie than a film about road movies (Capra's *It Happened One Night* (1934), Lumet's *The Fugitive Kind*), with character and action largely pasted together from cinematic cliche. The terrains of subjectivity mapped out in the classical road narrative are ignored for an exclusively filmic topography. The critical notion of personal freedom is obsolete on this travel through a decidedly Baudrillardean hyperreality. Lynch, like Baudrillard, is on the road to nowhere, casually cruising across a cinespace of affectless signs.

The key intertextual reference in *Wild at Heart* is of course to the yellow brick road in *The Wizard of Oz*. Characters and actions are spliced together ostentatiously (Lula is Dorothy, Marietta is the Wicked Witch, whilst the Good Witch plays herself). This is a film that belongs to Lynch's favourite decade, the tranquillised 1950s, by default (as John Alexander notes, its initial reception at the end of the Depression, on the eve of war was not that impressive – it was subsequently canonised through endless television reruns that began in the Eisenhower era) (Alexander 1993, p. 116). The Victor Fleming film ends with an unashamedly schmaltzy sentiment, as Dorothy proclaims at the end of her journey:

> If I ever go looking for my heart's desire again, I won't look any further than my own backyard, because if it isn't there, I never really lost it to begin with.

*Wild at Heart* echoes this ending with a characteristically Lynchian affectionate tribute to sentimental closure. Sailor proposes to Lula by singing a favourite Elvis Presley number – but the family do not appear to have anywhere to go. This is why they conclude the film in the back of their car. Home has become associated with psychosexual perversion and the yellow brick freeway itself is the site of one's heart's desire. As in all road narratives and their prototypes, from *Huckleberry Finn* onwards, the trouble starts when the journeying stops.

Whilst in *Wild at Heart* the protagonists define themselves in relation to cinematic texts, in *Twin Peaks* the frame of reference is more obviously indebted to televisual traditions. Characters and sets are immediately recognisable as media cliches appropriated from police and FBI dramas (especially *The Untouchables*), from daytime soap operas, teen romances and 1950s commercials. *Twin Peaks* assimilates these with *noir* and Gothic film codes, with media stylisations of pre-media mythologies and with references to earlier Lynch productions. The mechanical robin at the close of *Blue Velvet* becomes the 'real' robin in *Twin Peaks*' opening credits. These credits echo the opening montage of *Blue Velvet* in that we have migrated from the suburbs to nature – or rather nature as the Great American Outdoors, the Northwest photographed as backdrops from a Sears and Roebuck catalogue. As in Lumberton, as the camera moves beyond the surface serenity signified in these opening shots, a dark secret is discovered at the heart of the American small town. The Lynch landscape always contains its pockets of venality that must be patrolled and contained by honest cops, kindly doctors and lumberjacks. In this instance, as in Pynchon's *Vineland*, the evil threatening the community on the edge of the Ghostwood forest is twofold: both terrestrial and supernatural. First, there is a capitalist real estate project that involves arson attacks and industrial espionage and which threatens environmental devastation. This, however, becomes simply the backdrop to a manichean melodrama introduced by Laura Palmer's murder and Deputy Hawk's recounting of a native American legend concerning the Black and White Lodges, home to a primal Good and Evil.

Lynch's Northwest *noir* is clearly indebted to two films of 1944: Otto Preminger's *Laura* and the original *Twin Peaks*. Preminger's film, concerning the mysterious murder of a beautiful young woman and the effect that her picture has on various men, is generally regarded as the work that initiated the more mature *film noir* of the late 1940s. Lumet's *The Fugitive Kind* was based upon the Tennessee Williams play, *Orpheus Descending* and retained some of that drama's echoes of classical mythology. In *Twin Peaks* Lynch gestures towards a range of non-media mythologies – Greek and Nordic legend (Cooper's quest into the Underworld to rescue Annie, his Eurydice, the giants and dwarves), native American and Tibetan folk lore, astrology and New Age mysticism. But, like his cinematic and televisual references, these gestures are largely throwaway, they offer the pleasure of recognition whilst pointing to the fact that no one grand narrative can fix spatial and temporal relations. All history is a junkyard for casual reference. The spectator is presented with the media equivalent of Malraux's Imaginary Museum, an infinite installation of depthless images that exchange exclusively amongst themselves, promising endless self-referential signification and the glazed ecstasy of *jouissance*.

## Lynch's mappings and the New Right

Lynch uses incessant references to the dream factories of Hollywood and also to the unconscious as interpreted by psychoanalysis and painting. By framing place and people through pop psychoanalytical cliche and surrealist art the Lynch text remaps American geography as an unchartable dreamscape. The scene from *Blue Velvet* in which Jeffrey watches Frank and Dorothy from the cramped space of her closet in the Deep River apartments is a prime example of this. It is so loaded with psychoanalytical possibilities that it threatens to become a parody of significance. The camera focuses upon key props and players in the Oedipal drama (mouths and vaginas, scissors and guns, an umbilical cord fetish, voyeurism, castration anxiety, scopophilia and sadomasochism). Lynch redraws the Freudian family romance as a cartoon with Frank/Jeffrey as Daddy/Baby and Dorothy at the apex of their Oedipal triangle as the dangerous object of male desire. The cumulative effect of this Oedipal overdetermination is, however, a flattening out, a jeopardising of the modernist hermeneutic of suspicion. Freud's declared aim was the *interpretation* of dreams. *Blue Velvet* offers a mock, hyperbolic Oedipality, not as a depth model articulation of psychosexual tensions within the nuclear family, but as a Freudian farce. Lynch himself declares that he was unable to contain his amusement on the set during the shooting of this scene, comparing Frank to 'a dog in a chocolate shop' (cited in Alexander 1993, p. 76). As in Scott's *Alien*, the self-conscious appropriation of psychoanalytical orthodoxy by film-makers both anticipates and threatens to make obsolete the application of a Freudian critical paradigm. Jeffrey plans different means of access to the secrets of Deep River until he stumbles across a key. Psychoanalysis is offered within the text itself as an interpretative key (rather than as its latent content), but one that ensures that the mysteries remain locked up.

Dreams are central to all of Lynch's films to date, from the extended surrealist montage that is *Eraserhead*, to the memorable dream sequence in *Fire Walk With Me*. Whilst his landscapes exhibit the colloquial corniness of Norman Rockwell and the subtle menace of Edward Hopper, his main frame of reference is to European surrealism. Lynch's surrealism manifests itself not simply in the specific use of the dream sequence, but in a general inversion of the classical Hollywood prioritisation of narrative over image. The image in Lynch's work consistently seeks to extricate itself from its narrative context, to float free, as ambient visual pleasures are privileged over linear plot progression.

Classical surrealism's irrationalism was a potentially subversive antidote to dominant ideology. Lynch's irrationalism, however, acts as a cover for the consonance of his work with dominant ideology. Core impulses within surrealism could be interpreted as politically radical in terms of their attempt to extricate the creative imagination from the restrictions of Enlightenment rationality within an increasingly administered society. Lynch's surrealism serves no such grandiose function. Alongside his intertextuality, it simply enables the extraction of place from its material historical context and its conversion into an array of empty signs that offer mindless pleasures best described by Baudrillard:

> There is a kind of primal pleasure, of anthropological joy in images, a kind of brute fascination unencumbered by aesthetic, moral, social or political judgements. (Baudrillard 1987, p. 15)

In *A Cinema without Walls* Timothy Corrigan responds to this kenosis thus: 'In David Lynch's *Blue Velvet* there are no politics because there are only illegible social configurations' (Corrigan 1991, p. 71). Lynch's surreal, intertextual mappings of a hyperreal America appear to offer a purely visceral pleasure, unencumbered by moral or political judgement. But the hegemony of the illegible image is of course itself a profoundly political development.

'I love these honest film-films [B-movies] which don't have any purpose other than being a film ... I see films more and more as separate from whatever kind of reality there is anywhere else' (Lynch, cited in Kaleta 1993, p. 85). Despite Lynch's efforts to deny the rootedness and cultural instrumentality of his work, it has to be noted that the core concerns and impulses in his work, beyond the seductive surfaces of narcissistic self-absorption, are largely consonant with dominant ideology. The Lynch text denies its rootedness in history, but to understand it fully it must be returned to its specific material circumstances and its relation to hegemonic discourses in contemporary America surrounding religion, sexuality, the family, nostalgia, race and class.

One of the cornerstones of the New Right's rise to political ascendancy was a dramatic resurgence in religious fundamentalism. Beneath the flamboyant intertextuality and surrealism, conventional Christian tropes figure centrally within the Lynch *mise-en-scène*: images of angels, fire, darkness and light which are suggestive of the persistence of an essentially manichean sensibility beneath the persona of the postmodern player. Throughout *Twin Peaks* and *Fire Walk With Me* domestic violence and sexual abuse are associated with possession by evil spirits, thus deflecting responsibility from the Moral Majority's privileged and fetishised nuclear family unit. The collision between the forces of pure Good (embodied in uniformed Law officers) and pure Evil (embodied in denim, youthful rebellion, foreigners and criminal masterminds) also echoes the New Right's mappings of the moral landscape. This can be read as a knowing postmodern appropriation of gothic convention, but the degree to which it reproduces the contemporary recodification of social ills in religious terms is remarkable: sexual abuse, teenage rebellion, drug trafficking and intellectualism are correlated with an elemental Evil.

The reinvention of Original Sin in Lynch's work parrots the rhetoric of the fundamentalist lobby. Evil is understood as an elemental malignity. There is no attempt to *explain* it, it simply *is*. Jeffrey's critical question, 'Why are there men like Frank in the world?' cannot be answered. Similarly, with all of Lynch's villains from Baron Harkonnen to Bob, there is no *why*, these things simply are. Presenting evil as a pre-social force reinforces the revisionism of the New Right, with its effort to overturn progressive orthodoxies institutionalised in the 1960s, concerning the socioeconomic and psychological roots of deviance. In Lynch's strange world, like that reviled by the moral majority, perverts, drug traffickers and criminals do not need to be understood, they simply require punishment. Evil is thus mystified, shrouded in metaphysical enigma and positioned outside the auspices of rational explication.

There is a range of other symptoms of a fundamental consonance between the Lynch *oeuvre* and the New Right. The politics of return are reproduced in Lynch's insatiable nostalgia for the 1950s; that is, the mythology of the Eisenhower era suitably screened of Cold War hysteria, imperialist aggression, social and racial repression. Lynch's landscapes are patrolled by Sheriffs called Harry S. Truman, dominated by 1950s diners seen from 1950s cars whilst wearing 1950s clothing. Lynch's cinema performs the fantasy time-travel promised by Reagan's backs to the future politics of return. Turning the clock back in this way in film and political rhetoric has the consequence of erasing the disastrous consequences for traditional power groups of Civil Rights activism, feminism and gay rights, Viet Nam and Watergate. The aim here is to will a collective return to a time when America's virtue and strength seemed assured, when its authority figures could be trusted (as they can in Lynch's world), when women knew their place (as many do in Lynch and those who do not are usually punished or 'redeemed'), when racial and ethnic minorities were practically invisible to most white Americans (as they are consistently in Lynch's work). The New Right's insistence that many of the problems confronted by the working class were of their own making (too many children, sloth, 'lack of initiative') reverberates in Lynch's work with a demonisation of the disempowered. Lynch's anti-feminism, anti-environmentalism (reduced to a comical 'Save the Pine Weasel' campaign in *Twin Peaks*), his evasion of urban crisis, racial crisis, class hostility and the conditions of labour, alongside his essentially religious representation of crime as sin, are all indices of the consonance, beneath the glossy postmodern stylistics, between his work and the dominant ideology in the Reagan–Bush era.

At heart, Lynch's cartography of postmodern America is far from wild. In fact it is profoundly right-wing and driven by an voracious lust for order, control and stability. It is structured around sublimely tidy geographical oppositions: Lumberton suburbs and Lumberton night town; white lodge and black lodge; middle-class home and working-class city; House Atreides and House Harkonnen. Narrative interest is provided by the crossings between these spaces of a Good male protagonist (Henry, Frederick, Paul, Jeffrey, Sailor, Dale). These places are refracted through media cliche and a parodic psychoanalysis, but the insistence is always upon their polarisation and the fact that these places can be experienced but never known.

Essentially, Lynch's cinema is informed by the sensibility of the tourist. The tourist industry in Snoqualmie, the setting for *Twin Peaks*, wasted little time before cashing in on its recognisability. Since Lynch's visit, tourists have flocked to sample 'Dale Cooper coffee' and cherry pie and to be photographed on the banks of the Columbia river wrapped in plastic like the corpse of Laura Palmer. Similar pleasures are offered to the Lynch spectator – pleasures reminiscent of the heady admixture of aestheticism and decadence that erupted in European art in the 1890s. Lynch is best described as a *fin de siècle* film-maker who, like the millennial prophet Baudrillard, produces images of space imbued with a gleefully apocalyptic nihilism, images that testify ultimately to the triumph of style over substance.

CHAPTER 14

# Conclusion: From Geographies of Abjection to the *Mundus*

Phenomena intersect; to see but one is to see nothing.
Victor Hugo, *The Toiler of the Sea*,
cited in Least Heat-Moon (1991), p. 64

To return to the questions posed in my introduction: what are the dominant, residual and emergent features of the geographical imagination in its postmodern phase? And do its cartographies constitute a decisive break from the mappings produced within previous phases of American cultural history? To illustrate my answer to these questions it is necessary to turn to one of the canonical figures in the literary history of representing space: James Fenimore Cooper. R.W.B. Lewis, in *The American Adam*, was one of many critics to comment upon the flourishing of the geographical imagination in Cooper's writing. Lewis describes the character at the heart of the Leatherstocking novels as

> the hero in space, in two senses of the word. First the hero seems to take his start outside time, or on the very edges of it, so that his location is essentially in space alone; and, second, his initial habitat is space as spaciousness, as the unbounded, the area of total possibility. (Lewis 1955, p. 90)

A passage from *The Last of the Mohicans,* in which the hero in space and his party look down towards the ramparts of Fort William Henry, illustrates Lewis' point well:

> The mountain on which they stood, elevated perhaps a thousand feet in the air, was a high cone, that rose a little in advance of that range which reached for miles along the western shores of the lake, until meeting its sister piles beyond the water, it ran off far towards the Canadas, in confused and broken masses of rock, which were thinly sprinkled with evergreens. Immediately at the feet of the party, the Southern shore of the Horican swept in a broad semicircle, from mountain to mountain, marking a wide strand, that soon rose into an uneven and somewhat elevated plain. To the north stretched the limpid, and, as it appeared from that dizzy height, the narrow sheet of the

'holy lake', indented with numberless bays, embellished by
fantastic head-lands, and dotted with countless islands. At the
distance of a few leagues, the bed of the waters became lost among
mountains, or was wrapped in the masses of vapour, that came
slowly along their bosom, before a light morning air. But a narrow
opening between the crests of the hills, pointed out the passage
by which they found their way still further north, to spread their
pure and ample sheets again, before pouring out their tribute
into the distant Champlain. To the south stretched the defile,
or rather broken plain, so often mentioned. For several miles
in this direction, the mountains appeared reluctant to yield
their dominion, but within reach of the eye they diverged, and
finally melted into the level and sandy lands, across which we
have accompanied our adventurers in their double journey.
Along both ranges of hills, which bounded the opposite sides
of the lake and valley, clouds of light vapour were rising in spiral
wreaths from the uninhabited woods, looking like the smokes
of the hidden cottages, or rolled lazily down the declivities, to
mingle with the fogs of the lower land. A single, solitary, snow-
white cloud floated above the valley, and marked the spot,
beneath which lay the silent pool of the 'bloody pond'. (Cooper
1990, p. 140)

Like many of Cooper's landscape descriptions this passage suffers
somewhat from a superabundance of information: by providing so
much detail he makes it practically impossible for the reader to
visualise the scene at hand effectively. But there is a second possible
explanation as to why this passage is not particularly effective as
landscape description, and this is the point at which the essential
continuity between Cooper's mappings and postmodern cartography
becomes apparent.

Considering the above passage from the perspective of psychoanalytical theory, certain features in the landscape are clearly
foregrounded: there is a sensualisation, or to be more specific, a
feminisation of space taking place here. Cooper is indulging in the
classic romantic trope of feminising the land, of imagining space
as Mother Nature. The shapes that he focuses upon – the curves,
bosoms, openings and narrow passages – have a distinct resonance
at the level of sexual symbolism. This is combined with references
to beds, sheets and a number of verbs that might connote sexual
activity (rising, stretching, spreading, wrapping and melting). Space
is perceived as dizzy, confused and overpowering. At the centre of
this passage there is a critical change of wording: 'To the south
stretched the defile, or rather, broken plain, so often mentioned.'
This is a textbook example of parapraxis: in geographical terms a
defile, as a noun, signifies a narrow pass or gorge, but, as a verb,

'defile' also carries connotations of making something dirty, of violating chastity. It is these connotations that encourage Cooper to change his mind, since by using this term he is getting dangerously close to the absent centre of this passage.

Throughout *The Last of the Mohicans* Cooper devotes a considerable quantity of prose to homoerotic descriptions of the male physique which reinforce the cultural codes of masculinity. At the same time he consistently shies away from the facts of female sexuality. Cooper has to imply that the Dark Lady of his tale, the mulatto Cora Munro, is both the object and subject of desire through a sequence of visual exchanges that he can barely bring himself to describe. What we see in the course of his landscape descriptions therefore is a return of the repressed corporeal geographies of female sexuality. In this context the bloody pond at the foot of the passage brings to mind the references made throughout the text to Cora's mixed blood, which always appears 'ready to burst its bounds' (*ibid.*, p. 19) and provides another dimension to the unspecified 'curse' with which she is afflicted: menstruation as opposed to miscegenation.

As mentioned in my introduction, one of the ruling metaphors used by colonialists when referring to the New World, was 'Virgin Land'. Cooper confirms this trope in the above passage and throughout his writing. His land is often feminised, seen as something that needs to be conquered, controlled and civilised. This feminisation of the land is entirely appropriate because *The Last of the Mohicans* is fundamentally concerned with the struggle between white men and red men for the possession of women's bodies (the narrative is structured around a series of kidnappings) and it is set against the historical backdrop of the struggle between white men and red men for possession and ownership of the wilderness. In a book obsessed with crossings, this is something which unites white culture with some elements of the native population, for in Cooper's world both the land and women are seen essentially as forms of male property.

The postmodern cartographies surveyed in this study are separated from *The Last of the Mohicans* by almost a hundred and fifty years. And yet, if these texts can be taken as in some sense representative, there are key correlations that suggest a degree of continuity in the workings of the geographical imagination. Lines of power continue to be inscribed in space. Landscapes are still seen through the ideological lens of cultural codes that are firmly embedded in social power structures. The dominant power structures of Cooper's milieu – capitalism, patriarchy and white racial hegemony – may have assumed different shapes, but are still determining forces on the postmodern landscape. These continuities stretch back further than the Age of Jackson.

The postindustrial mappings of Bell, McLuhan and Baudrillard clearly displayed instances of what Pynchon terms the 'Puritan reflex' of seeking orders behind the visible. When Daniel Bell contemplates the white-collar landscapes of the campus and the downtown business district, like Oedipa Maas' 'odd religious instant' poised above San Narciso, he achieves a semi-mystical vision of a conflict-free society embodied in the built environment. Marshall McLuhan goes even further to divine the transubstantiation of a new spiritual community, the Global Village, in the second nature of electronic technologies that have displaced the Puritan's wilderness. Jean Baudrillard, approaching this scene from an Old World, non-Puritanical perspective, actually comes closest to the spirit of Cotton Mather, by reinventing a malign force, the reign of objects, shaping New World topography and destiny. Although there are spectacular differences between these mappings, the core impulse at the heart of the geographical imagination here, the practice of *reading the landscape*, remains constant.

The postmodern cartographies explored in this study do not then constitute a decisive break from the dominant traditions of landscape representation. Rather, they represent a reworking of the raw materials that have always been central to the American geographical imagination. Recent mappings offer a reinscription of established concerns into contemporary discourse formations, so that the dominant tendencies have remained largely constant. First, and most importantly, the concern for space itself has not diminished across time. From conservative mappings of the postindustrial landscape to the spatial vogue amongst Marxists, to images of nature, second nature and the body, insides and outsides in recent fiction and film, the impulse to engage with space is as strong now as it has ever been. These spaces continue to be responded to as texts in which the lines of power imprinted by capital and class, gender and sexuality, race and ethnicity, can be followed. Within recent representations the gravitation towards utopian (Bell's 'Salomon's House', McLuhan's 'Global Village', Pynchon's 'Territories of the Spirit', Lynch's 'Cherry-Pie Heaven') and dystopian antipodes (Baudrillard's 'Hyperreal America', Morrison's 'House of the Master', New Age science fiction's 'City of the Future') continues to be a conspicuous feature. Alongside the utopian/dystopian dynamic, postmodern cartographies, like their predecessors, return consistently to the dynamic interaction between natural and wo/man-made spaces. Although, given that less than 2 per cent of North America in the 1990s is officially classified as wilderness, there has been a shift in emphasis from the machine in the garden to the garden in the machine. The associated concept of a second nature of technological forms is of course far from unique to postmodern mappings (it was initially institutionalised in modernist urban folk lore). Finally, in terms of residual elements within the postmodern geographical imagination, the search for sacred spaces goes on. As wildly divergent as they are, the quest for holy ground and the echoes of paganism in the work of Morrison, Pynchon, Auster, Lynch and McLuhan, can each be traced back through transcendentalism, to the early settlers and explorers and on into pre-Columbian mythology.

In the process of drawing lines of continuity between diverse cultural practices in different eras, it is clearly of paramount importance that one avoid reductive generalisation. By concluding this synthesis with a recognition of those elements that unite the geographical imagination in its postmodern phase with the representation of space in previous periods of cultural history, I do not intend to diminish the significance of those critical nuances, those emergent elements, that characterise contemporary mappings. The impact of technology upon space continues to be a concern but new varieties are constantly appearing. Emphasis is shifting from the romantic and modernist concern for industrial technologies of production to postindustrial technologies of reproduction. The concern for the relationship between space and its reproducible image in the work of McLuhan, Baudrillard, Pynchon and Lynch is representative of this trend.

The intensification of concern for corporeal cartographies that recurs throughout contemporary cultural production is another key emergent element. In her study of romantic, modern and postmodern images of the land, *The Green Breast of the New World*, Louise Westling charts the passage from Emerson to Baudrillard and Octavia Butler as a 'continuum of symbolic practice' (Westling 1996, p. 6). However, given the frequency with which bodies are spatialised and spaces epidermalised in contemporary cultural production, from Gaia-inspired yearnings in Pynchon and Morrison's reclamation of the black body, to the monstrous feminine in recent science-fiction films, the term 'continuum' may distract from the dramatic nature of the upsurge in this particular practice. The importance of this emergent impulse is underscored by Lefebvre's assertion in *The Production of Space*:

> Any revolutionary project today, whether utopian or realistic, must, if it is to avoid hopeless banality, make the reappropriation of the body, in association with the reappropriation of space, into a non-negotiable part of its agenda. (Lefebvre 1991, pp. 166–7)

Strains of nihilism were discernible within transcendentalist topographies (associated primarily with the annihilation of the ego in mystic union with the Over-Soul manifest in Nature) and some modernist mappings (typically in the form of a redemptive purging of the waste land). In some postmodern cartographies these strains have mutated into a full-blown nihilistic drive. The intense impulses towards self-erasure in the mappings of Baudrillard, Auster and Lynch represent one of the most disturbing emergent facets within the contemporary geographical imagination. One recent development that makes this wilful negation of meaning so disturbing is an increasingly pervasive placelessness across postmodern landscapes: the rising hegemony of standardised, undifferentiated spaces, areas depleted of history, drained of the possibility for relations, identity, narrative and significant social action. Kenotic cartographies by cultural critics, novelists and film-makers only serve to reinforce the increasingly infective menace of what Marc Augé terms 'non-place' (Augé 1995).

Another of the most significant determining differences to the geographical imagination in its postmodern phase is its enhanced preoccupation with the faculty of remembrance. In postmodern cartographies memory too has become spatialised:

> Memory as a place, as a building, as a sequence of columns, cornices, porticoes. The body inside the mind, as if we were moving around in there, going from one place to the next, and the sound of our footsteps as we walk, moving from one place to the next. (Auster 1991, p. 82)

Throughout contemporary American fiction and film there is a passionate sensitivity to the presence and absence of memories inscribed in space. One must note, however, a distinct gender orientation towards inside and outside within this practice. Whilst Pynchon, Auster and Scott tend to focus upon the urban landscape and nature, Morrison, like Phillips, is more often attuned to the politics and poetics of domestic space. The common denominator in each instance however, is a profound hostility towards the commodification of both interiors and exteriors; an insistence on the distinctions between knowing places and owning spaces.

The extent to which memory is valorised in the process of reproducing space is a critical distinguishing feature for each of the texts I have examined. At one end of the spectrum there is the inestimable value placed upon re-memory in the writing of Morrison and Phillips, with Pynchon not too far behind. At the other end of the scale, there is the forgetfulness that typifies postindustrial mappings and the forceful assault upon memory enacted in the films of David Lynch. Auster's 'City of Glass', alongside New Age science-fiction cinema, with its conviction that 'the future ain't what it used to be', falls somewhere between these two poles. An essential division to be drawn then between variants of postmodern cartography centres upon those that seek to disavow memory and narrative and those that insist upon the importance of telling stories. Ultimately there can be no geographical knowledge without historical narrative. To know one's place and to change places it is necessary to listen to the meanings buried deep and wide across the storied earth.

The final emergent feature to the geographical imagination that I should like to consider is the increasing centrality of forms of waste. Few, if any, contemporary critics have written with as much elegant urgency about waste as Julia Kristeva. In her theories of abjection she has explored the complex social and psychological dynamics determining reactions to and relations with waste:

> Excrement and its equivalents (decay, infection, disease, corpse etc.) stand for the danger to identity that comes from without: the ego threatened by the non-ego, society threatened by its outside, life by death. (Kristeva 1982, p. 71)

> Living with the other ... confronts us with the possibility, or not, of being an other. It is not simply – humanistically – a matter of being able to accept the other but of being *in his place* and this means to imagine and make oneself other for oneself. (Kristeva 1991, p. 64)

This willingness to make oneself other for oneself and thus come face to face with both the potentially threatening and the potentially liberating instabilities of identity, is another critical means of distinguishing between postmodern cartographies. On one side there are the mappings of Morrison, Phillips, Pynchon and, to a lesser extent, Auster and recent science-fiction films, that show an openness to varieties of waste across the postmodern landscape, all that and those which have been, in Kristeva's terms, abjected – rubbish, trash, bodies, women, races, classes and the geographies with which they are intimately associated. There is an attempt in the mappings of these figures, with varying degrees of success, to invert centre-margin structures, to recover the abject, to bring back excluded objects, people and places. Pynchon, Scott and Auster show an explicit concern for waste products as spatial allegories of the underclass. Phillips similarly tries to bring in from the margins those social groups treated as 'trash' by the dominant culture. Morrison shows how the African-American body and community has been abjected by white culture and offers the hope of locating alternative centres.

On the other side of this spectrum there are those whose representations of space have worked largely to sustain hegemonic centre-margin structures, by reproducing the dynamic of abjection, relegating certain people and places to the periphery, either explicitly or by omission. The postindustrial mappings of Bell, McLuhan and Baudrillard conform to this description, excluding spaces and social groups that interfere with their utopian, or gleefully dystopian visions. Postindustrial cartographies tend to hinge upon a highly selective and closed spatial paradigm that denies the fluid contingency of space, the structural independence between core and periphery. David Lynch and certain science-fiction films permit forms of waste to enter their mappings, but only to reinforce their exclusion elsewhere, typically through association with the corporeal geographies of the monstrous-feminine.

Both the foregrounding and the neurotic expulsion of waste in many of the mappings charted here testifies to the efficacy of Kristeva's comments on the dynamics of abjection. Abjection functions not simply at the corporeal and psychological level, but at the sociospatial, being extended to places and people. This is, of course, a central concern of recent postcolonial theory, in examining the relations between colonisers and the colonised. That which has been abjected needs to be brought back to the centre, not least to reveal the margins' centrality to the identity of the core, to its sense of self and functioning. The geography of identity is consistently defined in relation to the 'not-here', the 'not-us'. But only by recognising the structural inseparability of the core (dominant cultures) and their abjected periphery (devalorised objects, bodies, territories) can the boundaries of alienation and oppression begin to be dismantled. Progressive mappings of postmodern space, those that aim to deconstruct, physically and ideologically, all geographies of abjection, might begin to achieve their imperative through a recognition of the possibilities of a space which Lefebvre defines in his description of the *mundus*:

> The *mundus*: a sacred or accursed place in the middle of the Italiot township. A pit, originally – a dust hole, a public rubbish dump. Into it were cast trash and filth of every kind, along with those condemned to death, and every newborn baby whose father declined to 'raise' it ... A pit, then, 'deep' above all in meaning. It connected the city, the space above ground, land-as-soil and land-as-territory, to the hidden, clandestine, subterranean spaces which were those of fertility and death, of the beginning and the end, of birth and burial ... The pit was also a passageway through which dead souls could return to the bosom of the earth and then re-emerge and be reborn. As locus of time, of births and tombs, vagina of the nurturing earth-as-mother, dark corridor emerging from the depths, cavern opening to the light, estuary of hidden forces and mouth of the realm of shadows, the *mundus* terrified as it glorified. In its ambiguity it encompassed the greatest foulness and the greatest purity, life and death, fertility and destruction, horror and fascination. (Lefebvre 1991, p. 242)

The *mundus* might be an inspirational symbolic site for future counter-hegemonic cartographies, radical mappings that endeavour to bring the abjected back to the centre, recovering its power and potential. Lefebvre's description of spaces of waste essentially as a site of ambiguity, 'deep above all in meaning', specifically recalls Kristeva's model:

> We may call it a border: abjection is above all ambiguity. Because, while releasing a hold, it does not radically cut off the subject from what threatens it – on the contrary, abjection acknowledges it to be in perpetual danger. (Kristeva 1982, p. 9)

Whilst several of the mappings examined here threaten to drift towards a mesmerised sense of powerlessness and passivity before a dizzying postmodern hyperspace (I am thinking here, in particular, of moments in the writing of Jameson, Baudrillard and Auster), Kristeva proposes that resistance can continue, that the centre is in perpetual danger, it is not as unified and unassailable as it may appear to be: 'And yet, from its place of banishment, the abject does not cease challenging its master' (*ibid.*, p. 2). This challenge can be seen in those deviant or 'counter-spaces' located most forcibly in the work of Morrison, Phillips and Pynchon (Lefebvre 1991, p. 367). Power cannot exist in isolation. To rephrase Foucault, there are no spaces of power without spaces of resistance. And one of the most effective means of consolidating these is through continuing to uncover and create progressive cartographies of postmodern space.

Having insisted at the outset of this study on the importance of locating the nothings, the significant omissions that are present in all cartographies, it seems appropriate that I should conclude by mentioning some of the many from which my own study is composed. Three of the most exciting fields in recent geographical studies, eco-criticism, 'cartographies of diaspora' and what Gill Valentine terms the 'heterosexing of space', I have had, regrettably, neither the space nor the skill to explore effectively (see Brah 1996, Duncan 1996, Valentine 1996). Given the scale of the synthesis attempted here my own lacunae are inevitably numerous, but one of the guiding principles throughout this study has been that no map can ever be final or complete (it is precisely those that claim this distinction which ought to arouse most suspicion). Cartography is less a conclusion than an ongoing process. For, as Lefebvre has persuasively inquired:

> How many maps, in the descriptive or geographical sense, might be needed to deal exhaustively with a given space, to code and decode all its meanings and contents? ... It is not only the codes – the map's legend, the conventional signs of map-making and map-reading – that are liable to change, but also the objects represented, the lens through which they are viewed, and the scale used. (Lefebvre 1991, pp. 85–6)

Maps are always provisional then and this fact enhances rather than diminishes their significance. Some critics in the burgeoning field of feminist geography have argued that cartography is inherently authoritarian, tainted by its association with a prohibitive Enlightenment metaphysic that ensures the abolition of difference, automatic complicity with authority and the imposition of standardised patterns of order. This seems to me an entirely appropriate criticism of the dominant cartographic tradition, but this is precisely why, in Harley's terms, maps are simply too important to be left to cartographers alone. There are as many varieties of map-making as there are spaces to represent and map-makers to represent them. Maps are about experiences and can be a heuristic device for acquiring, rather than imposing, the requisite knowledge to enable change. Any failure to continue the process of mapping postmodern space would entail a terrible impoverishment of the geographical imagination and the consolidation of oppressive geographies of abjection.

# Bibliography

Adorno, T. (1990) 'Culture industry reconsidered', in Jeffrey C. Alexander and Steven Sedman (eds), *Culture and Society* (Cambridge: Cambridge University Press, 1990).

Alexander, J. (1993) *The Films of David Lynch* (London: Letts).

Augé, M. (1995) *Non-Places: Introduction to an Anthropology of Supermodernity*, trans. by John Howe (London: Verso).

Auster, P. (1987) *The New York Trilogy* (London: Faber).

—— (1982) *The Art of Hunger and other essays* (London: The Menard Press).

—— (1991) *The Invention of Solitude* (London: Faber).

Barnes, T. and Duncan, S. (eds) (1992) *Writing Worlds: Discourse, Text and Metaphor in the Representation of Landscape* (London: Routledge).

Barthes, R. (1972) *Mythologies* (London: Paladin).

Baudelaire, C. (1964) 'The Painter of Modern Life', in *The Painter of Modern Life and Other Essays*, trans. by Jonathan Mayne (London: Phaidon Press).

Baudrillard, J. (1967) Review of *Understanding Media*, in *L'Homme et la Société*, no. 5.

—— (1968) *Le système des objets* (Paris: Deneol-Gonthier).

—— (1975) 'Design and Environment, or How Political Economy escalates into Cyberblitz', in *For a Critique of the Political Economy of the Sign* (St Louis: Telos).

—— (1981) *The Mirror of Production* (St Louis: Telos).

—— (1983) *Simulations* (New York: Semiotext(e)).

—— (1984) *Fatal Strategies* (London: Semiotext(e)/Pluto Press).

—— (1987) *The Evil Demon of Images* (Sydney: Power Institute).

—— (1988a) *America*, trans. by Chris Turner (London: Verso).

—— (1988b) *Symbolic exchange and death*, in Mark Poster (ed.), *Jean Baudrillard: Selected Writings* (Cambridge: Polity Press).

Bell, D. (1949) Review of George Orwell's *1984*, *New Leader*, November 1949.

—— (1952) *The Background and Development of Marxian Socialism in the United States*, in Donald Drew Egbert and Stow Persons (eds), *Socialism and American Life*, Volume I, (Princeton: Princeton University Press).

—— (1960) *The End of Ideology: On the Exhaustion of Political Ideas in the Fifties* (Illinois: Free Press).

—— (1974) *The Coming of Post-Industrial Society: A Venture in Social Forecasting* (London: Heinemann).

—— (1987) 'The Third Technological Revolution', *New Society*, January 1987.

Benjamin, W. (1982) *Illuminations* (Suffolk: Fontana).

Berger, J. (1971) *Selected Essays and Articles: The Look of Things* (London: Penguin).

196      POSTMODERN CARTOGRAPHIES

Berman, M. (1982) *All That Is Solid Melts Into Air: The Experience of Modernity* (London: Verso).

Berry, P. (1990) 'Deserts of the Heart', *Times Higher Education Supplement*, 28 December.

Biga, T. (1987) *'Blue Velvet'*, *Film Quarterly*, no. 41(1).

Bjork, P. (1992) *The Novels of Toni Morrison: the Search for Self and Place* (New York: Peter Lang).

Borden, L. (1986) 'The World according to David Lynch', *Village Voice*, 23 September.

Bradbury, M., (1984) *The Modern American Novel* (Oxford: Oxford University Press).

Brah, A. (1996) *Cartographies of Diaspora: Contesting Identities* (London: Routledge).

Bundtzen, L. (1988) 'Don't look at me! Woman's Body, Woman's Voice in *Blue Velvet*', *Western Humanities Review*, no. 42(3).

Bush, C. (1989) '"Gilded Backgrounds": Reflections on the Perception of Space and Landscape in America', in Mick Gidley and Robert Lawson-Peebles (eds), *Views of American Landscapes* (Cambridge: Cambridge University Press).

Callinicos, A. (1984) *Against Postmodernism: A Marxist Critique* (Oxford: Polity Press, 1984).

Caws, M. (ed) (1991) *City Images: Perspectives from Literature, Philosophy and Film* (New York: Gordon and Breach).

Channel 4 Television (1995) *The Wild West: the way the American west was lost and won, 1845–1893* (London: Channel 4 Television).

Clark, M. (1986) 'Remembering Vietnam', *Cultural Critique*, no. 3.

Cohan, S. and Hark, I. (eds) (1993) *Screening the Male: Exploring Masculinities in Hollywood Cinema* (London: Routledge).

Cooper, J.F. (1990) *The Last of the Mohicans* (Oxford: Oxford University Press).

Corrigan, T. (1991) *A Cinema without Walls: Movies and Culture after Vietnam* (London: Routledge).

Creed, B. (1990) *'Alien* and the Monstrous-Feminine', in Annette Kuhn (ed.), *Alien Zone: Cultural Theory and Contemporary Science Fiction Cinema* (London: Verso).

Davis, M. (1985) 'Postmodernism and the Spirit of Urban Renaissance', *New Left Review*, no. 151, April–May.

—— (1990) *City of Quartz: Excavating the Future in Los Angeles* (London: Verso).

—— (1991) Interview, *The Late Show*, BBC 2, 7 February.

De Certeau, M. (1984) *The Practice of Everyday Life* (Berkeley: University of California Press).

Denzin, N. (1991) *Images of Postmodern Society; Social Theory and Contemporary Cinema* (London: Sage).

di Lampedusa, G. (1960) *The Leopard*, trans. by Archibald Colquhoun (London: Collins and Harvill).

Duncan, N. (ed.) (1996) *Bodyspace: destabilizing geographies of gender and sexuality* (London: Routledge).

Eco, U. (1987) *Travels in Hyperreality* (London: Picador).

Emerson, R.W. (1990a) *Nature*, in Paul Lauter *et al.* (eds), *The Heath Anthology of American Literature*, Volume I (Lexington, Mass.: D.C. Heath & Co.)

——— (1990b) 'The Poet', in Paul Lauter *et al.* (eds), *The Heath Anthology of American Literature*, Volume I (Lexington, Mass.: D.C. Heath & Co.).

Esch, D. (1991) 'Things Can't Go On Like This: a Beggar's Itinerary', in Mary Ann Caws (ed.), *City Images: Perspectives from Literature, Philosophy and Film* (New York: Gordon and Breach).

Farris, W. (1991) 'The Labyrinth as Sign', in Mary Ann Caws (ed.), *City Images: Perspectives from Literature, Philosophy and Film*, (New York: Gordon and Breach).

Faulkner, W. (1940) *The Hamlet* (New York: Random House).

Fitzgerald, F.S. (1993) *The Great Gatsby* (London: Everyman).

Foucault, M. (1980) 'The Eye of Power', in C. Gordon (ed.), *Power/Knowledge; Selected Interviews and Other Writings, (1972–1977)* (New York: Pantheon).

Genette, G. (1982) *Narrative Discourse* (Oxford: Oxford University Press).

Gidley, M. (1989) 'The Figure of the Indian in Photographic Landscapes', in Mick Gidley and Robert Lawson-Peebles (eds), *Views of American Landscapes* (Cambridge: Cambridge University Press).

Gidley, M. and Lawson-Peebles, R. (eds) (1989) *Views of American Landscapes* (Cambridge: Cambridge University Press).

Gregory, D. (1986) 'Spatial Structure', in R.J. Johnston *et al.* (eds), *The Dictionary of Human Geography*, 2nd edn (Oxford: Blackwell).

Haliwell (1989) *Film Guide*, 7th edn (London: Paladin).

Harley, J.B. (1992) 'Deconstructing the Map', in Trevor J. Barnes and James S. Duncan, (eds), *Writing Worlds: Discourse, Text and Metaphor in the Representation of Landscape* (London: Routledge).

Harvey, D. (1989) *The Condition of Postmodernity: An Enquiry into the Origins of Cultural Change* (Oxford: Blackwell).

Haug, W.F. (1984) *Critique of Commodity Aesthetics: Appearance, Sexuality and Advertising in Capitalist Society* (London: Macmillan).

Hawthorne, N. (1990a) 'The Custom-House', in Paul Lauter *et al.* (eds), *The Heath Anthology of American Literature*, Volume I (Lexington, Mass.: D.C. Heath & Co.).

——— (1990b) *The Scarlet Letter*, in Paul Lauter *et al.* (eds), *The Heath Anthology of American Literature*, Volume I (Lexington, Mass.: D.C. Heath & Co.).

Heller, M. (1991) 'The Cosmopolis of Poetics: Urban World, Uncertain Poetry', in Mary Ann Caws (ed.), *City Images: Perspectives from Literature, Philosophy and Film* (New York: Gordon and Breach).

Jameson, F. (1981) *The Political Unconscious: Narrative as Socially Symbolic Act* (London: Methuen).

——— (1984a) 'Postmodernism, or, the Cultural Logic of Late Capitalism', *New Left Review*, no. 146, July/August.

——— (1984b) 'Progress Versus Utopia: or Can We Imagine the Future?', in Brian Wallis and David R. Godine (eds), *Art After Modernism: Rethinking Representation* (New York: Putnam).

—— (1986) 'Reification and Utopia in Mass Culture', *New Left Review*, no. 162, August.

—— (1990) *Late Marxism: Adorno, or the Persistence of the Dialectic* (London: Verso).

—— (1991) *Postmodernism, or, the Cultural Logic of Late Capitalism* (London: Verso).

Jancovich, M. (1992) *Horror* (London: Batsford).

Jeffords, S. (1993) 'Can Masculinity be terminated?', in Steven Cohan and Ina Rae Hark (eds), *Screening the Male: Exploring Masculinities in Hollywood Cinema* (London: Routledge).

Kaleta, K. (1993) *David Lynch* (New York: Twayne).

Karl, F. (1983) *American Fictions: 1940–1980* (New York: Harper and Row).

Kavanagh, J. (1990) 'Feminism, Humanism and Science in *Alien*', in Annette Kuhn (ed.), *Alien Zone: Cultural Theory and Contemporary Science Fiction Cinema* (London: Verso).

Kellner, D. (1989) *Jean Baudrillard: From Marxism to Postmodernism and Beyond* (Oxford: Polity Press).

Kolko, G. (1988) *Vietnam: Anatomy of a War* (Bloomington: Indiana University Press).

Kristeva, J. (1982) *Powers of Horror* (New York: Columbia University Press).

—— (1991) *Strangers to Ourselves* (New York: Columbia University Press).

Kuhn, A. (ed.) (1990) *Alien Zone: Cultural Theory and Contemporary Science Fiction Cinema* (London: Verso).

Kumar, K. (1978) *Prophecy and Progress: The Sociology of Industrial and Post-Industrial Society* (London: Penguin).

Lasch, C. (1979) *The Culture of Narcissism: American Life in an Age of Diminishing Expectations* (New York: Abacus).

Lauter, P. *et al.* (eds) (1990) *The Heath Anthology of American Literature*, Volume I (Lexington, Mass.: D.C. Heath & Co.).

Lawson-Peebles, R. (1988) *Landscape and written expression in Revolutionary America: The world turned upside down* (Cambridge: Cambridge University Press).

Least Heat-Moon, W. (1991) *Prairyerth* (London: Picador).

Lefebvre, H. (1991) *The Production of Space*, trans. by Donald Nicholson-Smith (Oxford: Blackwell).

Lewis, R.W.B. (1955) *The American Adam: Innocence, Tragedy and Tradition in the Nineteenth Century* (Chicago: Chicago University Press).

Macherey, P. (1978) *A Theory of Literary Production*, trans. G. Wall (London: Routledge & Kegan Paul).

McHoul, A. and Wills, D. (1990) *Writing Pynchon: Strategies in Fictional Analysis* (London: Macmillan).

McLuhan, M. (1964) *Understanding Media: The Extensions of Man* (London: Routledge).

Madsen, D. (1991) *The Postmodern Allegories of Thomas Pynchon* (Leicester: Leicester University Press).

Mailer, N. (1968) 'A Note on Comparative Pornography', in *Advertisements for Myself* (London: Granada).

Malcolm X (1990) 'Definition of a Revolution', in John Henrik C. Clarke (ed.), *Malcolm X: the Man and his Times* (New Jersey: Africa World Press).

Maltby, P. (1991) *Dissident Postmodernists: Barthelme, Coover, Pynchon* (Philadelphia: University of Pennsylvania Press).
Mandel, E. (1975) *Late Capitalism* (London: Verso).
Marcuse, H. (1966) *One-Dimensional Man* (Boston: Beacon Press).
Milton, J. (1968) *Paradise Lost*, Book I, ed. Alastair Fowler (London: Longman).
Moi, T. (1985) *Sexual/Textual Politics: Feminist Literary Theory* (London: Methuen).
Moore, M. (1979) 'New York', in *The Norton Anthology of American Literature*, Volume I (New York: Norton).
Morrison, T. (1970) *The Bluest Eye* (London: Chatto & Windus).
—— (1973) *Sula* (Harmondsworth: Plume/Penguin).
—— (1978) *Song of Solomon* (London: Chatto & Windus).
—— (1981a) 'City Limits, Village Values: Concepts of the Neighbourhood in Black Fiction', in Michael Jaye and Ann Chalmers Watts (eds), *Literature and the Urban Experience* (New Brunswick: Rutgers University Press).
—— (1981b) *Tar Baby* (London: Chatto & Windus).
—— (1987) *Beloved* (London: Picador).
—— (1989) 'Unspeakable Things Unspoken: The Afro-American Presence in American Literature', *Michigan Quarterly Review*, vol. 1, no. 28.
—— (1992a) Interview, *The Late Show*, BBC 2, 21 October.
—— (1992b) *Jazz* (London: Chatto & Windus).
Neale, S. 'Issues of Difference: *Alien* and *Blade Runner*', in James Donald (ed.), *Fantasy and the Cinema* (Essex: B.F.I.).
O'Donnell, P. (ed.) (1991) *New Essays on The Crying of Lot 49* (Cambridge: Cambridge University Press).
Olson, C. (1967) *Call Me Ishmael* (London: Jonathan Cape).
Penley, C. (1989) *The Future of an Illusion: Film, Feminism and Psychoanalysis* (London: Routledge).
—— (1990) 'Time Travel, Primal Scene and the Critical Dystopia', in Annette Kuhn (ed.), *Alien Zone: Cultural Theory and Contemporary Science Fiction Cinema* (London: Verso).
Petillon, P.-Y (1991) 'A Re-cognition of Her Errand into the Wilderness', in Patrick O'Donnell (ed.), *New Essays on The Crying of Lot 49* (Cambridge: Cambridge University Press).
Pfeil, F. (1990) *Another Tale to Tell: Politics and Narrative in Postmodern Culture* (London: Verso).
Phillips, J. (1984) *Machine Dreams* (London: Faber).
Philo, J. (1907) *Uberweg; History*, in *The American Encyclopaedic Dictionary*, Volume III (London: Cassell).
Pile, S. and Keith, D. (1993) *Place and the Politics of Identity* (London: Routledge).
Poster, M. (ed.) (1988) *Jean Baudrillard: Selected Writings* (Cambridge: Polity Press).
Pynchon, T. (1975a) *Gravity's Rainbow* (London: Picador).
—— (1975b) *V* (London: Picador).
—— (1979) *The Crying of Lot 49* (London: Picador).
—— (1985) *Slow Learner* (London: Picador).
—— (1990) *Vineland* (London: Secker & Warburg).

Relph, E. (1976) *The Placelessness of Place* (London: Pion).

Rilke, R.M. (1987) 'The Black Cat', in *The Selected Poetry of Rainer Maria Rilke* (London: Picador).

Rose, G. (1993) *Feminism and Geography* (Oxford: Polity Press).

—— (1991) Review of *Postmodern Geographies* and *The Condition of Postmodernity*, *Journal of Historical Geography*, vol. 17, no. 1.

Ryan, M. and Kellner, D. (1988) *Camera Politica: The Politics and Ideology of Contemporary Hollywood Film* (Bloomington: Indiana University Press).

Schwarzenegger, A. (1992) Speech at a Republican Party rally.

Seattle, Chief (1855) 'Speech delivered at the signing of the Port Elliot Treaty', in Paul Lauter *et al.* (eds), *The Heath Anthology of American Literature*, Volume I (Lexington, Mass.: D.C. Heath & Co.).

Skelton, R.A. (1972) *Maps: A Historical Survey of the Study and Collecting of* (Chicago: University of Chicago Press).

Smith, P. (1977) *The Syntax of Cities* (London: Hutchinson).

Soja, E. (1989) *Postmodern Geographies: The Reassertion of Space in Critical Social Theory* (London: Verso).

Stanton, D. (1986) 'An Interview with Jayne Anne Phillips', *Croton Review*, no. 9, Spring–Summer.

Stein, G. (1996) *The Letters of Gertrude Stein and Thornton Wilder*, eds Edward M. Burns and Ulla E. Dydo (London: Yale University Press).

Stepto, R. (1977) 'Intimate Things in Place: A Conversation with Toni Morrison', *Massachusetts Review*, September.

Stevens, W. (1984) 'The Snow Man', in *Collected Poems* (London: Faber and Faber).

Tanner, T. (1971) *City of Words* (London: Jonathan Cape).

—— (1987) *Thomas Pynchon* (London: Methuen).

Tasker, Y. (1993a) 'Dumb Movies for Dumb People: Masculinity, the Body, and the Voice in Contemporary Action Cinema', in Steven Cohan and Ina Rae Hark (eds), *Screening the Male: Exploring Masculinities in Contemporary Hollywood Cinema* (London: Routledge).

—— (1993b) *Spectacular Bodies: Gender, Genre and the Action Movie* (London: Routledge).

Taubin, A. (1992) 'Invading bodies: *Alien*[3] and the Trilogy', *Sight and Sound*, vol. 2, no. 3, July.

Thoreau, H.D. (1979) *Walden, or Life in the Woods*, in Nina Baym et al. (eds), *The Norton Anthology of American Literature*, Volume I (New York: Norton).

Turner, F.J. (1972) 'The significance of the Frontier in American History', in George Rogers Taylor (ed.), *The Turner Thesis: Concerning the Role of the Frontier in American History* (Lexington, Mass.: D.C. Heath & Co.).

Valentine, G. (1996) '(Re)negotiating the heterosexual street: lesbian productions of space', in Nancy Duncan (ed.), *Bodyspace: Destabilizing Geographies of Gender and Sexuality* (London: Routledge).

Westling, L. (1996) *The Green Breast of the New World: Landscape, Gender, and American Fiction* (Athens: University of Georgia Press).

Whitman, W. (1990a) Preface to *Leaves of Grass*, in Paul Lauter *et al.* (eds), *The Heath Anthology of American Literature*, Volume I (Lexington, Mass.: D.C. Heath & Co.).

—— (1990b) 'Song of Myself', in Paul Lauter *et al.* (eds), *The Heath Anthology of American Literature*, Volume I (Lexington, Mass.: D.C. Heath & Co.).

Wood, R. (1984) 'An introduction to the American horror film', in Garry Keith Grant (ed.), *Planks of Reason: Essays on the Horror Film* (New Jersey: Scarecrow/Methuen).

—— (1986) *Hollywood From Vietnam to Reagan* (New York: Columbia University Press).

Zukin, S. (1991) *Landscapes of Power: From Detroit to Disney World* (Berkeley: University of California Press).

# Filmography

*Alien* (Ridley Scott, Twentieth Century Fox, 1979).
*Aliens* (James Cameron, Twentieth Century Fox, 1986).
*Alien*[3] (David Fincher, Twentieth Century Fox, 1992).
*Back to the Future II* (Robert Zemeckis, Warner Bros, 1986).
*Blade Runner* (Ridley Scott, Warner Bros, 1982).
*Blue Velvet* (David Lynch, Twentieth Century Fox, 1986).
*Dune* (David Lynch, Warner Bros, 1984).
*The Elephant Man* (David Lynch, Universal, 1980).
*Eraserhead* (David Lynch, Polygram, 1977).
*E.T.* (Stephen Spielberg, Warner Bros, 1982).
*Fire Walk With Me* (David Lynch, New Line Cinema, 1992).
*The Terminator* (James Cameron, Carolco, 1984).
*Terminator 2: Judgment Day* (James Cameron, Carolco, 1991).
*The Thing* (John Carpenter, Warner Bros, 1982).
*Twin Peaks* (David Lynch, Warner Bros, Screened on British TV, 1989–1991).
*Wild at Heart* (David Lynch, Polygram, 1990).

# Index